Reason's Disciples

Reason's Disciples
Seventeenth-Century English Feminists

HILDA L. SMITH

UNIVERSITY OF ILLINOIS PRESS

Urbana   Chicago   London

© 1982 by the Board of Trustees of the University of Illinois
Manufactured in the United States of America

This book is printed on acid-free paper.

LIBRARY OF CONGRESS CATALOGING IN PUBLICATION DATA

Smith, Hilda L., 1941–
Reason's disciples.

Bibliography: p.
Includes index.
1. Feminism—England—History—17th century.
2. Women authors.   I. Title.
HQ1599.E5S62   305.4'2'0942   81–14834
ISBN 0–252–00912–6   AACR2

For Tom, Gregory, and Christopher
and
To the Memory of my Mother

Contents

Preface

Scholars, when tracing the history of feminism, have seldom ventured back beyond the writings of Mary Wollstonecraft. While there have been studies of isolated writers interested in the status of women, such as Christine de Pisan and Anna Maria van Schurman, few historians have discussed the development of either feminist ideology or groupings before the eighteenth century. Early expressions of feminist thought are normally seen as idiosyncratic, and revelant only for the culture out of which they sprang. Rarely are these works related to the continuing historical development of feminist thought and action.[1]

These chronological limitations have often bound historical studies of feminism, limiting their perspective to the realities out of which nineteenth-century feminism arose. Scholars have concerned themselves with two basic issues: what are the social and economic factors that lead women to develop feminist goals and organizations, and which set of ideas most clearly represents a feminist ideology? In answering these questions, historians have usually looked only at their group of feminists and derived very general answers. Since much of the study of feminist history has focused on the nineteenth century, and a large portion of that scholarship on the origins of the women's rights movement in the United States, we have most information and theorizing about why feminism developed during the third and fourth decades of the 1800s in this country. Thus many of the judgments on feminism's origins stress the urban moral reform movements, the abolitionist crusade, or the industrial revolution and familial alterations of early nineteenth-century America. Although similar issues are addressed by historians of English feminism, there has simply been much less written about the emergence of the women's movement there. This emphasis on particular expressions of feminism has both limited awareness of it in other settings and, to a degree, hidden its roots in the continuing restrictions of women's traditional role.[2]

The chronological narrowness of the scholarly consideration of feminism is also reflected in the studies of ideology. Work has been done on what separates feminism from women's rights and what constitutes the fundamental beliefs of feminist organizations. Significant attention, however, has yet to be focused on an analysis of the common denominator of feminist thought and action in different times or places, or on pinpointing historically recurrent social and economic situations that might be conducive to feminist activities. This study, by examining a period normally thought antecedent to accepted feminist activity, has by necessity probed both the social and intellectual origins of feminist writings and the nature of these writings in light of our knowledge about later developments in feminist thought and action. It suggests that feminism has had a more varied existence than is generally recognized, and that by looking at one of its prior manifestations we can gain a clearer sense of the conditions that gave it rise, nurtured it, and influenced its decline.[3]

Little specific work has been done on seventeenth-century England as a setting for feminism. Some attention has been paid to women's status during this period and to the prescriptions about proper roles for females, but such work has centered on the political and religious issues relevant to the general society. Despite some studies of women in the radical sects of the Civil War, especially Quakers, and some works on women's treatment by political theorists and Puritan writers, almost no attention has been given to women's having developed an independent criticism of their situation outside of the revolutionary and religious ideologies and groupings formed between 1640 and 1660 and later during the Glorious Revolution.[4]

It is the dual purpose of this work to identify and analyze feminist views produced in seventeenth-century England and to link them to a central theme of later feminist movements—namely, the understanding of women as a group with identifiable sociological characteristics. A small number of female authors, fewer than twenty including both the known and the anonymous, came to write about women as a group during the second half of the seventeenth century. The vast majority of these authors were royalists and later Tories, and their views about women did not spring from any attachment to either political or religious resistance to the crown, or from broader criticism of the structure of English society. The impact of the revolution on feminist thought, aside from supplying some adaptable rhetoric, was almost wholly negative, reminding these women who opposed its goals that the leaders of the revolution had little interest in improving the status of women, within either the home or the state.[5]

A feminist realization of women's group identity, which was increasing steadily among a small band of writers after the 1650s, evolved from a series of seventeenth-century influences. The revolutionary questionings, even if unacceptable to the feminists, provided an intellectual and political climate favorable to those raising fundamental questions about social relationships, including relationships between the sexes. The growing importance of rationalist and scientific thought both encouraged and provided the tools of argument to individuals questioning customary and providential justifications for social relationships. Isolated demographic studies suggest in more practical terms a number of factors which could have encouraged women to think of their lives differently: a growing number of spinsters, later ages at marriage for women, smaller families, and an increasingly negative sex ratio. Economically, the increase in commercialization, decline in small landholdings, and shifts from local to national markets diminished women's traditional economic functions. For the genteel classes, a greater emphasis on the London season and on social and cultural accomplishments reduced the important managerial functions of the lady of the manor. Many of these changes, especially the demographic and economic, were regional rather than national and certainly each of these alterations would touch the lives of a minority of women. Yet taken as a whole, they provided a climate of change and a significant common experience for those critical of women's lives during the late seventeenth century.

Not only were changes occurring in the lives of seventeenth-century women generally, but we can pinpoint a number of important alterations in both the reality and the image of educated women from the sixteenth and early seventeenth centuries to the period after 1650. From materials gathered from a survey of women listed in the *Dictionary of National Biography* who were born during the years 1525 through 1675, there emerges a clear movement away from the aristocratic lady who was praised for her linguistic skills and translations to women authors from more divergent social backgrounds who were included for their original writings. Female entries for the sixteenth century fall almost entirely into three categories—members of the court or aristocracy, religious figures (normally Protestant or Catholic martyrs), and learned ladies of the upper class. Those born between 1625 and 1675, who came to maturity during the second half of the century, represented a broader class background, although one still heavily weighted in favor of the upper classes. Those noted for their learning are included much more often for original writings than for classical translations.

This movement is significant because it suggests that educated women during this period were being recognized not merely as students, as passive repositories of learning, as patrons of male scholars, or as translators of past and current classics, but as authors developing their own ideas and publishing their own works. The female intellectuals of the seventeenth century were quite different from their sixteenth-century predecessors. During the 1500s the daughters of Anthony Cooke were noted for their learning and their prominent mates; Mary Sidney, Countess of Pembroke, and Queen Catherine Parr were remembered primarily for their support of (or connection to) important men, and other learned women, such as Margaret Roper or Lady Jane Grey, were notable for their close ties to the court. After 1650 women came from a wider social circle and applied their minds to more varied intellectual topics.[6] One illustration of the growing breadth and social-relatedness of women's writings after 1625 is that for the earlier period only men wrote significant works outlining what the educational and social role of women should be. After 1625 women writers never relinquished a substantial role in describing and prescribing their sex's position.

It is true that women intellectuals continued to do translations and to be praised for their mastery of foreign languages, but unlike their earlier sisters they wrote treatises on all kinds of subjects: midwifery, cookery, household management, science and philosophy, women's education, religious controversies, and the proper rules for private meditation. They wrote poetry, drama, and fiction in increasing numbers near the end of the century as well. There is not only an increase in the number of women included in the DNB (forty-three women born from 1550 to 1625, seventy-nine for the period 1625–75) but the number of poets increased from none to six and the number of writers from ten to seventeen. Anne Conway and the duchess of Newcastle wrote philosophical treatises; Katherine Evans, Margaret Fell Fox, and a number of other Quaker women composed both religious and political treatises defending the Quaker faith and denouncing the government for religious intolerance; and Jane Sharp and Elizabeth Cellier authored medical works for midwives, defending the profession against attack by physicians. Lady Rachel Russell, a prolific letter writer, stressed religious values, while a large number of female mystics, including Jane Lead, Anne Docwra, and Eleanor Douglas, described their personal communion with God. Several other women took up poetry, including Katherine Philips, Anne Killegrew, and, of course, Aphra Behn. In short, women in increasing numbers produced a variety of intellectual works based on their own experience and expressing opinions about their individual interests and those of English society generally.

The image of the female intellectual was changing as well. She was no longer so exceptional in terms of rank or ability. Katherine Philips was praised as an average housewife writing poetry, and middle-class women were encouraged to develop their intellect by the editors of popular periodicals such as the *Athenian Mercury*. The image of the learned female was altered as well in those works encouraging women's education during the late 1600s. In the sixteenth century the educated woman, as portrayed by Sir Thomas Elyot and John Aylmer, had been an exceptionally talented scholar who spent a portion of her young life learning languages and imitating the wisdom of the ancients, before her marriage. To emphasize this image of exceptionalness, supporters of women's education produced long lists of outstanding women from Scripture, the classics, and mythology. If only the modern women could imitate the ancients' amazing accomplishments, they could obtain comparable fame.

Feminist writers during the seventeenth century not only encouraged women generally to pursue learning, but their focus on women as a group led them commonly to omit the lists of past "women worthies" and to speak of the equal rational abilities of the sexes.[7] While the sixteenth-century defenders of women's learning had fought their opponents on their opponents' terms, the feminists refused to compose lists of heroic females to compete with the catalog of base women developed by the opposition. They instead shifted the arena of the debate from the qualities of individual women to the natures of men and women. Thus the female scholar of the late seventeenth century came to be seen not as a single example and worthy follower of the great biblical and classical heroines, but simply as an individual woman who, through her example, demonstrated the intellectual capabilities of her sex.

This work will not argue, however, that seventeenth-century feminists were alone in questioning the relationships between the sexes or the nature of marriage during the 1600s. An increasing number of authors came to criticize marriage as an institution in which the male had greater freedom of action than the female and in which parents dominated their children's choice of mate destructively. Numerous tracts criticized men for viewing marriage only as a prison and for failing to appreciate the importance of having a worthy life companion in their wife. Much of their criticism, however, was not written from the wife's perspective. Women were advised to realize that theirs was the more difficult marital existence and that they would simply have to prepare for and accept that reality. The best-known example of an author's understanding women's plight without suggesting it could or should be changed was Lord Halifax's *Advice to a Daughter*, but a similar sensitivity to women's special troubles within marriage was revealed in the following comment by the Puritan Richard Baxter, who also failed to advocate any change in sexual relationships:

> *Women* especially must expect so much suffering in a married life, that if God had not put into them a natural inclination to it, and so strong a love to their children, as maketh them patient under the most annoying troubles, the world would ere this have been at end, through their refusal of so calamitous a life. Their sickness in breeding, their pain in bringing forth, with the danger of their lives, the tedious trouble day and night which they have with their children in their nursing and their childhood; besides their subjection to their Husbands, and continual care of family affairs: being forced to consume their lives in a multitude of low and troublesome business. All this and much more would have utterly deterred that Sex from marriage, if *Nature* itself had not enclined them to it.[8]

Feminists shared much of this evaluation of a woman's lot, but insisted that it was the result not of "Nature" but of social patterns and choices that both could and should be changed. That insight, the sociological definition of sex roles, was to be their most significant contribution.

NOTES

1. Biographies of Mary Wollstonecraft by Eleanor Flexner (*Mary Wollstonecraft: A Biography* [Baltimore: Penguin Books, 1972]) and Margaret George (*One Woman's "Situation": A Study of Mary Wollstonecraft* [Urbana: University of Illinois Press, 1970]) do not place her writings in the context of earlier feminist expressions and, rather, view her essentially as a maverick establishing the issues of debate for the modern feminist movement. For studies of earlier women concerned about the treatment afforded women in society see an older work, Una Birch Pope-Hennessey's *Anna van Schurman, Artist, Scholar, Saint* (London: Longmans, Co., 1909), which deals broadly with Schurman's life but does include a chapter on her resentment of women's enforced ignorance, and a more recent article by Susan Groag Bell, "Christine de Pisan (1364–1430): Humanism and the Problem of a Studious Woman" (*Feminist Studies* 3 [1976]: 173–84), which focuses, as well, on the demand for women's education by an early female scholar. Carolyn Lougee, in her important analysis of seventeenth-century French feminism, *Le Paradis des Femmes: Women, Salons, and Social Stratification in Seventeenth-Century France* (Princeton, N.J.: Princeton University Press, 1976), employs a definition of feminism relevant only for that setting.

2. Building upon the classic treatment of American feminism by Eleanor Flexner (*Century of Struggle: The Woman's Rights Movement in the United States* [Cambridge, Mass.: Harvard University Press, 1959]) and an early and important article by Gerda Lerner ("Women's Rights and American Feminism," *American Scholar* 40[1971]: 235–48), a number of recent works have analyzed why feminism developed in this country when it did. See Barbara J. Berg, *The Remembered Gate: Origins of American Feminism: The Woman and the City, 1800–1860* (New York: Oxford University Press, 1978); William H. Chafe, *Women and Equality: Changing Patterns in American Culture* (New York: Oxford University Press, 1977); Nancy Cott, *The Bonds of Womanhood: "Woman's Sphere" in New England, 1780–1835* (New Haven, Conn.: Yale University Press, 1977); Ellen C. DuBois, *Feminism and Suffrage: The Emergence of an Independent Women's Movement in America, 1848–1869* (Ithaca, N.Y.: Cornell University Press, 1978); and Keith Melder, *Beginnings of Sisterhood: The American Woman's Rights Movement, 1800–1850* (New York: Schocken Books, 1977). Works on the history of the women's movement in England have focused less on its origins and more on the nature of militancy and the interaction of working-class movements with suffrage activity. For a discussion of militancy see Andrew Rosen's *Rise up Women! The Militant Campaign of the Women's Social and Political Union, 1903–1914* (London: Routledge and Kegan Paul, 1974), and for a study of the suffrage movement from a socialist perspective, concentrating on the efforts of working-class women for the vote, see *"One Hand Tied Behind Us": The Rise of the Women's Suffrage Movement* (London: Virago Press, 1978) by Jill Liddington and Jill Norris.

3. There is a need to distinguish between activist and theoretical feminism more clearly and to realize that the socioeconomic conditions or political values necessary for the establishment of an organized women's movement may differ from the circumstances encouraging a single writer, or a group of writers, to argue the need for change in women's status.

4. Older works such as Alice Clark's *Working Life of Women in the Seventeenth Century* (1919; reprint ed., London: Frank Cass and Co., 1968) and Doris Mary Stenton's *The English Woman in History* (London: Routledge and Kegan Paul, 1957) contain useful information about women's lives during the 1600s, as does a newer comparative work, Roger Thompson's *Women in Stuart England and America* (London: Routledge and Kegan Paul, 1974). Keith Thomas's important article, "Women and the Civil War Sects" (*Past and Present* 13 [Apr. 1958]: 42–62) places women's quest for improved status within the radical Protestantism of the English Civil War. There is little explicit discussion of the feminism that developed during the 1600s, however, except for isolated and sometimes questionable comments about Mary Astell and the duchess of Newcastle in Thompson's work (see esp. pp. 12–13) and a brief section on the subject (pp. 336–41) in Lawrence Stone's *The Family, Sex and Marriage in England, 1500–1800* (New York: Harper and Row, 1977). There have appeared, after the completion of this work, articles on a number of individual seventeenth-century feminists. These include: Mary Ann McGuire, "Margaret Cavendish, Duchess of Newcastle, on the Nature and Status of Women," *International Journal of Women's Studies* 1 (1978): 193–206; Joan K. Kinnaird, "Mary Astell and the Conservative Contribution to English Feminism," *Journal of British Studies* 19 (Fall 1979): 53–75; and Katharine Rogers, "Anne Finch, Countess of Winchilsea: An Augustan Woman Poet," in *Shakespeare's Sisters: Feminist Essays on Woman Poets*, ed. Sandra M. Gilbert and Susan Gubar (Bloomington: Indiana University Press, 1979). More recently two additional essays on seventeenth-century feminists have appeared in *Female Scholars: A Tradition of Learned Women before 1800*, ed. J. R. Brink (Montreal: Eden Press, 1980); they are J. R. Brink's "Bathsua Makin: Educator and Linguist (English, 1608?–1675?)," pp. 86–100, and Mary Elizabeth Green's "Elizabeth Elstob: The Saxon Nymph (English, 1683–1765)," pp. 137–60. The volume is useful for those interested in early female scholarship and includes essays on Christine de Pisan and Anna Maria van Schurman, among others.

5. See the Introduction to this work for brief biographies of seventeenth-century feminists and for a discussion of why their feminism emerged from sources other than the revolutionary forces of mid-seventeenth-century England.

6. To develop a listing of women in the *DNB* and their particular interests I extracted those individuals born during three periods—1525–75, 1575–1650, and 1650–1725—and noted both the descriptor given first in their entry, i.e., "poetess," "courtesan," etc., and the additional information about their lives contained in the *Concise Dictionary of National Biography: Part I, From the Beginnings to 1900* (Oxford: Oxford University Press, 1969). Changes in de-

scriptors and general biographical information suggested that both the actual lives of these women and the evaluations of later commentators altered. In particular, there is a noticeable shift in those women selected for inclusion in the *DNB:* from the learned ladies of the sixteenth century to the authors or partici-pants in religious communities of the seventeenth century to bluestockings, frequenters of salons, and acquaintances of important literary figures during the eighteenth century. A fuller discussion of the educated woman of the eighteenth century is given in the Conclusion of this work.

7. The term "women worthies" is discussed in Natalie Z. Davis's article, "Women's History in Transition: The European Case," *Feminist Studies* 3 (1976): 83–103.

8. George Savile, Marquis of Halifax, *The Lady's New-Years Gift; or, Advice to a Daughter* (London, 1688). Halifax's popular work stressed the necessity of a wife's forming her character to meet the wishes of her husband and of preparing herself for possible neglect and harsh words. It contained compas-sion but little hope for the newly married bride. By 1741 Halifax's volume had gone through twelve editions. Richard Baxter, *A Christian Directory; or, A Summ of Practical Theologie, and Cases of Conscience*, 2d ed. (London: Printed by Rob't White, for Nevil Simmons, 1678), p. 8.

Acknowledgments

I would first like to thank collectively that group of women historians which has, over the last decade, come together to form feminist organizations within the profession and labored to create the current field of women's history. Without the help of these historians, scholars such as myself, both as graduate students and as faculty, would have had to pursue the nearly impossible task of developing careers and research in a vacuum. In particular I am grateful to Berenice Carroll for providing me with her scholarly insights and her personal support throughout the various stages of my academic career. Natalie Davis has also given both intellectual enlightenment and professional support over the years.

I would like to thank Charles Gray for encouraging me to pursue my initial interest in women's history and for helping to shape my historical understanding. He has generously given personal and professional support throughout my career. I also appreciate the scholarly advice of William Monter and Leonard Krieger in the preparation of this work in its dissertation form.

A number of individuals have been most generous with their time and exceedingly helpful through their readings of the several versions of this manuscript. I would like to thank Sharon Nell-Williams and Eleanor Melamed for suggestions about the work's stylistic and organizational difficulties. Elly especially has helped me during long hours discussing the broader historical implications of this study. Sam Merrill and David Grimsted also provided useful suggestions for improving the clarity of this work in its final stages, for which I am most grateful. I also want to thank Alfred Moss, Madeline Zilfi, Gabrielle Speigel, Claire Moses, and Carol Pearson for sharing with me their academic insights, their friendship, and their support as colleagues.

Finally, I greatly appreciate the support given me by Richard Went-
worth and Carole Appel of the University of Illinois Press. In collecting
the materials for this work I am indebted to the reference staffs of the
British Library; the Newberry Library; the Folger Shakespeare Library;
the Bodleian Library, Oxford University; the Houghton Library, Harvard University; and the research facilities of the Library of Congress.
Also, the secretarial staff of the Department of History at the University
of Maryland has shown continual kindness toward me, and I appreciate
the efforts of Vera Blenkiron and Darlene King in typing the numerous
versions of this work. I also thank Cynthia Requardt for perparing the
index.

Reason's Disciples

Introduction
Feminism and Its Seventeenth-Century Adherents

During the second half of the seventeenth century a group of English women began to write critically about their exclusion from educational institutions and positions of importance within English society and the restrictions placed upon women within the home. They also urged all financially able women to become serious scholars, to use their minds to their full potential, and to give up decorative, lesiurely, and inconsequential existences. This is a study of that group, twelve seventeenth-century feminists including Margaret Cavendish, Duchess of Newcastle; Bathsua Makin; Hannah Woolley; Jane Sharp; Elizabeth Cellier; Mary Astell; Elizabeth Elstob; Lady Mary Chudleigh; Anne Winchilsea; Elizabeth Singer Rowe; Sarah Fyge Egerton; and Margaret Fell Fox. Some discussion is also included of two other writers, Katherine Philips and Aphra Behn, whose literary successes influenced the development of feminism but who were primarily concerned with other issues.

Though all were educated, these feminists came from a rather wide spectrum of English society. One was a duchess, one was a servant who later advanced to the post of personal secretary, three were either governesses or teachers in girls' schools at periods in their lives. Most were part of the leisured upper or upper-middle classes. Of the ten about whose identity we are certain, eight were married and three had children. They were predominantly Anglican in their religious beliefs and Tories politically.

These seventeenth-century women fall into two groups. The first group presented their ideas in essays and in introductory materials to cookbooks, scientific works, and general literary efforts from 1655 to 1675. They wrote mostly on the subject of education, and their numbers included the duchess of Newcastle, Bathsua Makin, and Hannah Woolley. Only the duchess wrote about women's general position within society, while her contemporaries focused almost exclusively on the topic of education. The second group of writers, publishing between 1690 and 1710, raised more general questions about women's position within the family and how that position restricted the development of their talents. These later writers included Mary Astell, Elizabeth Elstob, and the anonymous author of *An Essay in Defence of the Female Sex*. Four feminist poets also wrote in this period, most extensively during the first decade of the eighteenth century: Anne Winchilsea, Lady Mary Chudleigh, Elizabeth Singer Rowe, and Sarah Fyge Egerton.

This study contends that these women were the first group of modern "feminists"—that is, individuals who viewed women as a sociological group whose social and political position linked them together more surely than their physical or psychological natures.[1] This view led them to favor a number of changes in the relationship between the sexes. First, because they believed that women were men's intellectual equals whose potential had been thwarted by exclusion from institutions of higher learning, they argued for the establishment of a women's college, advanced secondary schools for girls, and the furtherance of learning by women in their own homes. More important, they endeavored to change the attitudes of both women and men about female intellectual capacity and to challenge the popular belief that women should be educated only on less advanced philosophical, scientific, or theological subjects.

Their demands for change were not limited to the intellectual realm; they argued just as strongly against women's secondary role within the home. These feminists viewed marriage in general, and the relationship between husband and wife in particular, as an institution which operated for the benefit of men. They termed the wife an "upper servant" and argued that until the marriage relationship was more nearly equal women could not fulfill their potential as human beings.[2] Wives led trying existences filled with repetitious chores and often irrational husbandly demands, with little escape from family duties. Further, husbands were legally political lords, with full control of finances during the marriage. Under these conditions there was a necessary conflict between a woman's personal and intellectual needs and her duties as wife and mother.

Seventeenth-century feminists fitted these two major points—intellectual restriction and domestic subordination—into a general system of protest against men's total control of the public and private institutions of English society. These women desired to change the sexual balance of power. They did not simply criticize women's position in society, but saw social change as necessary to restoring women's rightful opportunities.

This desire to change women's lives, rather than simply to recognize isolated injustices, separated the feminists from other sixteenth- and seventeenth-century critics of women's role in society. Humanist writers such as Juan Vives and Sir Thomas More, for example, urged stronger intellectual training for women, but rested this call for expanded education on the view that a mentally trained woman would not merely modify but would improve the traditional sexual relationship by becoming a better companion for her husband and mother for her children. More warned his own daughter that her learning should never be made public but should be kept for the enjoyment of her husband and father. Vives's "expanded" education for women stressed piety, modesty, and obedience, and eschewed advanced learning as unsuitable to females. And for both writers, female education meant tutoring for the few who could afford to be trained privately. There were to be no institutions comparable to those available to males to bring the "new learning" to women.

Seventeenth-century French writers who dealt with the question of women's secondary status favored expanding women's education and increasing their role in the salon and the court, but held that women's public role was to be enhanced for the benefit of men and society more than for women. Although they decried women's inadequate education and the waste of their talents within the home, these French writers believed in inherent sexual differences and in a different educational agenda for women. They wanted to retain the positive qualities of "femininity," while giving an opportunity for the intellectually talented and socially cultivated aristocratic woman to be free from the stifling

controls of her family. Their program combined intellectual with social
and sexual liberation, so that this special kind of woman could mingle
freely with males of like interests and sophistication.[3]

Seventeenth-century feminists, in moving beyond these "improvements" in a few women's lives, spoke not of the single or exceptional
woman, but addressed all women of the educated classes. To be sure,
they did not speak to the daughters of the poor, urging them to higher
educational goals, but they did ask all women of their class to devote time
and talent to advanced learning and to utilize their full intellectual
capacities. They spoke of women, or of ladies, in their writings, but not of
individual women, no matter how talented. And, although in reality
these "women" referred only to a small minority of the female sex,
feminist works were little different in this regard from the general works
of social and political theory of the period, in which "men" meant only a
minority of the male members of society.

The feminism of these women was rooted in the intellectual currents
of their century. Seventeenth-century rationalism, particularly René
Descartes's writings, provided the crucial ingredient for these feminists'
proof of women's essential equality and gave incentive to work for a
society where women could employ their powers to the fullest to understand truth, both godly and secular.[4] By coming to the realization that
women were thinking individuals and not a historical, unchanging species whose sexuality defined them as more emotional, weaker, and less
intellectual than men, they rejected inherent sexual differences. Moreover, in looking for other answers to the question of why and how
women were "inferior," these feminists developed a new understanding
of women's basic identity as a sociological group.

An understanding of the feminist view of women as a sociological group
is essential to grasping the thought processes of individual seventeenth-
century feminists and to placing them into a continuum of feminist
ideology reaching from that century to our own. A feminist ideology can
incorporate a number of interests focusing on women and divergent
viewpoints about women's position within a given time and place, but it
must include some understanding of women as a group whose lives have
differed from men's on account of their sex. The move toward such a
group-centered understanding of women is especially important for an
initial expression of feminist thought.

The thoughts and writings of individual seventeenth-century feminists reveal the budding and growth of such ideas. The imagery and the language used in sixteenth-century works on women did not concentrate on women's group identity. Rather, the writers argued that individually talented females should pursue intellectual interests, and they supported this view by examples of earlier great women who had revealed exceptional intellectual or moral character. From the various defenses of women's abilities in the sixteenth century, such as Agrippa's *Nobilitie and Excellencye of Woman Kynde* or Sir Thomas Elyot's *The Defence of Good Women*, to Thomas Heywood's mid-seventeenth-century history of women, defenders of the sex repeated similar lists of "women worthies" to demonstrate that individual women could rise above the general limitations of the sex. But the seventeenth-century feminists seldom supported their belief in women with evidence culled from the accomplishments of past exceptional (and often mythical) females; rather, they argued from the axiom that men and women were given equal rational abilities. By the late seventeenth century, they took this position as a given and then asked why the equal abilities of both sexes had led to such divergent results in intellectual accomplishment. In developing their explanation of this apparent paradox they came to argue that women's unity did not come from likenesses based on physiology, that women had to be seen not only as a biological but also as a sociological group.[5]

Seventeenth-century feminism was important because it implicitly worked out a definition of feminism that was continuingly relevant. This sociological definition was an initial step crucial to the development of a feminist chain of thought. There are a number of ideas commonly connected to feminism: belief in the equality of the sexes, desire to end arbitrary sex-role divisions, support for equal public and legal rights for both sexes, and understanding of the relation of women's inferior role in the family to general social restrictions placed upon them. These components of feminist thought imply not only recognizing unjust restrictions but acting upon them as well. They also rest on a basic premise which views women as a group whose status is subject to change. If women are only isolated individuals, there can be no theory about them as a whole. If they form a group only by reason of their sexual functions or supposed psychological peculiarities, such differences are either good, functional, or essentially unalterable. The assumption that women are a socially defined group is essential to a hope that their lives may be socially altered.

Coming to this realization was especially important for feminist ideology in its earliest stages. When the necessary assumptions become matter of course, particular groups may effectively focus more on action than on ideology, because fundamental feminist principles have already been formulated. Yet feminists could neither expand their efforts nor refine their arguments while constantly debating first principles: Are women truly oppressed? Is there a basic equality of the sexes? Is women's circumscribed social role the result of physiological necessity?

A number of corollaries flow from the feminist view of women as a sociological group. The view implies the existence of a group, namely men, with the means and desire to establish social and political controls over women's lives. Seventeenth-century feminists, and those who followed, were adamant in arguing that men excluded women from positions of power for their own ends, and that they instituted a "private tyranny" in the home. Men had stressed women's biological and psychological differences to exclude them from training so that females could not compete successfully for dominance within society and could be held to traditional roles of providing sexual and domestic services.

If women's inferior opportunities are socially derived, they are of course not necessarily permanent. Feminists during the 1600s established a pattern, followed by their later counterparts, of arguing that there was nothing sacred, natural, or necessary about women's secondary role within the home or society generally. They insisted that women must better equip themselves, both intellectually and practically, to compete with men. Women must first come to a realization of their own worth and then demand that society alter its institutions to represent their needs and interests more fairly. These early feminists urged their sisters to use their minds to the fullest, while at the same time criticizing society for restricting women's chances in both school and home. And they stressed that men must change—that they must give up their position of domination and share society's rewards more equally with women.

Feminists have traditionally assumed the general sisterhood of all women. One seventeenth-century feminist, Mary Astell, spoke of herself as being a "lover of my sex," and another Sarah Egerton, of "being too much a woman" to ignore the plight or wishes of other members of her sex. Despite recognition of class, racial, or national differences among women, feminist writers have always stressed the similarities rather than the differences in women's lives, noting a common core among all women based on shared experiences. The largest numbers of women marry into an institution that requires more time and commitment from the wife than from the husband; a large majority have children for which they provide the primary care; and all are raised in cultures in which masculine activities and achievements are more highly valued than feminine ones. To stress the unity of women is not to deny vast personal and social differences, but merely to stress the central importance of such shared realities.

Thus by seeing women as a sociological group and by using that vision to establish programs and viewpoints which work to end the inequalities in women's status as a group, feminists separate themselves from those who do not concern themselves with changing the lives of all women. It is the uniting of the experience of one woman, or a group of women, to a general understanding of women as a whole that is the beginning of a feminist chain of thought and action. Those seventeenth-century feminists, then, by linking their personal experiences to those of women generally and by speaking of women's past and present relationships with men in terms of one sex's treatment of the other, established that feminist construct which became the model for later feminist theorists.

Why these early feminists moved toward their views is, of course, a complex social and ideological question. The conditions of seventeenth-century England were obviously conducive to the attempt to develop new ideas about the relationships between the sexes. The general social and political turmoil of the English Civil War created a favorable setting for people questioning traditional relationships. Essayists and authors of tracts were continually debating the meaning of tyranny and the rights of freeborn Englishmen. The Levellers criticized the domination of the large landowners in both the national and local political and social structure. Religious sectarians questioned the authority of the ministers and the religious orthodoxy of the Anglican and Presbyterian establishments. The Baconians attacked the universities' rigid academic curricula while expanding the purview of what was properly called learning. Educational reformers, drawing their program heavily from the ideas of Comenius, wanted to open up English education to those outside the triumvirate of grammar school, university, and the Inns of Court. In this time of profound social questioning, it is not surprising that a few women began contemplating aspects of sexual inequality.

It was a period of intellectual as well as political stirrings, and the feminists could draw upon a wide range of ideas to aid them in formulating a new explanation for women's current status within society. The literature of the mid-seventeenth century was commonly prescriptive, encouraging readers to think in terms of right and wrong and of desirable or possible social change. General essays calling for social or political reforms almost never addressed the status of women, but they obviously helped establish an intellectual milieu which encouraged the questioning of the fundamental principles which bind a society together. The ideas of the feminists were always outside the liberalism or radicalism of those advocating change during the 1640s and 1650s, but their political and religious conservatism perhaps made them especially aware of, and pleased to point out, how sexually circumscribed were the glowing definitions of liberty which emerged from that period.

The political and social writings of the left during the Civil War at once encouraged and restricted the efforts of feminists. The feminists, predominantly royalist and Anglican, were unsympathetic to the viewpoints of most of the country's diverse revolutionaries: Puritans, common lawyers, Levellers, sectarians, and communal groups. Each of these groups pointed out the threat to English liberties implied by the unjust restrictions placed upon constituencies such as soldiers, small and medium-sized landowners, sectarians, Puritans, lawyers, and freemen generally. Yet none of these reformers concerned themselves with the rights of women, though they deified the rights of individual Englishmen to govern their own families and their own property against the arbitrary power of the king.[6] These Anglican and Tory women could justify their own political, religious, and feminist position by sharply asking why the likes of John Milton, concerned about English freedom, did not "cry up liberty to poor females slaves" in the home.[7] Such rhetoric obviously drew on this revolutionary ideological tradition even while attacking its basic lacunae. Concern for the rights of Englishmen had obscured, not included, those of English women.

If the ideas of seventeenth-century political and social reformers did not address themselves to the needs of women, feminists found two things which they could use as a positive basis for their thought. Their observations on the lives of English women in their century, their own and their sisters', gave direction to feminist concerns. Furthermore, in seventeenth-century rationalism, most clearly represented in Cartesian thought and scientific ideas, they found intellectual principles on which to build their ideas.

Although our knowledge of the lives of English women is limited, we have some information about the conditions that angered the feminists. Contemporary historical accounts agree that women were losing some of the social roles they traditionally had held. Social changes decreased upper-class women's useful functions on family estates and encouraged their becoming social ornaments and gadabouts. This wasteful and empty existence was a major target of feminist ire. The same basic process went on at other social levels. With the beginnings of professionalization in medicine and the decline of women's status within the guilds, women who were trained as medical practitioners, midwives, or skilled artisans found it more difficult to get a fair wage for their skill or to function as independent workers. Feminists who were midwives or teachers made clear the financial and social plight of this group of women.[8] Similarly, the growing specialization of agriculture in some regions lessened the woman's traditional role as a partner in the family enterprise. It was becoming more and more difficult, also, for women to receive a fair economic settlement upon marriage, especially at the highest social ranks, because of the larger numbers of suitable female partners for upper-class men. Feminists wrote much about the economic powerlessness of women in landholding families. Finally, women at all class levels were more poorly educated than their brothers, and their talents were seldom utilized to the fullest; the waste of women's intellectual talents was a central theme of feminist writings.

Only isolated facts about the lives of individual feminists remain, making it difficult to link their writings directly to what we know of the lives of seventeenth-century women. Yet their experiences as women with decreasing social power and, among the upper class, more leisure time, obviously encouraged them to raise basic issues about the general devaluation of women's usefulness during the late 1600s.

The development of rationalism as a complement to the use of faith in discovering truth provided the feminists with a significant method to analyze the relationships between the sexes. They spoke of reason in both general and specific Cartesian terms. Generally, they saw custom as an often irrational and unjust foundation for social relationships, though, like any number of seventeenth-century thinkers, they employed the term "right reason" loosely, as if it were a self-defined concept. When speaking of women, however, they were clear that custom, or any continuing action whose only justification was its historical precedence or longevity, was no guide. They would not accept the view that women's role in the family or society was justified because women had always held that position in England. Rather, they argued, women's role in the family and in society should be based on two premises: that God had created women as human beings with rational souls which he expected to be developed, and that men and women had equal rational abilities.

Seventeenth-century feminism expanded and deepened its feminist perspective over the course of the second half of the century. The earliest feminist writers—Newcastle, Makin, and Woolley—often wrote cautiously, and, in the case of the duchess, contradictorily. Later feminists, on the other hand, were more systematic and rigorous in their denunciation of women's subordinate role in society. Finally, the feminist poets, writing predominantly between 1700 and 1710, added an element less easily discernible in the earlier works—personal anger and frustration at the unlikelihood of change in either the attitudes of men or the lives of women.

The duchess of Newcastle was, in many ways, the most difficult to fathom of these feminists writing during the 1600s. Writing first, she often argued the most extreme case of women's familial and social subordination, and she just as often drew back from the implications of her feminism. The idea of sex division as a means of ordering society dominated her works; she constantly reminded her readers that she was a woman and that this meant she was poorly educated, had little chance for lasting fame, and was subject to an inferior status within marriage and society. She also stressed women's frustrations in rearing children for men's glory. Newcastle realized that women were not citizens, and she pointed with bitterness to the subordinate wifely relationship as the only significant political role open to women.

Yet her own childless marriage was a happy one. It was true that she failed to gain for her writings the acclaim that she desired so strongly. But if she lived under a masculine despotism, it was surely a mild one, coming from a husband who gave her constant encouragement in her intellectual pursuits and who accepted her ineptitude in the management of a household. Perhaps even more puzzling was the lack of any obvious intellectual influences leading her to an understanding of the importance of sexual division in structuring society. She was very much the theorist moving in new directions, with little guidance from either her contemporaries or past writings. She often faltered on the route to a feminist analysis, veering from blaming women for their incompetence or weakness to arguing that men falsely denied women's strength and purposely would "hide them in their houses or beds as in a grave." Often she seemed unable to make up her mind about the reasons for women's lack of intellectual success. But as a true pioneer in feminist thought, she often expressed far-ranging and insightful analyses of women's position within society. Her works highlight the possibilities of an individual woman's coming to a feminist understanding of society with little personal or intellectual encouragement other than her own shrewd observations.

Her contemporaries, Bathsua Makin and Hannah Woolley, focused more narrowly on questions of education. Woolley's educational concerns were of a practical kind, geared generally to the needs of housewives of divergent social ranks. She provided, along with a feminist analysis of women's position, practical advice on medical needs, children's education, social etiquette, and cooking. Her work was directed as well toward servants and governesses who would perform a portion of such wifely duties. Her own background as a servant and a teacher often led her to sharper and more earthy expressions than those employed by Bathsua Makin, who had served as governess to the daughters of Charles I. Makin wanted women to pursue advanced training in their secondary schools, comparable although not identical to what boys were receiving at grammar schools. She lamented and deplored the decline in the prominence of the "learned lady" of the Elizabethan court and wanted women of her generation and later to return to the serious intellectual endeavors of the former century. Her work on the education of gentlewomen was sometimes daring, but more often it was a conservative document arguing the benefits to men of educated companions. She encouraged wifely obedience, as did Woolley, and simply wanted the wife's role to include adequate educational preparation before marriage and an opportunity to use her mind after she wed.

Makin's work was published in 1673; the next significant feminist work did not appear until 1694, in the form of Mary Astell's *Serious*

Proposal to the Ladies. Astell continued the demand for quality education for women, even calling for the establishment of a women's college.
However, her major contribution to seventeenth-century feminist
thought was her systematic analysis of the reasons women lacked a
proper education, the kinds of bad decisions this led them to make in
terms of marriage, and the inequities that constricted a married woman's
intellectual and personal growth. She wrote works on both marriage and
education and revealed more clearly than had her predecessors how
women's lack of serious intellectual interests was integrally linked to the
kind of role they were expected to play as wives. An Anglican and Tory,
her conservative political and religious views sometimes hampered her
critique of women's place within the home and society generally, but she
clearly provided the broadest intellectual bases for women's need and
right to develop their minds and personal characters fully.

The Astell's friend, Elizabeth Elstob, was a scholar and a feminist whose
prefaces to her Anglo-Saxon translations lamented women's miserable
education and pushed for its improvement on lines similar to those of
Makin and Astell. Through her informal relationship with Oxford University, because of her brother's presence there, she was acutely aware of
what she missed as a female scholar excluded from England's universities.

The four feminist poets of the early eighteenth century—Winchilsea,
Chudleigh, Rowe, and Egerton—wrote personal and polemical verse
hitting at women's unfair treatment in the England of their day. They
seldom wrote poems to men, although Egerton and Rowe discussed the
enticements of heterosexual relationships. Winchilsea and Chudleigh, on
the other hand, spoke much about retreating from society and developing perfect, platonic friendships with other women. They actively argued
with those they deemed to be women's enemies—insensitive playwrights,
obtuse and arrogant scholars, and self-righteous and foolish clergy.
Rowe and Egerton throughout their poems either toyed with or agonized
over their relationships with men, but both rejected such relationships in
the end. All of these poets developed their views of men and women from
a basically feminist perspective. They continually revealed a high degree
of anger at both the personal and public treatment of women by men and
divided their literary efforts between outlining women's unjust oppression and suggesting their own solutions to this imbalance of sexual
power. Often the most impatient of the feminists of their time, these

poets revealed both feminist anger and a strong commitment to the interests of women.

These seventeenth-century feminists did not have a lasting impact on the lives of women in the following century or a direct influence on feminist writings in the future. Yet it is possible to measure their impact in a number of areas of late seventeenth-century and early eighteenth-century English society and culture. Women's periodicals were appearing in increasingly large numbers at the turn of the eighteenth century. From John Dunton's *Athenian Gazette* of the 1690s to Richard Steele's collection, *The Ladies Library*, in 1714 there were considerable numbers of publications aimed at the educated woman. Also, these learned females often revealed their interest in feminist topics through poems or letters to the editors submitted to the various publications. Further, although not built directly upon feminist principles, the charity schools of the 1690–1720 period took pride in educating poor girls along with their brothers.

The heroines of Restoration comedy sometimes expressed feminist ideas, and when these heroines did not speak directly in feminist language, they still displayed the independence of spirit that the feminists tried to instill in their sisters generally. There were too a number of male authors, including most significantly Daniel Defoe, who also developed ideas and plans with strong feminist overtones. Defoe's plan for a female academy was quite close to Mary Astell's serious proposal to her sex. William Walsh and Nahum Tate wrote tracts with strong prowoman sentiments, though with some gushy language and imagery that undercut their ideas.

This turn-of-the-century feminism was to fade when faced with eighteenth century values that embraced sentimentality and feeling rather than reason. Serious feminist thought did not mesh well with the more subtle and less confrontational advances made by heroines in the early eighteenth-century novels. Nor would the seventeenth-century feminists have approved the bluestockings' intermingling with the literati of their day on an accepted but clearly inferior level. The salon allowed intellectual women to display their talents during the early eighteenth century, but it did not encourage them to raise such indelicate issues as the exclusion of women from educational institutions or the basic oppressiveness of the husband-wife relationship in contemporary marriages. The isolated, somewhat embittered, but principled feminist of the late seventeenth century would have felt sorely out of place in the polite society of the literary and educated elite of eighteenth-century London. Her feminism was too much a product of the political questioning and rationalism of the 1600s to move forward into a more sentimental setting, and such thoughts were seldom publicly urged again until Wollstonecraft's writings near the end of the 1700s.

Seventeenth-century feminism, then, evolved out of the experiences of a group of women who were aware of the conditions of their sisters' lives and who realized that the vision of seventeenth-century reformers did not include women. Upon a rationalist base they built a new understanding of women as a group, intellectually equal to men but socially and politically separate from them. In this sense they were the earliest individuals to develop a theory of women as a sociological group, capable of, and in need of, fundamental change in their lives. If their influence was historically truncated, still their ideas retain continuing relevance.

NOTES

1. The term *sociological group* is not used in any technical sense here. It is used to indicate a connection between individuals—in this case women—that is based on social, political, and economic characteristics, rather than on biological or physical ones. Members of such a group view one's allegiance to the group as primary and identify one's interests with the interests of its other members. In the case of these seventeenth-century feminists, their primary interest and personal identity were tied to other members of their sex. They consistently analyzed social and political institutions from the perspective of their treatment of women and their impact on the lives of women.

2. The concept of an "upper servant" was developed in Mary Astell's *Serious Proposal to the Ladies*, published first in 1694. Lady Mary Chudleigh, another seventeenth-century feminist, echoed this judgment in a line from one of her verses: "Wife and Servant are the Same, but only differ in the Name," in *Poems on Several Occasions* (London: Printed by W. B. Lintott, 1703), p. 40.

3. For the most thorough account of the development of feminist ideas in seventeenth-century France see Carolyn Lougee, *Le Paradis des Femmes*. Lougee makes clear that feminism during the 1600s in France was a phenomenon separate from later feminist movements, and her definition of the term reveals these limitations. "The term 'feminism' is used to denote nothing other than the positive response to the question whether women should play a public role in French society. Designed merely as a shorthand expression for the defenses of women's participation in salons, it carries no other connotations than those

developed within this study." The author makes clear that women were expected to help socially mobile males as part of their duties within the salon. She states: "The salon played a central role in the process of social assimilation because within the salons ladies taught the social graces which covered the new rich with the 'parfum de l'aristocratie.' " Finally, the explicit nature of such efforts is made clear in the following: "Ladies made gentlemen, then, in an existential sense. This was the social mission of women in seventeenth-century France" (pp. 53–54).

4. Baconian efforts in seventeenth-century England, at least as they are primarily remembered, took the form of institutional reform and were therefore of little practical use for women living during that period. For a fuller discussion of the relationship between the scientific revolution and the growth of feminism during the seventeenth century see Ch. II.

5. Ch. II, on the intellectual background of seventeenth-century feminism, discusses the humanist views of women's education; Natalie Davis develops the concept of "women worthies" at some length.

6. Such an analysis of the development of Puritanism during the seventeenth century is presented in Michael Walzer's *Revolution of the Saints* (Cambridge, Mass.: Harvard University Press, 1965). He contends that the Puritan man's sense of worth inceased because of his membership in God's elect. This sense of group identity gave him an increased belief in his ability to confront the king as an individual whose stance had been validated by a higher authority. Thus his membership in the sainthood enhanced his stature in the political realm of seventeenth-century England. The feminists, as well, enhanced the value of the rational powers of an individual woman by grounding women's limited intellectual productivity in the social existence of all women and, thus, developed the argument that only through understanding women's group limitations could one appreciate their abilities as individuals.

7. The phrase appears in Mary Astell's *Serious Proposal*. See Ch. IV for elaboration.

8. Elizabeth Elstob, Hannah Woolley, and Bathsua Makin were all teachers or governesses, while Elizabeth Cellier and Jane Sharp were midwives.

CHAPTER I

"Barbarous Custom to Breed Women Low"
The Social Setting

Mid-seventeenth-century England was an exciting and challenging place for those unprecedented numbers of people gaining university and legal educations, for those forming new religious congregations, for those challenging traditional political relationships, and for those consolidating land or commercial holdings. Women were either totally excluded from such opportunities, or, in the case of religious efforts, were followers rather than leaders. Women's exclusion from such phenomena was, of course, the norm, and most women did not question men's right to alter public institutions without involving women in their efforts. Still, a number of society's patterns were being challenged—social inferiors did not always defer to the wishes of their superiors, subjects sometimes failed to obey their monarch, and those destined to be followers often forgot their place. Thus a precedent was established for women to question their status as well.

Women of the educated classes saw men of inferior social status gaining educations they could never receive. While the value of a sound education was widely touted, no woman was able to obtain advanced training. And for many men, training was socially rewarding. Many of the middling classes, after receiving their educations, were able to find positions in the expanding professions of grammar school instructor and minister.

These realities constituted a pattern of relative deprivation, of the kind sociologists see as the primary motive for protest movements, for middle- and upper-class women during the middle and late seventeenth century. Although women's lives were not worsening in absolute terms in the period, they were not improving at the same pace as those of the more favored members of society, men. Thus, women experienced a loss of status in relation to this more favored group at a time when questions of individual rights were in the fore. The perception of the unfairness of their particular lot led them to analyze and attack the distinction between the opportunities afforded themselves and those open to an increasingly large part of the male population. In this sense seventeenth-century English feminists fit closely the explanation later scholars have given of "why men rebel." This explanatory framework works for women too and helps to explain both the current interest in women's liberation and the feminism of women living in seventeenth-century England.[1] Yet providing the evidence for such a pattern during the seventeenth century is something of a challenge.

Seventeenth-century women can still be seen only obliquely through fragments of information about a few women, statistical generalizations about women living in particular locales, and analogous materials from women living in similar conditions throughout early modern Europe. What is lacking is that base of institutional documents—military, political, religious, educational, and economic—much more readily available for different segments of the male population. Women's work was seldom recorded in guild records, their education in academic rolls, or their market and social gatherings in town or club minutes. We are only beginning to create a portrait of their lives through isolated remarks in contemporary letters and diaries, or the eulogistic information in funeral sermons on women, and to gain some sense of the more general characteristics of women's life cycle and life expectancy from demographic materials.[2] But these scanty sources do reveal a growing division and, in some cases, an overt tension between the changes in the lives of men and women during the seventeenth century.

The gap in educational opportunities between men and women most angered the feminists. The educational opportunities were limited for women at both ends of the social scale. Lower-class women had few chances for any training which could provide them with the skills or contacts necessary for social mobility; upper-class women were excluded from those most important educational institutions, the universities and the Inns of Court, where upper-class men preserved their status and where middle-class men could advance. Education was linked to vocation; for the poorer students it was the vocation of minister or teacher, and for the wealthier it was the vocation of courtier or country gentleman. Further, the universities themselves were too closely connected to a religious vocation to make a place for women. The separation between teaching and ministering was not clear-cut, and university instruction remained securely linked to the priestly function. Although women such as Elizabeth Elstob were able to establish informal intellectual relationships with a number of Oxford scholars, it would simply have been unthinkable for them to have attended institutions of higher education as students.[3]

On the other hand, the educational opportunities for Englishmen were expanding in two different directions during the early and mid-seventeenth century. Vastly increased numbers of students, especially plebeians, were attending the universities during the 1620s and 1630s and, to a lesser extent, during the 1650s and 1660s. At the same time, those who established the Royal Society or argued for expanding education to the poor touted less traditional modes of scholarship. Educational reformers such as Samuel Hartlib and John Dury were combining the need for educational and religious change with arguments that only through establishing a "spiritual brotherhood" of educated men could one hope to reform the morals of English society generally.[4]

There was significant growth in numbers of university students during the first half of the seventeenth century. This growth took place both among poorer students, who were most often destined to find their future careers as ministers or as teachers in grammar schools, and among the children of the gentry, who were more apt to manage their own estates, become courtiers, or perhaps try their hand at the law, following a brief stay at the university. Many of these "gentlemen scholars" came to Oxford and Cambridge only to acquire a grounding in the classical curriculum and then dropped out before completing their degrees—the period from 1580 to 1640 featured a belief in the need for gentlemen to be tutored in the classics before they took up community and family duties.[5]

The pool of qualified applicants to the universities grew during the early seventeenth century because of the significant increase in the numbers of grammar schools (about 800 new grammar schools were established between 1480 and 1660) and the expanding practice by local ministers of preparing boys in the classics on a more informal basis. During the early seventeenth century, the sons of plebeians filled the need for growing numbers of ministers. Over 50 percent of the university student body came from plebeian origins during the 1570s and the 1630s, and further, these students came predominantly from quite modest homes. Two Cambridge college registers recorded fathers' occupations as being "husbandmen, clothworkers, tailors, drapers, glovers . . . etc.," and the universities made provisions for poor students by establishing 500 scholarships between 1560 and 1640. Funds were also available to a poor boy through support from a local gentleman or bishop, or through his performance of services for the wealthier students and the dons.[6]

These opportunities led to a tremendous growth in degrees awarded during this period; the numbers of students gaining first degrees grew sixfold between the 1520s and the 1620s, the period of fastest growth in Oxford's entire history, and advanced degrees increased proportionately.[7] Englishmen training to be the professionals, leaders, politicians, and landlords of the mid-seventeenth century gained university educations in unprecedented numbers. And many used this education as a means for social mobility, moving from backgrounds of artisan, small farmer, and shopkeeper to the lower ranks of the professions.[8]

Expanding male educational opportunities existed outside the universities as well. Puritan educational reformers wanted to establish new schools for poor boys and to set up informal networks among scholars to further social and religious change. Samuel Hartlib was perhaps the leading Puritan educational advocate who tried to reform the universities and to establish academies along Comenius's lines with equal emphasis on the empirical and spiritual. But even his close ties to John Pym were not enough to get parliamentary approval, and the movement resulted only in private tutoring or expanded scholarships. Yet the need for broader and better male education was strongly and widely urged.[9]

The largest growth in the numbers of men entering the universities and the greatest educational agitation occurred before the seventeenth-century feminists wrote. Yet the social results of these changes were clearest just at the time the duchess of Newcastle, Bathsua Makin, and Hannah Woolley were first writing about women's inadequate educations. Those men obviously benefiting from educational opportunities would have been the contemporaries of these early feminist writers—the university scholars, grammar school instructors, ministers, and other professionals who were using their talents in ways women could not, while incidentally often prescribing proper domestic spheres for women. Though feminists born after 1660 did not experience these patterns of change, they were equally or even more conscious of the central social truth they represented: universities were open to men who had less ability and were from lower social strata than many of the women who were systematically denied an advanced education.

Women concerned about their social and educational lot could hardly fail to notice that educational reforms, either proposed or implemented, had little to do with women's lives. Girls from families with sufficient income to provide some additional training were taught at home, boarded out in private homes, or sent to the increasing numbers of boarding schools that opened up during the seventeenth century. Their course of study was similar in each of these settings: reading, writing, household management, limited medical training, French, needlework, music, and dancing.[10]

Girls' greatest educational gains, unsurprisingly, given the sexual ideologies of the age, came at the lowest levels. Although the largest growth in charity schools awaited the eighteenth century, a number of schools were established to educate poor boys and girls during the sixteenth century and the first half of the seventeenth. The girls were taught mostly to sew and, unlike the boys, were seldom prepared for apprenticeships which could aid them in improving their social status. Rather they were destined to become servants or to hold "dead-end employment in some trade." At the few charity schools modeled on Christ's Hospital girls learned such trades as "pin-making, silk-weaving, and linen-weaving," and one of the major concerns of school authorities was that the girls' work should pay for their maintenance. At the Red Maids' school in Bristol the students were indentured to the mistress, who taught them reading and sewing and then sold their goods for her own profit. Although masters normally gained financially from the work of apprentices, the latter also gained from the arrangement by acquiring a skill which made them financially independent in later life. For the girls, commonly destined for servanthood, such was not the case. As one author noted, "it is easy to see why schools of this type often produced a system under which unpaid labour was shamefully exploited." [11]

Girls were also educated in the dame or parish school and learned the basic rudiments of the English language for a fee of three or four pence a week, which effectively excluded the children of the poorest members of society. There was little uniformity in the organization of these dame schools and the level of instruction varied greatly depending on the skill and training of the local teacher. Although boys and girls were both taught, for girls this was apt to be their last opportunity for formal education. Isolated grammar schools may have admitted a few female pupils, but such practice was far from the norm.[12]

How many girls' boarding schools existed is impossible to say. One contemporary observer noted "several large houses" in the Chelsea area. Hackney and Putney also had several such schools for girls, and they existed in Manchester, Oxford, Exeter, and Leeds as well. One of the better-known Hackney schools was administered by a Mrs. Salmon. Katherine Philips, who later became a poet of some reputation, was a pupil there after a relative had taught her basic skills. Mrs. Perwich's academy, following its establishment in 1643, educated 800 girls before its closing in 1660. The school specialized in all kinds of musical and dancing accomplishments, as well as excelling in the teaching of handicrafts. A Chelsea school, run originally by a Mr. Bannister and a Mr. Hart, taught its students embroidery and the technique of making wax models. After Josiah Priest became director of the school, he asked his friend Henry Purcell to write an opera for his pupils, and Purcell wrote his *Dido and Aeneas* for the occasion. These schools emphasized social arts and graces and paid little attention to more academic subjects, but their whole influence was perhaps not negative. At least it seems likely that groups of girls in such schools may have been touched with aesthetic or intellectual interests, learned that their aspirations and sense of frustration were shared, and moved into their larger social world again with some feminist awareness. These finishing schools, though, conflicted with Puritan values and declined with the Interregnum. It remains debatable, however, whether Puritan or royalist attitudes produced the most educational opportunities for girls. As one historian characterized them, Puritan values led to "the devout, stay-at-home housewife," while Restoration values encouraged "the elegant, accomplished woman of the world who might have a pretty wit but was often empty-headed." Seventeenth-century feminists decried the educational limitations on both sides.[13]

Distinctions in levels of literacy for men and women also reveal women's unequal educational preparation. One study contends a quite high literacy rate for men—approximately 30 percent for England as a whole and up to 60 percent for London—immediately before the English Revolution, but, of course, there is much less explicit information about women. Recently, however, some attention has been given to women's literacy. A summary of findings by the Cambridge Group for the Study of Population and Social Structure has noted striking differences between the abilities of men and women to read and write during the 1600s. Yet the figures for each sex are not comparable, for the existing records, whether they be marriage registers or depositions taken of witnesses to the ecclesiastical courts, fail to list the occupation or social rank of women. Therefore, although one can correlate men's social class with their literacy level, one cannot for women, who are lumped together as a group. Nonetheless, Table 1 documents the sharp divergence between male and female literacy rates.[14]

TABLE 1

ILLITERACY IN DIOCESE OF NORWICH, 1580–1700[15]

Occupation	Number Sampled	Percentage of Illiteracy
clergy/professional	332	0
gentry	450	2 ± 1
yeomen	944	35 ± 3
tradesmen/craftsmen	1838	44 ± 2
husbandmen	1198	79 ± 3
laborers	88	85 ± 7
all women	1024	89 ± 2

It is reasonable to assume that female witnesses to the ecclesiastical courts, like the group recorded in Table 1, would fall within the general class distribution of male witnesses. Thus, there is no reason to believe that the women were poorer than their male counterparts, but their total illiteracy level was higher than that of the lowest rank of male workers.

Such a distinction is generally substantiated by Norwich wills as well, in which women as a whole had a higher rate of illiteracy than any other single rank of men except laborers. Although the illiteracy rate for laborers was 12 percent higher than that for women in the sample of Norwich wills, the percentage of illiteracy for all men was 56 percent while it was 88 percent for all women.[16] This same discrepancy in the ability to write was also apparent for sixteenth- and early seventeenth-century Cambridgeshire.[17] There was an illiteracy rate of 70 percent for men in rural seventeenth-century England, "with the home counties and metropolitan areas somewhat better." For women, however, the figures were much higher. The highest female illiteracy rate, among those regions studied, was in East Anglia, where between 1580 and 1640 95 percent of the women were unable to sign their names, and even in London "between 1580 and 1640 ninety ± 3 percent could not sign." However, the late Stuart period saw a significant growth in the rates of female literacy, particularly in the cities. By the 1690s urban female illiteracy was reduced to 52 percent ± 6, "while it lingered around eighty percent in the provinces."[18]

A number of factors probably contributed to this growing literacy of women in London. The vastly increased demand for female servants during the second half of the century gave an opportunity for large numbers of lower-class girls to grow to maturity in literate households where they were more likely to learn to read than in their parents' homes. Further, the importance of Puritan values in mid-century London encouraged the spread of Bible-reading to larger segments of the urban population. It was normally the ambitious individual who traveled from distant parts of England to the capital, and such a person was most apt to acquire the skills necessary for advancement in society, such as literacy. Finally, the growth of charity schools and boarding schools during the second half of the seventeenth century encouraged a growing literacy among both lower- and middle-class girls.[19]

This growing literacy among London women during the later seventeenth century provided an enlarged audience for the feminist writings being published during the 1690s, and a sharpened awareness of the remaining discrepancy. This greater awareness of injustice suggests a major corollary of the relative-deprivation thesis: a sense of social anger commonly depends less on loss of status than on unfulfilled "rising expectations" created by modest or minor improvements. Such was the situation in women's education during the span of the 1600s.

Of course, in areas besides education, women's lives were also changing in complex ways that may have contributed to the development of feminist ideology. There were probable gains as well as losses, and both may have contributed to the new ideas. Women were most likely losing ground economically to men; they were probably losing status within the family; and, although their legal status did not worsen, they were omitted from the legal reforms proposed during the Interregnum. Yet it is difficult to be sure of women's relative decline in areas from which they were not completely excluded, as they were from higher education.[20]

Even though women were not directly a part of the isolated efforts toward agricultural specialization, the growth of joint stock companies and overseas trade, or the greater accumulation of wealth among certain groups during the second half of the century, presumably they were members of families that gained financially from these advances. Marriage was a union of two persons and each did not necessarily gain the same rewards from economic change. An expansion of liquid capital during the later seventeenth century was more apt to improve a husband's financial position at the expense of his wife's because he was given the right to manage both of their holdings during the marriage. Her interests were tied to a dowry or jointure, which she was desirous of preserving in case of his death. Thus her interests were not always served by venture capitalism. If her husband were successful in his adventures, and she gained equitably from this success, then her position was indeed enhanced. If, on the other hand, he was not successful she could lose those funds which would be her only protection should he die. She simply possessed less economic maneuverability than her husband and was less able to make up any losses through her own efforts. This often led seventeenth-century women, especially of the landholding classes, to hold economically conservative positions. To the degree that women shared in familial economic prosperity they probably gained leisure, which in some cases provided incentive to desiring more intellectual opportunity.[21]

In her important study, *Working Life of Women in the Seventeenth Century*, Alice Clark overstated the case for industrialization during the 1600s.[22] Agricultural modernization was still in its infancy, and, despite the growth of shipping and foreign trade especially to the American colonies, the basis of the economy was still overwhelmingly agricultural.[23] Yet in those areas where numbers of smallholders were decreasing, women's role within the rural economy also declined. Any increase in the numbers of mobile agricultural workers undercut women's ability to add to the family's income by growing vegetables or caring for livestock and selling their products in local markets. Wives and others also were hurt by the decline of women's position within the guilds. The exact timing and extent of the change varied with the trade or occupation under discussion. The one area, medicine, where women's professional position was most clearly undercut provided the most specific incentive to the feminist argument.[24]

Patriarchal authority was most likely increasing near the middle of the seventeenth century. There were demographic realities which encouraged such a development. The ability of gentlemen to marry beneath them without social penalty and thereby bring into the family a wealthy merchant's daughter, a flexibility that was denied to their sisters, who would have lost their gentle status by marrying down, gave men an advantage in establishing prenuptial agreements because it increased the pool of available partners. As a result fathers paid more in dowry to receive the same amount of jointure as the century progressed. Men were also encouraged to take their authority as husbands and fathers more seriously by a massive body of political theory and Puritan theology which argued that such authority was necessary for the efficient and just operation of society. Also, with the declining influence of the extended family and diminution of the importance of the needs and wishes of kin, the individual householder was more able to govern his family without outside interference. Seventeenth-century feminists pointed out that marriage, intended as a partnership between two people who were to respect each other, had become subverted so that the husband had come to rule the home, but whether they were describing a newly strengthened reality or a traditional pattern is less certain.[25]

During the second half of the seventeenth century women either remained single or married later than they had earlier, which also had some effect on the development of feminism. An analysis of 100 parish records reveals that the lowest average family size from 1547 to 1821— 4.00 persons per household—occurred during the second half of the seventeenth century and the first half of the eighteenth. Thus, either because of the greater migration of men to the new world, the especially skewed sex ratio of later seventeenth-century London, or the social custom that allowed men to marry below them more easily than women, large numbers of women married late or not at all during the period in which feminists wrote. Thus women as a group had more time to gain an education before marriage, and married women of the middle and upper classes had more time for their own interests.[26] It also seems probable that these demographic realities encouraged greater numbers of women, especially among the middle classes in London, to form friendships with each other. One such circle formed around Mary Astell, and other groups may have been encouraged to read and discuss feminist ideas as well.

Women's legal status did not deteriorate noticeably during the second half of the seventeenth century, unless the continual demise of the widow's dower rights as the century progressed can be counted as deterioration. But even in that matter, women may have gained from the replacement of dower rights by jointures. With jointures, they were able to guarantee themselves more than the dower third of their husband's estate following his death. Obviously, women's legal status was not enviable during any period of the seventeenth century. A single woman seldom had legal rights identical to those of a single man, and should she marry, her legal independence ended. The complicated structure of an essentially restrictive common-law tradition offset by a more liberal policy grounded in principles of equity makes any definitive statement impossible. Certainly in a period which saw an increase in proposals for legal reform, virtually no one questioned women's inferior legal status. The legal situation in many ways paralleled the educational one: agitation about laws, inequities, and failings was prominent, and feminists were aware that the reform efforts wholly neglected the major injustices women faced.[27]

In some way all these changes contributed to the social background of feminist thought. In some economic areas, most clearly the guilds of medicine, women lost ground and felt anger. Inasmuch as some of them benefited from greater familial wealth, it brought those women leisure to develop their skills, to form closer ties with other members of their sex, and to recognize more keenly the limitations placed on them by inferior social opportunities. Later and fewer marriages and smaller families had largely the same effect. Agitation for general legal and political rights created awareness among thoughtful women that such reforms neglected the grosser inequities toward women. And the continuing, and often increasing, differences between male and female educational opportunities became the area of most conscious anger for a group of women whose rational capacities were the equal of men's but who found little chance to hone those abilities in educational institutions or to use them in a socially purposeful way. On such social foundations was built this seventeenth-century feminist ideology.

NOTES

1. Jo Freeman, in her *Politics of Women's Liberation* (New York: McKay, 1975), has outlined a model of relative deprivation as an explanation for the attractiveness of feminism to middle-class American women. Although these women may not have experienced as difficult an existence as their working-class sisters, in absolute terms, yet they feel more deprived vis-à-vis middle-class business and professional men than do poorer women. The latter do not compare themselves so readily with middle-class men, not being in close contact with them, and the status gap between working-class men and women is not as great as that for middle-class men and women. Middle-class women are comparing themselves with the more successful members of American society, those who are most apt to be educated and to be capable of economic and social mobility (pp. 15–17). The concept of relative deprivation was developed most systematically in Ted R. Gurr's *Why Men Rebel* (Princeton, N.J.: Princeton University Press, 1970). Although historians of women have not often explicitly employed a relative-deprivation model when discussing the lives of women, a number have discussed the ways in which women have lost ground to men during particular periods of the past. Gerda Lerner's classic "The Lady and the Mill Girl" (*American Studies Journal* 10 [Spring 1969]: 5–15) postulates a loss of status for American women during the Jacksonian period vis-à-vis men who were better able to take advantage of the economically expanding and socially fluid nature of their age; more recently Joan Hoff Wilson argues in "The Illusion of Change: Women and the American Revolution" (in *The American Revolution: Explorations in the History of American Radicalism*, ed. Alfred F. Young [De Kalb: Northern Illinois University Press, 1976], pp. 385–445) that American women lost ground during the American Revolution because they were not a part of that economically and politically sophisticated segment of the population capable of taking advantage of the changes concurrent with the colonies' separation from the mother country. Finally, both my analysis of Renaissance women's increasingly inferior education in "Feminism and the Methodology of Women's History" (in *Liberating Women's History: Theoretical and Critical Essays*, ed. Berenice A. Carroll [Urbana: University of Illinois Press, 1976]) and Joan Kelly-Gadol's broader treatment of the subject in her essay "Did Women Have a Renaissance?" (in *Becoming Visible: A History of European Women*, ed. Renate Bridenthal and Claudia Koonz [Boston: Houghton Mifflin, 1977]) argue that the sixteenth century was a period of growing relative deprivation for upper- and middle-class European women.

2. A general history of seventeenth-century women has yet to be written, but a number of secondary works do provide some narrative of their lives, as well as useful discussions of available sources. Roger Thompson's *Women in Stuart England and America* offers a solid, factual, although less interpretively acceptable, account of the demographic, educational, economic, and legal aspects of the lives of seventeenth-century English women (in comparison to their colonial counterparts). A newer work, *The Women of England*, edited by S. Barbara

Kanner (Hamden, Conn.: Archon Books, 1979), includes a bibliographic essay by Rosemary Masek on the secondary works and primary sources available on women during the Tudor-Stuart period. An extensive list of published materials by or about seventeenth-century women will appear in an annotated bibliography Susan Cardinale and I have compiled, *Women and the Literature of the Seventeenth Century: An Annotated Bibliography Based on Wing's Short-Title Catalogue* (Westport, Conn.: Greenwood Press, forthcoming).

3. There are a number of treatments of the English universities in the seventeenth century. For an institutional history of Oxford and Cambridge during the first half of the seventeenth century see Mark H. Curtis, *Oxford and Cambridge in Transition, 1558–1642* (Oxford: Clarendon Press, 1959). A more recent work, *Oxford and Cambridge from the 14th to the Early 19th Century*, vol. 1 of *The University in Society*, ed. Lawrence Stone (Princeton, N.J.: Princeton University Press, 1974), includes Stone's "Size and Composition of the Oxford Student Body 1580–1909" (pp. 3–110) and "Cambridge University and the 'Country' 1560–1640" by Victor Morgan (pp. 183–247). Hugh Kearney's *Scholars and Gentlemen* (Ithaca, N.Y.: Cornell University Press, 1970) gives most attention to the interaction between the universities and the political and religious movements of the sixteenth and seventeenth centuries. Each of these works provides ample information on the connections between university education, the professions, and men's public activities.

4. There has been a great deal written on the links between education and social mobility during the late sixteenth and early seventeenth century. Joan Simon argued in "The Social Origins of Cambridge Students" (*Past and Present* 26 [Nov. 1963]: 58–67) that the evidence was too slight to conclude that there was a massive influx of the sons of the gentry into Cambridge colleges from 1603 to 1649 or a decline in those from lower-class families. Lawrence Stone in his important article "The Education Revolution in England, 1560–1640" (*Past and Present* 28 [July 1964]: 41–80) contended that the early seventeenth century saw an unprecedented growth in university students, especially those from plebeian backgrounds. See also David Cressy's more recent reassessment of the controversy over the degree of educational opportunity open to seventeenth-century Englishmen, "Educational Opportunity in Tudor and Stuart England" (*History of Education Quarterly* 16 [Fall 1976]: 301–20). Somewhat less attention has been paid to the educational reformers of the seventeenth century, but there has been substantial study in this area as well. Four of the more important works include Charles Webster's introduction to his source collection, *Samuel Hartlib and the Advancement of Learning* (Cambridge: Cambridge University Press, 1970); the section on educational reform in his larger study *The Great Instauration: Science, Medicine and Reform, 1626–1660* (New York: Holmes and Meier, 1975); John E. Sadler's *J. A. Comenius and the Concept of Universal Education* (London: George Allen and Unwin, 1966); and Robert F. Young, ed., *Comenius in England* (Oxford: Oxford University Press, 1932).

5. Stone, "Oxford Student Body"; see esp. pp. 3–11 for a discussion of the major growth in the numbers of students during the early seventeenth century,

the social backgrounds from which they came, and the value society placed upon university training during this period.

6. Ibid., pp. 12–23. Poor students who were unable to benefit from the increasing financial aid available during the period could survive at Oxford by being either battelers or servitors. The former were students who were taught at a college but who brought their own food rather than eating in the commons; servitors ate from the leftovers of the dining halls and made money doing errands for the wealthier students or university dons.

7. Ibid., pp. 18–21. Although the general trend outlined by Stone presents an accurate picture of the real growth among university students at this time, there are some qualifications to be made. First, as Mark Curtis noted, even though this was a period of the greatest production of B.D.'s, the absolute numbers were still small and had little relation to the increased numbers of lower-level clergy. This point is made in much greater detail in Rosemary O'Day's *The English Clergy: The Emergence and Consolidation of a Profession, 1558–1642* ([Leicester]: Leicester University Press, 1979). She argues that if one looks at the clergy itself, rather than focusing on university students, the numbers of lower-class men becoming clergymen—especially those who were able to rise through the church hierarchy—represent a small minority of the total. See especially her chapter on "The Career Structure of the Clergy" for a discussion of the limited social and professional mobility available for the lower ranks of clergymen. David Cressy's treatment of educational opportunities in the early seventeenth century also suggests that the increased numbers at universities may not have led to social mobility of the scope indicated by Stone. Educational theory, he contends, was seldom linked to goals of increasing opportunities for social mobility. David Cressy, "Educational Opportunity in Tudor and Stuart England," pp. 304–7.

8. Stone, "Oxford Student Body," pp. 24–30. It should be remembered that the increasing importance of the university during this period was not due only to the growth of the number of plebeians, but also to the great value placed upon a university education by gentry families. As Stone notes, at no other time "has the social elite been so determined to give their children a truly academic education before they went out into the world . . ." (p. 25).

9. Webster, Introduction to *Samuel Hartlib*, pp. 6–35. For a discussion of Comenius's views on the need for a general reformation of education both structurally and ideologically see Sadler's *J. A. Comenius and the Concept of Universal Education*, pp. 60–96, 164–209, 213–39. For the most succinct discussion of Parliament's reaction to Hartlib's proposals see Webster, *Samuel Hartlib*, pp. 25–38, 43–50. Webster presents a thorough integration of educational reform into the general intellectual currents of the mid-seventeenth century in *The Great Instauration*. Here he argues that the views and efforts of Hartlib's circle were more influential on the establishment of the Royal Society and the development of the dissenting academies than has heretofore been acknowledged. Many of the Puritans, who had been ejected from their academic posts with the Restoration, turned to nonconformist educational institutions to teach

and to further their goals of educational reform. These academies provided a refuge for the more practical and scientific studies favored by the reformers, and students had an advantage over those from Anglican homes "whose sons suffered the fate of exposure to the decaying scholastic tradition of the universities" (pp. 242–45). Webster concedes the small attention paid to women's education by the reformers, who, when speaking of women, state that "they were to be educated separately, and according to their different vocational requirements" (pp. 219–20).

10. Information about the education of girls in the seventeenth century is highly limited. There are few records of the boarding schools that existed for girls, and the records that do exist are mostly from literary sources. There is a more solid statistical basis for the study of poor girls in charity schools, at least for the numbers of schools and the ratio of male to female students. However slight the institutional records are for the education of men during the seventeenth century, they are considerably more ample than those available on women's education. Secondary works on the history of women's education in the seventeenth century include Josephine Kamm's *Hope Deferred: Girls' Education in English History* (London: Methuen and Co., 1965); Dorothy Gardiner's older work, *English Girlhood at School: A Study of Women's Education through Twelve Centuries* (Oxford: Oxford University Press, 1929); and slight attention is given to the subject in Phyllis Stock's recent general work, *Better than Rubies: A History of Women's Education* (New York: G. P. Putnam's Sons, 1978).

11. Kamm, *Hope Deferred*, pp. 63–66. For a more thorough evaluation of the education of girls in early eighteenth-century charity schools, see my conclusion.

12 Ibid., p. 66.

13. Ibid., pp. 69–73; Gardiner, *English Girlhood*, pp. 206–46.

14. Lawrence Stone's "Literacy and Education in England, 1640–1900" (*Past and Present* 42 [Feb. 1969]: 69–139) gives little attention to the literacy of women; his graphs are devoted almost entirely to the literacy rates of bridegrooms or adult males, depending upon the sources of his evidence. Also R. S. Schofield's "The Measurement of Literacy in Pre-industrial England" (in *Literacy in Traditional Societies*, ed. Jack Goody [Cambridge: Cambridge University Press, 1968]) gives little attention to women's level of literacy. For more information on female literacy consult David Cressy, "Literacy in Seventeenth-Century England: More Evidence," *Journal of Interdisciplinary History* 8 (Summer 1977): 141–50.

15. Cressy, "Literacy," p. 145.

16. Ibid., p. 146.

17. Margaret Spufford, "The Schooling of the Peasantry in Cambridgeshire, 1575–1700," in *Land, Church and People*, ed. Joan Thirsk (Reading: Museum of English Rural Life, 1970), pp. 112–47. The village schools were established to teach boys and adolescents to write, read, and cast accounts, according to one contemporary. The teachers for the schools were particularly well trained, with nearly two-thirds of those licensed to teach being university

graduates. It is particularly telling that girls were excluded when one realizes the social sweep of the schools. For instance, in 1593 in the village of Willingham residents who subscribed toward the establishment of a town school gave very small amounts of money, but many, including cottagers and landless laborers as well as yeomen, gave. Only five of the subscribers gave over 2£; the total amount for 102 donors was 102£ 7s 8d (pp. 127–32).

    18. Cressy, "Literacy," pp. 146–47.

    19. Social-mobility studies for seventeenth-century England (as elsewhere) have concentrated on the geographic movements and changes in the career patterns of males. It is possible, however, to utilize the studies of seventeenth-century London to determine the high percentage of servants in wealthier parishes, to note the large percentage of women among urban servants, and thus to determine the growing numbers of women moving into London after 1650 and taking on the duties of urban servants. For the importance of London during this period see E. A. Wrigley's classic article "A Simple Model of London's Importance in Changing English Society and Economy, 1650–1750," *Past and Present* 37 (July 1967): 44–70. For an analysis of the role of urban servant as a means of social mobility for women see Theresa M. McBride, *The Domestic Revolution: The Modernization of Household Service in England and France, 1820–1920* (New York: Holmes and Meier, 1976). For discussions of the Puritans' emphasis on the growth of literacy see Richard Schlatter's *Social Ideas of Religious Leaders* (1940; reprint ed., New York: Octagon Books, 1943); L. L. Schucking's *Puritan Family* (New York: Schocken Books, 1969); and William Haller's *Rise of Puritanism, 1570–1640* (New York: Columbia University Press, 1938).

    20. It is difficult to discover any discernible trend in women's economic status during the seventeenth century. The major problem lies in the economic and family histories that discuss economic change, but do not link it to the lives of women. Women are discussed almost exclusively as family members, and most often in their role as childbearers. Obviously, we have most information about women's demographic characteristics, but too great a focus on this topic obscures their independent economic functions. In works dealing theoretically with economic change and family relationships we do have some clues about the connection between women's role in the home and their general position within society, but such discussions are seldom placed into a dynamic framework. For instance, Jack Goody's "Inheritance, Property and Women: Some Comparative Considerations" (in *Family and Inheritance: Rural Society in Western Europe*, ed. Jack Goody et al. [New York: Cambridge University Press, 1976]) treats women's status as essentially static, and rather compares the inheritance pattern of European women to that of women in other geographic regions. In the same volume, essays by Joan Thirsk and Margaret Spufford include useful information about the position of daughters and younger sons relative to that of eldest sons on questions of inheritance during the seventeenth century, but they limit their discussions about change in inheritance policies to issues other than women's position. See Margaret Spufford, "Peasant Inheritance Customs and Land Distribution in Cambridgeshire from the Sixteenth to the Eighteenth Centuries," in

Family and Inheritance, pp. 156–77; and Joan Thirsk, "The European Debate on Customs of Inheritance, 1500–1700," in ibid., pp. 177–91. Although Thirsk's interest is primarily the relative positions of the eldest and younger sons, she does make clear that seventeenth-century Puritanism did support the traditional rule of primogeniture in inheritance. A work such as David Levine's *Family Formation in an Age of Nascent Capitalism* (New York: Academic Press, 1977) is more useful, particularly in his connection between a decline in the woolen industry, especially around Colyton, which led to women's later marriage and their movement to a more independent economic occupation, with the growth of the lacemaking industry. This is, unfortunately, not a well-developed point in his work (pp. 134–38).

21. Although Alice Clark includes a chapter on female entrepreneurs, and isolated women are noted in economic histories of England, there is no systematic or recent treatment of the economic history of women. There is no comparable work, either, on women's contribution to the family economy like, for instance, Olwen Hufton's "Women and the Family Economy in Eighteenth-Century France" (*French Historical Studies* 9 [Spring 1975]: 1–22). Louise Tilley and Joan Scott, although focusing on a later period, also discuss at some length the importance of women to the family economy (*Women, Work, and Family* [New York: Holt, Rinehart and Winston, 1978], pp. 31–60). Recently, there has been opposition to overvaluing such a role by Mary Beth Norton in her introduction to *Women of America* (New York: Houghton, Mifflin, 1978).

22. Alice Clark, *Working Life of Women*. Clark argues a general loss of economic status both among upper- and lower-class women and within agriculture, the professions, and the skilled trades. She does support these contentions with isolated examples such as the Barber Surgeons of Salisbury's attempt in 1614 to prevent women from exercising their trade (pp. 259–560) and the severe difficulties experienced by unemployed female laborers who were forced to rely upon local poor-law authorities (pp. 66–73). She also presents a history of women's loss of status within the guild structure, contending that, with the decline of guild control over a particular trade and with fewer numbers of men being able to reach the status of master, the wife was not able to continue in the partnerlike arrangement she had had as wife of the master. The major faults with Clark's work, although they are far from invalidating her thesis, are her exaggeration of the degree of industrialization in seventeenth-century England and her failure to distinguish the different degrees of change among the various regions of England.

23. The general outline of economic change during the seventeenth century can be found in works such as Ralph Davis's *The Rise of the Atlantic Economies* (Ithaca, N.Y.: Cornell University Press, 1973) and in Sybil M. Jack's introduction to her source collection, *Trade and Industry in Tudor and Stuart England* (London: George Allen and Unwin, 1977). Davis notes that important economic changes coincided with the large growth in population during the sixteenth century and the early part of the seventeenth century. Such changes altered commercial relationships in ways that fundamentally affected the working life of

women. Davis summarizes them as follows: "Urbanization and rural specialization brought an increasing part of production into market transactions; greater distances and more complicated trading organization made necessary a proliferation of middlemen between purchasers and ultimate consumers" (p. 98). His discussion of women, however, is limited to their late age at marriage in western Europe (p. 91). Jack's discussion of development and change among seventeenth-century industries stresses, primarily, their primitive nature. She notes the small amount of coal available for industrial production, and that, although the greatest technological change took place in the iron industry, still production continued to be quite limited (pp. 66–79). Her analysis of the cloth industry tells us somewhat more about what was happening to women's work in the seventeenth century. The introduction of the "new draperies" after the 1620s was a retrogressive development "and labour intensive, since the worsted yarn they used had to be spun on a spindle and distaff" rather than a spinning wheel. It did mean that more people could be hired in the woolen industry, but at low-paid, traditional tasks. Other positions within the cloth trade—such as stocking knitting—may have employed as many as 90,000 to 110,000 people, most of whom were women (pp. 101–5). Thus women were not among those gaining commercially from changes in the woolen trade, and their position was seldom improved through innovations such as the production of "new draperies."

24. A number of works trace economic changes in particular areas during the seventeenth century. Ralph Davis in his *Rise of the English Shipping Industry* (London: Macmillan and Co., 1962) outlines a major growth in English trade and shipbuilding from 1560 to 1689, with only short-term declines during periods of recession or war (pp. 1–21). This trade was tied to the growth of London both as the center for the importation and exportation of goods and as a growing national market for internal production (pp. 16–18). In a discussion of the marketing of wool in *The Wool Trade in Tudor and Stuart England* (London: Macmillan and Co., 1962), P. J. Bowden points to the central importance of credit as the basis for the relationship among growers, manufacturers, and middlemen and argues that these relationships became more complex with the seventeenth century (pp. 95–106). He does not include women in his account, and one must extrapolate from his description of the changes in the sources of wool thread throughout the seventeenth century some understanding of what was happening to women. He notes that both the London and the Essex wool industries were drawing their supplies from larger and larger areas, and thus merchants were shipping wool further distances. Just what effect such developments had on female spinners scattered throughout the wool-producing regions is less clear (pp. 64–72). Finally, those works which discuss change within agriculture provide additional hints at change in women's traditional work patterns during the seventeenth century. Margaret Spufford outlines the disappearance of the small landowner in Cambridgeshire during the seventeenth century in *Contrasting Communities: English Villagers in the Sixteenth and Seventeenth Centuries* (New York: Cambridge University Press, 1974) and she explicitly notes the custom of either providing the widow a life interest in the

holding or at least providing her space within the home of one of her children until her death. Such provision, of course, became more problematic; during "the first thirty years of the seventeenth century there was a noticeable diminution in the number of customary tenants . . . and a corresponding increase in the size of the larger holdings, and in the number of cottagers" (p.118). In "Seventeenth-Century Agriculture and Social Change" (in *Land, Church and People*, ed. Joan Thirsk [Reading: Museum of English Rural Life, 1970]), Joan Thirsk outlines the general decline of the smallholder in areas of good arable land, and the enclosure of lands in grazing areas where wool production predominated. "The decline of small landowners in the seventeenth century, then, was a feature of specialized arable regions, and also of vale lands newly enclosed for pasture, not . . . of traditional pasture-farming districts. The smaller farmer was being driven out by a combination of factors, notably the technical economies possible in large-scale cereal production, or in conversions to pasture, sluggish grain prices, and the high cost and quantity of labour in corn growing" (p. 157). This essay outlines most thoroughly the link between changes in agricultural production and the economic and social conditions of particular regions. Although the author does not focus on questions of women's status, she does make clear that the seventeenth century was a difficult time for the small landholder. In summary, there is evidence that the traditional economy of the small landowner in which women played such an important role was declining with the seventeenth century; however, it is not until the eighteenth century that one can pinpoint anything like an agricultural revolution in England, and, because most modern authors ignore women's economic functions, we can only surmise the negative impact such changes had on their lives. See Ch. III for the link between midwifery and feminism.

25. Stone, *Family, Sex and Marriage*, pp. 151–218. For a succinct discussion of the demographic realities for seventeenth-century women see Roger Thompson's chapter on the sex ratio for Stuart England in *Women in Stuart England and America*, pp. 21–59. The classic presentation of European women's late marriages and the high percentage of spinsters is by J. Hajnal in his "European Marriage Patterns in Perspective: The Uniqueness of the European Pattern," in *Population in History*, ed. D. V. Glass and D. E. C. Eversley (Chicago: Aldine, 1965), pp. 101–10. A number of studies have pointed out, as well, a particularly late marriage age for women during the second half of the seventeenth century. E. A. Wrigley in "Family Limitation in Pre-Industrial England" (*Economic History Review*, 2d ser. 19 [1966]: 82–107) contends both late marriages and small families for women in the village of Colyton from 1647 to 1710. Peter Laslett, in "Mean Household Size in England since the Sixteenth Century" (in *Household and Family Size in Past Time*, ed. Peter Laslett and Richard Wall [Cambridge: Cambridge University Press, 1972], pp. 125–58), notes that for the 100 parishes analyzed for this study household size was at its lowest point for the period 1650–1749, dropping to only about 4.00 persons per household. Katherine Gaskin, in "Age at First Marriage in Europe before 1850: A Survey of Family Reconstitution Data" (*Journal of Family History* 2 [1978]: 23–36), points out an increase of about one year in the mean ages of marriage for

women during the last half of the seventeenth century and the first portion of the eighteenth century. Her seventeenth-century figures come mostly from English materials (pp. 23–26). Peter Laslett's *Family Life and Illicit Love in Earlier Generations* (New York: Cambridge University Press, 1977) builds upon the materials gathered in his earlier work on the size of households. Besides updating the collection of data by the Cambridge group, he includes more comparative materials (especially from pre-industrial France and Japan), but continues to lament the lack of exact data necessary for family reconstitution for English villages and maintains that newly collected evidence does not alter his earlier vision of the size or nature of English families during the modern period.

26. Peter Laslett, "Mean Household Size in England," pp. 125–58. For a discussion of circles of female friends around Mary Astell and Katherine Philips see Chs. IV and V. For a recent discussion of Puritan attitudes toward marriage see Kathleen M. Davies, " 'The Sacred Condition of Equality'—How Original Were Puritan Doctrines on Marriage?" *Social History* 5 (May 1977): 563–80. A number of works have dealt with the question of women's power within the household and the way in which it is affected by the influence of outside kin. For this discussion consult Stanley Chojnack, "Patrician Women in Early Renaissance Venice," *Studies in the Renaissance* 21 (1974): 176–203; David Herlihy, *The Renaissance Family in Italy* (St. Louis: Forum Press, 1972); and Diane Owen Hughes, "Urban Growth and Family Structure in Medieval Genoa," *Past and Present* 66 (Feb. 1975): 3–28. While Chojnack and Herlihy stress the importance of women in elite families, Hughes argues that the extended kin structure did not increase women's power and that, in reality, they had a more equal role in the nuclear-based artisan families of Genoa.

27. For a general discussion of women's legal status see Lenore Marie Glanz, "The Legal Position of English Women under the Early Stuart Kings and the Interregnum, 1603–1660" (Ph.D. dissertation, Loyola University of Chicago, 1973). For an analysis of seventeenth-century legal reform see Donald Veall, *The Popular Movement for Law Reform, 1640–1660* (Oxford: At the Clarendon Press, 1970).

CHAPTER II

"Women Yet May Be Informed with Few Words"

The Intellectual Background

The seventeenth-century feminists developed their ideas in the wake of the swirling intellectual and social currents of the postmedieval world. Renaissance England supplied a new concern and a welter of new ideas about education, some of which touched peripherally on women's training. Revolutionary England, political and religious, probed a broad range of social issues, which focused on rare occasions on questions relative to women's status. Yet feminists saw that the ideas raised in these movements were not only very tangentially tied to women but also encased in an acceptance of the traditional female social sphere and familial subordination that made them, even in their more generous forms, as much hindrance as help to the new position feminists were developing. However, in the new currents of scientific and especially rationalist inquiry, feminists found justifications for raising the issues that concerned them most and structures for asserting both women's innate equality and the justice of equal social and especially educational opportunity for their sex.

I

Renaissance England, the common account runs when it considers women as a group at all, was marked by a flowering of female scholarship and much enthusiasm for the better education of women. This stance needs review.[1]

The case for women's scholarly advances during the Renaissance rests on the achievements of no more than fifteen learned English women ranging from royal figures like Frances Brandon, Queen Elizabeth, and Queen Mary to daughters of aristocrats with a scholarly bent such as those of Sir Thomas More, Protector Somerset, or Sir Anthony Cooke.[2] The case for humanist enthusiasm for women's education rests on a group of writings, including those by Juan Vives, Sir Thomas Elyot, Roger Ascham, and Richard Hyrde, as well as Sir Thomas More's private comments on the intellectual training of his daughters. On the issue of educational goals, however, the humanist writings themselves circumscribed better opportunities for women to learn. The Renaissance was a period in which educational and public service opportunities were opening for men but remained closed to women.

Certainly humanist educational interests focused on male scholarly accomplishment much more than on female. The early and mid-sixteenth century was a period of substantial growth among grammar schools and at the universities. Humanists, particularly within the court, were endowing new colleges at Oxford and Cambridge, and local supporters of the "new learning" were setting up schools where boys could prepare themselves for the rising academic standards of the universities and eventually for the court bureaucracies. There was no concern for such institutional improvements for women, and this neglect insured that the gap between men's and women's educational chances steadily widened.[3]

A primary reason for this discrepancy was that humanist education was in large part pragmatic, concerned that intellectual training was to be related to social role. According to Douglas Bush's often echoed description of humanism: "All the English humanists, like the majority of continental ones . . . wished to produce citizens and statesmen, not scholars." The problem for women, of course, was that there was no logical end for their humanist training. They could not pursue goals of civic humanism because they could not hold public office or professional positions within either the university or the church. Latin and Greek, or knowledge of the ancient authors, did not prepare women for housewifely duties, their accepted sphere, and therefore only exceptional women—destined to hold princely office—needed such training. The strongest humanist educational emphasis was that training was to be related to social action, and since men's and women's spheres of activity sharply diverged, so should their learning.[4]

The purpose of education was to train men and women to be appropriately different from one another, not to present them with a body of knowledge the understanding of which would make them socially or intellectually equal. Two works in particular were crucial in preparing sixteenth-century men of the gentle classes for their future roles. They also made clear the social pragmatism of men's education. Castiglione's *Courtier* (1528) and Sir Thomas Elyot's *The Governour* (1531) emphasized that the complete gentleman would be "accomplished rather than learned" and be interested especially in those areas of politics and ethics connected with his future social duties and obligations. A landowner was educated to be a well-rounded gentleman skilled enough to carry out his tasks at court, in daily commerce, and at home. This theoretical union of the scholar and gentleman, to be fostered by attendance at universities and used in professional governmental service, perpetuated women's exclusion from any advanced training in sixteenth-century England.[5]

Humanist scholars believed that women's education had to be quite different because it, too, was to be linked to their vocation. Women's social function as wives and mothers, along with differences in physical and mental capacity, dictated an education that would provide them with chaste thoughts and household skills. Chastity was stressed as the essential quality for women, an emphasis that made even the staunchest defenders of a woman's potential recommend limits on her reading. Educational arguments occurred not over the general worthiness of the materials but over whether a particular work properly prepared women for a domestic vocation.[6]

Some of the limitations on women's thought in the Elizabethan era are suggested by the fact that no woman wrote significantly about women's proper role, that the job of discussing what females should do and learn was left to men. By far the most influential tract on women's education in the sixteenth century, Juan Luis Vives's *Instruction of a Christian Woman*, reflects well this general weakness. Following its publication in 1523, it underwent more than forty editions and translations before 1600.[7] Despite some disagreement, Vives's work was the representative view on the topic, and the one that prevailed.

Vives discussed the proper training for women most influentially in his *Instruction*, in the *Plan for Studies* (intended for the use of the Princess Mary, daughter of Henry VIII and Catherine of Aragon) and, most extensively, in a chapter of his *De Officio Marti* or *The Duty of*

Husbands. Two interrelated themes predominate in those works, the primacy of chastity for women and the importance of a woman's domestic vocation in defining her education. A chaste and modest woman, Vives contended, ensured the integrity of the family and provided a moral guide for the children in her charge. This social role demanded education very different from that of men: "Moreover, though the precepts for men be innumerable: women yet may be informed with few words. For men must be occupied both at home and abroad, both in their own matters and for the common weal. Therefore, it cannot be declared in few books, but in many and long, how they shall handle themselves, in so many and divers things. As for a woman, she hath no charge to see to, but her honesty and chastity. Wherefore when she is informed of that she is sufficiently appointed" (p. 34).

Given such basic notions it was more peculiar that Vives's ideas should have so dominated sixteenth-century discussion of women's proper education than that he gave so little attention to the subject. He organized his *Instruction of a Christian Woman* around the periods of a woman's life—maid, wife, and widow—for each of which he prescribed proper dress, behavior toward family members and friends, and proper moral and social habits. Of some 300 pages, 9 were devoted to formal educational concerns such as "What books to be read and what not." [8] Offering little more than a lengthy homily on the need for chastity and obedience in women, Vives emphasized his moral framework even when discussing scholastic pursuits. For the education of the maid, he advised that "when she is of an age able to learn anything, let her begin with that which pertaineth unto the ornament of her soul, and the keeping and ordering of an house" (p. 43).

Because the formation of character was the primary goal of a woman's education, the Scriptures and moral lessons were to be the primary reading matter, and intellectual content mattered little. She was to read the patristic authors, Christian poets, and selected ancient authors, under the guidance of men to ensure her proper understanding of the material (p. 62). Under no circumstances were women to teach. "A woman is a frail thing, and of weak discretion, and that may lightly be deceived, which thing our first mother Eve sheweth, whom the Devil caught with a light argument." Easily deceived herself, a woman must not be allowed to "bring others into the same error" (p. 56).

Vives, of course, spent more time on domestic than on scholarly education for women, though with some apologies that he would include such lowly matters. Yet if such things were unsuitable to male thought, they were important to any woman "though she be a princess or a Queen." He was especially enthusiastic about training in flax and wool weaving, "two crafts yet left of that old innocent world, both profitable and keepers of temperance." His concluding questions were obviously rhetorical: "For what can she do better, or ought to do rather, what time she hath rid her business in her house? Should she talk with men or other women? And what shall she talk of? Shall she never hold her peace? Or shall she sit and muse?" Eve had best spin, since her thought was so "unstable walking and wandering out from home" (p. 19).

Vives presented more positive attitudes toward education for women in his *Duty of Husbands*, intended for male readers. Here he argued for the advantages of an educated wife and defended women's abilities much more freely than in his writings addressed to women: "The woman, even as man, is a reasonable creature and hath a flexible wit both to good and evil, the which with use and counsel may be altered and turned. And although there be some evil and lewd women, yet that doth no more prove the malice of their nature than of men . . . Shall the woman, then, be excluded from the knowledge of all that is good, and the more ignorant she is counted better?" (pp. 197–99). Christian principles also urged that women "ought and would be instructed and taught, as we men be." Yet even here Vives was concerned more with defining a woman's education negatively rather than positively. She was to be prevented from reading any "superstitious" works, from "meddling with those curious and deep questions of divinity, the which thing beseemeth not a woman," and from studying those male subjects "grammar, logic, histories, the rule of governance of the commonwealth, and the art mathematical" (pp. 201–5).[9]

Finally, a woman was not to equal her husband in learning because he, as the ruler of the home, should excel in judgment over the other members of the family as did the monarch over the common people. The contention that Vives questioned the medieval assumption of the existence of a close relationship between female piety and ignorance is true only in a very limited way. To Vives, absolute ignorance was not good, but women's education should not go beyond basic literacy and homilies (pp. 21–22, 28).[10]

English humanists who wrote on women's education accepted

Vives's general argument but interpreted it somewhat more liberally. Richard Hyrde, who first translated Vives's work into English in 1529, attested in his preface to the great admiration in which both he and Sir Thomas More held the work. Though Vives's work was highly regarded in More's circle, More and Hyrde differed from him, especially in tone. They also spoke of the primacy of moral teachings and domestic duties, but their support of women's education was more positive. Quite simply, they apparently had faith in women's potential and did not favor their education merely to prevent them from doing evil.[11]

Hyrde took issue with those who would malign female character. If men would but "consider the matter equally" they would see that "women be not only of no less constancy and discretion than men, but also more steadfast and sure to trust unto than they." [12] Hyrde's agreement with Vives as to the substance of women's role created some tension in his thought, causing him to oscillate between the more negative arguments for training women and the more positive ones. Sometimes he supported Vives's argument for women's learning as a time-consuming device, but he was genuinely excited over Margaret Roper's work and often spoke glowingly of women's intellectual potential. Hyrde's ambivalence was revealed clearly in a strong defense of women's education connected to an equally strong defense of Vives's *Instruction*. He asked rhetorically, "for what is more fruitful than the good education and order of women, the one half of all mankind?" Also, the female half of humanity, because of their maternal role, had the most important influence "concerning the life to come." Yet, to encourage their education, Hyrde recommended Vives's ideas: "And surely for the planting and nursing of good virtues in every kind of woman, virgins, wives and widows, I verily believe there was never any treatise made, either furnished with more goodly counsels, or set out with more effectual reasons, or garnished with more substantial authorities, or stored more plenteously of convenient examples, not all these things to her more goodly treated and handled than Master Vives hath done in his book." [13]

If Hyrde exuded a greater enthusiasm for educating women than Vives, so did his "singular good master and bringer up," Thomas More. Although More was concerned explicitly with the moral substance of his daughters' education, this emphasis seemingly originated in a general sense of the importance of morality, rather than in a commitment to restrictions on the lives of women. "Though I prefer learning joined with virtue to all the treasures of kings," he wrote, "yet renown for learning when it is not united with a good life, is nothing else than manifest and notorious infamy; this would be particularly the case in a woman." [14]

His views on women's education were clear in the special instructions for his daughters contained in a letter to their tutor, William Gonell. After terming education for women "a new thing and a reproach to the indolence of men," he voiced his belief that should a woman "add to eminent virtue even a moderate knowledge of letters, I think she will have more real profit than if she had obtained the riches of Croesus and the beauty of Helen." [15] The two qualities he wanted stressed in the education of his children (three daughters and one son) were virtue and caution against pride. He suggested that his daughter Margaret's "high-minded disposition" should not be thwarted, but he did not want her to become prideful.

He then returned to the question of different abilities between the sexes and appeared to accept, with a touch of ambiguity, the equality of women's education and talent.

> Nor do I think that the harvest will be affected whether it is a man or a woman who sows the field, they both have the same human nature, and the power of reason differentiates them from the beasts; both, therefore, are equally suited for those studies by which reason is cultivated, and is productive like a ploughed field on which the seed of good lessons has been sown. If it be true that the soil of woman's brain be bad, and more likely to bear bracken than corn (and on this account many keep women from study), I think, on the contrary, that on the same grounds a woman's wit is to be cultivated all the more diligently, so that nature's defect may be redressed by industry.[16]

He instructed Gonell to teach the Church Fathers so that from them his daughters could learn the purpose of their studies in an educational hierarchy, embracing "virtue in the first place, learning in the second and their studies to esteem most whatever may teach them piety towards God, charity to all, and Christian humility in themselves." [17]

More prescribed these educational values for all, not merely women, and the letters he wrote to his daughters reinforced his support of their studies. There was a large element of the proud father in them, but within the expressions of lighthearted humor they showed earnest concern over, and encouragement of, his children's progress. He could joke easily with his daughters about the alleged infirmities of their sex, in a manner it would be difficult to imagine from a man such as Vives: "And how can you want matter of writing unto me, who am delighted to hear either of your studies, or of your play: whom you may even then please exceedingly, when having nothing to write of, you write largely as you can of that nothing, than which nothing is more easy for you to do, especially being women, and therefore prattlers by nature, and amongst whom daily a great story ariseth of nothing." [18] In a letter to Margaret before the birth of her child, More made clear his pride in her accomplishments. He'd prefer a grandson, but if it were a girl he hoped she would "recompence him by being an imitation of her mother's learning and virtues." He concluded, "such a wench I should prefer before three boys." [19]

More did not question a domestic vocation or wifely obedience for women and praised Margaret for her modesty in wishing to share her learning only with her father and husband. Yet these admonitions More applied much less restrictively than Vives. More's writings showed that Vives's general argument could be given a liberal twist, but actually his more humane educational program for his daughters conflicted in no fundamental way with the values of Vives.

Richard Mulcaster's 1581 educational treatise, *Positions . . . Necessarie for the Training up of Children*, made it clear that a limited vision such as Vives's persisted over the century. Mulcaster gave only cursory attention to women's education, and in that little he stressed how women's role in life made learning of little import. Since men governed, males could rightly claim "learning as first framed for their use and most properly belonging to them." Only "out of courtesy and kindness" need women be educated, despite women's rational capacity. Yet girls' aptness at learning suggested God had not intended to leave their minds idle, and "the custom of this country" allowed female learning, though not in public grammar schools or universities.[20]

Like Vives, he argued for the close relationship between a woman's family duties and her education, but did speak of giving a girl "some technical training" if she "must prepare for a definite calling." Despite some more generous emphases, Mulcaster followed in Vives's footsteps in stressing the permissibility of only "learning within certain limits, having regard to the difference in their vocation." Men's training was to be "without restriction either as regards subject-matter or method" because men's work was "so general," but women's functions were limited, "and so must their education be also." [21] The prevalent six-teenth-century view was that while some education for women was probably good, it had to be strictly limited to accord properly with women's sphere of social action.

The sixteenth century significantly opened public debate on women's education, but within a very confined sphere. Those who first discussed female training opposed advanced professional or university training for women. Sixteenth-century views of appropriate female education could never have logically gotten women out of the home and into scholarly pursuits, for that was not their intent. It was precisely the opposite.

The limitations on women stressed in educational tracts were equal-ly clear in two mid-century writings: Sir Thomas Elyot's *The Defence of Good Women* and John Aylmer's *An Harborow for faithful and trewe Subjects*. Both writers wrote with more political than social purpose. Elyot's 1545 work was a disguised defense of Queen Catherine in a period when it was dangerous to defend her openly, and Aylmer's was an attack on John Knox's criticism of female rulers. Both men argued within the general framework of women's special character, and each presented his case defensively, rather than on the basis of sexual equality. In Elyot's dialogue, traditional plaints about women's immorality, incompetence, and inconstancy based on classical authorities were met by attacks on the logic and authorities that supported this view. In the midst of this intellectual squabble over classical authorities Elyot introduced an edu-cated woman, skilled in both Latin and Greek, who had married late so she could study moral philosophy past the age of twenty. Her learning had taught this ideal woman that temperance and the good sense to know when to speak and when to remain silent were women's chief attributes, along with obedience to one's husband. She had, of course, discontinued her studies during her marriage for "good Lernynge" inculcated "suche circumspection" that for "the lyfe of my noble husband of famous memory, I was never herd or sene, saie or do any thynge, which mought not contente hym, or omytte any thyng, whiche shulde delite hym." Elyot's perfect educated woman proved her intellectual competence by never forgetting her proper role in life.[22]

John Aylmer's defense of Elizabeth was a strong plea "that no fyre brands of Sedition be cast into the houses of mens hartes," which in this case required somewhat grudging support of a female monarch. Though women were not "strong of body, or commonly so courageous of mind," a female monarch was an anomaly ordained by God, who took care, obviously, to select an especially talented woman for princely office. Aylmer asserted that "you can never shewe in al England synce the conquest, so learned a kyng as we have now a Quene." If men refused to stand in as much awe of a queen as of a king, "that is their faulte and not hers." [23] His case wholly concerned the particular instance, not women rulers, much less ordinary women, generally. Like the humanist educators, these theorists suggested the possibility of an exceptional woman, but limited their arguments because of their vision of the limited social sphere open to women.

Seventeenth-century feminists understood that it was not sufficient to argue for the intellectual equality of the sexes while maintaining a family structure which would prevent women from using their equal minds. They would not accept the basic educational and role distinctions sixteenth-century humanists made between men and women. The Renaissance emphasis on classical learning allowed the gentleman to move beyond medieval piety in ways that were denied to a woman. He was to develop his intellect and his activities in a more unrestricted way; she was to be pious and domestic. "The free, bright world into which we step when it is a question of education for boys," Ruth Kelso accurately writes, "vanishes on consideration of girls, and we move in an atmosphere of doubt, timidity, fear, and niggardly concession." [24]

II

While scholars have viewed the Tudor period, and especially the Elizabethan era, as the golden age for the English learned lady, they have seen the Jacobean period as an intellectual wasteland for women. There is as scant justification for the second idea as there is for the first. The writings and actions of James I, the proliferation of misogynist tracts, and the absence of any major women intellectuals have caused the negative assessment of the Jacobean age. Elizabeth's court, it is argued, encouraged female scholarship and led to the praise of women in general as a by-product of the glory and scholarship of the queen herself. James, on the other hand, did not favor educated women, and his court was not a comfortable place for a learned or outspoken female. [25]

Although one can question the degree of the court's influence on

English women generally, there is certainly little evidence of Jacobean encouragement of female scholarship. The numbers and virulence of tracts against women increased in the early seventeenth century, but any qualitative difference in serious works speaking of women's education and their social behavior from the sixteenth to the early seventeenth century was insubstantial.[26] The numbers of humorous but misogynistic diatribes about women's incompetence and untrustworthiness increased slightly in the Jacobean age, though there were earlier examples of the genre. The authors often remained anonymous or used obvious pseudonyms, and seemingly wrote for profit, often replying to their own misogynistic tracts with equally glib pro-women pamphlets. These works were quite popular, going through a number of printings and eliciting published responses, both pro and con.[27]

A sixteenth-century work attributed to Edward Gosynhyll was one of the earliest printed versions of this kind of attack.[28] A lengthy verse warning against the deadly effect of women, it combined scurrilous attacks on women's supposedly insatiable sexual desires with barbed references to their need to bring all men under their sway. The following lines are representative of the *Scholehouse:*

> Malyce is so roteth in theyr harte
> That seldome a man, may of them here
> One good worde, in a whole longe yere
> Moche they crave, and nought gyve agayne,
> As holesome for a man, is a womans corse
> As a sholder of motton, for a sycke horse.

Gosynhyll followed his *Scholehouse* with a work entitled *The Prayse of all Women*, termed an "apology," in which he proved by biblical example that men often accused women falsely of weakness and dishonesty. Obviously both were merely exercises, the former setting up arguments he could destroy in the latter to produce two lucrative tracts on a universal topic.[29]

Joseph Swetnam's tract on women's forward behavior, written during the early seventeenth century, conformed to the style Gosynhyll established during the sixteenth century. The work opened with: "Moses describeth a woman: At the first beginning (saith he) a woman was made to be a helper unto man, and so they are indeede, for she helpeth to spend and consume that which man painefully getteth." Swetnam then attacked the state of matrimony, relying on ancient philosophers who warned young men against being seduced by the wiles of women. Swetnam, like other writers in the genre, showed much less concern about argument than about clever similes, puns, and sexual innuendoes. Thus these works are hard to take seriously as arguments or as social evidence about women's status during a particular era. That they were popular diversions Swetnam made clear in his next to last paragraph when he urged married men who had "seene the troubles and felt the torments that is with women" to take his work "merrily, and to esteeme of this booke onely as the toyes of an idle head." [30]

Swetnam's work received a rather convincing answer in *Ester hath hang'd Haman; or, An Answere to a lewd Pamphlet, entituled, "The Arraignment of Women"* (1617), written by an anonymous author claiming to be a woman, Ester Sowernam. Refuting Swetnam's attack point by point, Sowernam blamed men rather than women for any difficulty in sexual relations. In defending Eve the author contended that "as *Eve* did not offend without the temptation of a Serpent; so women doe seldome offend, but it is by provacation of men." The tone is facetious, like that of the earlier work, suggesting it may have been written by Swetnam or a colleague in order to perpetuate a profitable controversy. The similarity of the pseudonyms, Swetnam and Sowernam, also encourages such a conclusion.[31]

Serious literature about women during the Jacobean age, the writings of James himself or such advice tracts as *Domesticall Duties* or *The English Gentlewoman,* showed basic ideas little changed from the prevalent views of the preceding century. The ideas James I expressed in his advice to Prince Henry concerning his selection and treatment of a wife differed little from Vives's or Thomas More's view of proper marital relationships. In addition, James strongly attacked the sexual double standard, a position generally credited to Puritanism. Warning his son against fornication as well as adultery, James admonished him to "keepe your bodie cleane and unpolluted, till yee give it to your wife," and attacked the world's view that male fornication was merely "a light and a veniall sin." Such opinions led a man to the deceptively self-serving position of measuring sin "by the rule of his lust and appetites, and not of his conscience." [32]

The king's traditional views about proper sex relationships within marriage were clear in a well-known passage: "Treate her as your owne flesh, command her as her Lord, cherish her as your helper, rule her as your pupill, and please her in all things reasonable; but teach her not to be curious in thinges that belonges her not, Ye are the head, she is your body: It is your office to command, and hers to obey; but yet with such a swete harmonie, as shee should be as readie to obey, as ye to commaunde; as willing to follow, as ye to go before: your love being wholie knit unto her, and all her affections lovingly bent to follow your will." [33] Because they were "the frailest sexe" women had to be protected from bad company and not be allowed "to meddle with the politick government of the commonweale." Her role was in the "Oeconomick rule of the house," and even in this area she was "to be Suject to your direction." [34]

This work has a matter-of-fact tone about it, with James simply advising his son in acceptable social and political customs without discernible animus toward women. James's perhaps mythical remark regarding a learned Jacobean lady—"Can she sew?"—reflected a conception of women's role that Elizabethan scholars shared, even while praising that rare female genius among them. The views of scholars and of social guides about the proper relationships between the sexes closely paralleled those of James.

Both William Gouge's *Of Domesticall Duties* (1622) and Richard Brathwait's *English Gentlewoman* (1631) showed a sanctimonious quality closer to Vives's tone than to More's. The third treatise, "Of Wives particular duties," in Gouge's massive tome was most telling. "The extent of wives subjection doth stretch it self verie farre," he began, "even to *all things*." Gouge, a Puritan minister, found the source for this extensive obedience in the Bible. What God ordained, nature seconded, creating a self-evident "eminence in the male over the female." [35] Gouge's corollary to this made clear how women could be injured by any new social mobility. Since the marriage bond cut across all other kinds of social differences, Gouge argued that no matter what the husband's strength, intelligence, or former social status vis-à-vis his wife, after the wedding ceremony he was her superior. "The husband is made the head of his wife, though the husband were before marriage a very begger, and of meane parentage, and the wife very wealthy and of a noble stocke; or though he were her prentise or bondslave . . . for the Scripture hath made no exception in any of those cases." [36]

English law wisely protected, Gouge pointed out, the total husbandly power God directed.[37] A wife had special duties as mother of children and mistress to servants, and in this position she must be competent to aid her husband in administering the household, but always as a subject, "not equall." Gouge thought it especially honorable for a woman to follow her husband's orders even though she thought them unquestionably wrong, because her "subjection is most manifested in such cases." Warning women against "overweening conceit of their own wisdom," Gouge spoke to the issue of proper education for women only by reminding wives that they must be prepared to conduct their household business. Gouge's account differed little from the sixteenth-century materials, except in its total focus on marital duties.[38]

Although Richard Brathwait's work was published a few years after the end of James's reign, it contained the same perspective as the works of Gouge and his predecessors. Brathwait wrote *The English Gentleman* in 1630 and followed it with *The English Gentlewoman* the next year. The contrast between these two works makes clear that the Renaissance distinctions between male and female education had not lessened by the 1630s. Education was most important for the gentleman because honorable social acts were, by necessity, grounded in a liberal education "for barren, fruitlesse and lifeless is that *Knowledge* which is not reduced to *Action*." [39] Action, of course, took place in a number of arenas, including centrally the family. "As every mans house is his Castle so is his *family* a private Common-wealth, wherein if due government be not observed, nothing but confusion is to be expected," Brathwait concluded.[40]

His lengthy work on the gentlewoman devoted much less space to education and, of course, none to governance, except as it could be applied to servants and children. In his introduction to the gentlewoman reader he claimed to be establishing a model gentlewoman for all to imitate. His reiterated theme was the need for humility and chastity for "so little doth shee favour her selfe, as shee preferres others censures before her owne; and in no one particular so much expresseth her owne true glory, as in the constant practice of Humilitie." Because humility was that most glorious feminine quality, "the princesse of Vertues, the conqueresse of Vices, the mirror of Virgins," Brathwait believed that women's education should be clearly limited to their domestic role.[41] His discussion of proper education was similar to Vives's and throughout his work he made references to the "learned Vives in his *Instruction of a Christian Woman*." [42]

Like Vives, Brathwait spent most of his time listing subjects women were to avoid: "To discourse of State-matters, will not become your auditory; nor to dispute of high poynts of Divinity, will it sort well with women of your quality. These *Shee-clarkes* many times broach strange opinions, which, as they understand them not themselves, so they labour to intangle others of equall understanding to themselves. . . . *Women* as they are to be no *Speakers* in the Church, so neither are they to be disputers of controversies of the Church." [43] Women were only to speak in their "household academies" or "where your owne sexe is onely conversant," but even here they must avoid showing "over-great ambition." [44]

If Jacobean writers slipped back less on the question of women's role and education than some historians have asserted, it is largely because Tudor theorists had moved forward so little. The questions and perspectives the seventeenth-century feminists were to raise had still to be broached.

III

Feminist ideas were directly related to the revolutionary ideology of the mid-seventeenth century, although their sources of immediate intellectual inspiration came from scientific questioning and rationalism. But such thought obviously interacted with that drawn from the revolutionary political currents that shook England between 1640 and 1690. Since the earliest feminist tracts appeared during the 1650s, some link would seem likely between the revolutionary turmoil of the mid-century and women's questioning of their subordinate legal and political status. Yet the Royalist-Anglican loyalties of most feminists suggest twists in this causal chain. [45]

On the parliamentary side, heroines such as Lucy Hutchinson were rare, and even her renown came more from her memoirs of her husband than from her own actions. Later commentators have noted women's role in the radical sects and, to a lesser extent, their support of the Leveller cause, particularly in demanding release of prisoners. Women's role within the sectarian movement came less from a political than a religious commitment, but of course these two areas were not distinct in the seventeenth century. When God's will was being thwarted on earth, it was the duty of the true believer to work to right this wrong, and such efforts often involved criticism of the established government. Although these religious efforts had political consequences, they were far removed from any support for the political rights of women, which were never directly raised as a public issue.[46]

Christoper Hill, in *The World Turned Upside Down*, postulates a two-part revolution occurring during the 1640s. The first was the Puritan- and gentry-led attack on the king's prerogatives which ultimately succeeded in bringing about parliamentary rule. The second was a radical revolution carried out by the Levellers and the extreme religious sects, which failed. Hill contends that the latter was considerably more favorable to women's political rights than the former.

Yet the kinds of social turmoil Hill sees as both promoting radicalism, as part of the second revolution, and decreasing deference affected only males directly. The greater mobility of large numbers of itinerant peddlers and agricultural workers, which Hill sees as the social basis of the revolution, involved males overwhelmingly. And the one organization which he argues had a real chance to create a truly radical revolution—the New Model Army—was, of course, made up entirely of males. Also, although enclosure and disafforestation harmed the poor generally (even if only in the short run), women suffered in particular ways. When part of the growing pool of wage laborers, they were paid consistently one-half the rate for men and had less mobility to extricate themselves from "embarrassing situations" by moving on. Though Hill speaks of women's sexual freedom being enhanced by the free-love doctrines of the communal religious groups—especially the Ranters—his evidence stresses masculine more than feminine pleasures, "a community of all wives," and the fact that itinerant preachers could practice sexual license without suffering the same consequences as their female partners.[47]

Patricia Higgins has recently argued convincingly that women petitioners during the 1640s believed they possessed political rights separate from their husbands. Yet her evidence comes more from women who were supporting masculine causes—particularly the release of political prisoners—than from those having any interest in their own political rights. And although she demonstrates that women petitioners may have believed in the propriety of women's political actions, Leveller leaders seem to have showed little enthusiasm. John Lilburne, in praising his wife's support for his cause, noted that her efforts combined "a gallant and true masculine spirit" while maintaining her "feminine" qualities.

An active life, particular bravery, or an outstanding intellect in a single woman had traditionally been praised as "masculine" attributes by male authors. Lilburne's judgments proved no exception; his wife's gallantry did not alter his conception of the nature of women generally or encourage the adoption of their political rights; it simply revealed that an individual woman could overcome the frailties of her sex temporarily.[48]

Women petitioners attacked economic hardship and religious oppression. A number of women involved in English manufacturing and handicrafts argued against the easy importation of foreign goods. Others called for the expulsion of the bishops from the House of Lords and a general reformation of the church. They were concerned about their rights as citizens and not specifically as women, but the two issues could not help merging at times. For instance, a petition of a group of Leveller women voiced dissatisfaction with the answer given earlier to their husbands concerning the state of Leveller prisoners and raised the question of women's public action:

> assured . . . also of a proportionable share in the Freedoms of this Commonwealth, we cannot but wonder and grieve that we should appear so despicable in your eyes as to be thought unworthy to Petition or represent our Grievances to this Honourable House. Have we not an equal interest with the men of this Nation, in those liberties and securities contained in the Petition of Right, and other good Laws of the Land? Are any of our lives, limbs, liberties or goods to be taken from us more than from Men . . . ? And can you imagine us to be so sottish or stupid, as not to perceive, or not to be sensible when dayly those strong defences of our peace and welfare are broken?
>
> Would you have us keep at home in our houses, when men . . . are forced from their Houses . . . as if we our lives and liberties and all, were not concerned? . . . No . . . we will never . . . cease to importune you.[49]

A more common position among such groups was to support women's equality within a religious but not a political context. Particularly Quakers and female members of other radical religious sects, as well as some Puritans, focused on the equality of men and women before God and the equal worth of their souls, but did not carry such views to the conclusion that male-female relations should alter within the family or within society generally. Women were considered empowered to act independently of their husbands only in instances of fundamental religious differences. If the husband were a sinner who denied his wife the right to attend church or to take communion, she could break her vows of obedience to him. Yet such views did not necessarily lead to an attack on, much less the overthrow of, the dominant-subordinate relationship dictated in Genesis.[50]

Women on the left during the Civil War were normally members of movements which had previously established organizational and ideological goals that left little room for the pursuit of women's political rights. The fight against episcopacy, presbyterianism, and general religious control on the one hand, and the cry for the rights of freeborn Englishmen on the other, absorbed the social and intellectual energies women devoted to public causes.[51]

Seventeenth-century political issues, external to the family and largely irrelevant to women, were also often cast in a backward-looking political ideology which spoke of the fundamental constitution of the land as the basis for the rights of English citizens. This essentially conservative justification for quite radical political actions, again, hardly encouraged the political rights of women.[52]

On the other hand, the radical movement suggested action and stressed ideas that could be related to women's issues if focused in that direction in later years. The need for the expansion of the franchise on a more democratic basis and for the legitimate religious expression of all individuals were two such issues. The radicals looked for their justification of political rights not to pre-Norman England but to earlier days in which all power and all property had been held communally, a primordial society in which women would have been equal. No one moved toward the application of these notions to questions of sexual-social roles explicitly, but such theories, with their implicit if neglected corollaries, were raised.

The ideological origins of seventeenth-century feminism emerged with the fundamental questioning of society during the 1640s and 1650s, but did not follow a straight path from radical or reformist views to feminist ones. The feminists were not radicals in areas relevant to the revolution, but applied the earlier questioning and questing to other fundamental human relationships, particularly sex roles and family relationships. The revolutionaries focused on the interaction between the individual householder and his landlord, his social betters, and his government; they seldom spoke critically of his relationship to his wife.

Mary Astell criticized Milton for not "crying up liberty to poor female slaves," but even she did not pursue or even mention the political rights of women, though some feminists used the phrase "free-born English-women" in the early eighteenth century.[53] It was not until the end of that century, in the wake of "inalienable rights" theories tied to the American and French Revolutions, that Mary Wollstonecraft's writings urged the enfranchisement of women.

Despite the richness and variety of seventeenth-century political theories, they all proved unhelpful to nascent feminism. Monarchical theory, outlined most thoroughly by Robert Filmer, stressed authority flowing from a natural, God-ordained patriarchal principle. As the father ruled his family and household at God's will, so the king held sway over his larger, national family. Both roles had their ultimate justification in Adam's injunction from God that he should rule over his wife and later his children, under the directive of the Fifth Commandment.[54] This theory, which most suited high Tory sentiment, least fitted any form of feminist thought.

The two outstanding political theorists of the seventeenth century, Thomas Hobbes and John Locke, took exception to this patriarchal vision of the formation of government. Hobbes accepted the unrestricted power of the monarch but did not rest it on biblical patriarchal injunctions. Instead he envisioned a wholly opposite "social" reality: "In the state of nature," Hobbes contended, "every woman that bears children, becomes both a *mother* and a *lord*." The notion that the father gained power was contradicted, Hobbes said, by the fact that "the inequality of their natural forces is not so great, that the man could get the dominion over the woman without war," while tradition showed that "women namely Amazons, have in former times waged war against their adversaries, and disposed of their children at their own wills. And at this day, in diverse places women are invested with the principal authority; neither do their husbands dispose of their children, but themselves: which in truth they do *by the right of nature*. . . . And also, that in the state of nature it cannot be known who is the *father*, but by testimony of the *mother;* the child therefore is his whose the mother will have it, and therefore her's."[55] Hobbes's stress on women's superiority within the state of nature certainly did not evolve from any belief on his part in their political rights, but evolved logically from his view of individual prerogative dictating power within the state of nature.

Certainly his theory about the natural dominance of mothers disappeared in his discussion of society, which he saw formed "not in the mutual good will men had towards each other, but in the mutual fear they had of each other." He even excluded women from the family, which he defined as "a *father* with *sons* and servants, grown into a civil person by virtue of his paternal jurisdiction," or a "civil government" between husband and wife where "the children are the father's." [56] The female domination in Hobbes's state of nature, which might have given some grounding to feminist politics, then disappeared in his civil society. He made women's brief natural superiority end in unquestioned civil subordination.

John Locke's criticism of patriarchalism, if less fundamental than Hobbes's, was also sexually egalitarian. Rather than attacking the natural superiority of fathers, Locke, in his *First Treatise of Government*, took exception to Filmer's misuse of the Fifth Commandment in upholding patriarchal rule within the family and upon the throne. Questioning Adam's supremacy over Eve and later over his children, Locke contended that the Fifth Commandment revealed how men and women equally were due respect from their children. Locke asked rhetorically: "Can the Father, by this Soverignty of his, discharge the Child from paying this Honour to his Mother? . . . I think no Body will say a Child may withhold Honour from *her*, though his Father should command him to do so, no more than the Mother could dispense with him, for neglecting to Honor his Father." [57]

The sexual egalitarianism of his attack on Filmer, however, disappeared in the positive theory of his *Second Treatise*, where government became the creation and basically the possession not of all persons resident in an area but of landowners who banded together to protect their property. "The greatest and chief end therefore of Mens uniting into Commonwealths, and putting themselves under Government," he insisted, *"is the preservation of their Property."* [58] This private property he saw emerging from an individual's mixing his labor with the land to produce goods, the fate which God had decreed for Adam. The creation and control of property was thus a man's ordained social lot, while scripturally Eve's was to obey her husband and to suffer pain through childbirth. In Locke, as in Hobbes, a sexually egalitarian attack on Filmer ended with women restored to conventional social subordination.

The theories of Hobbes and Locke in some ways left women further from political rights or opportunities than they were in the medieval world, where position essentially conferred status upon its holder. In the medieval world many upper-class women controlled their husbands' estates in their absence or upon their death and even governed large territories and organized armies, not because of their rights as women but because the holding of a particular trust carried with it specific functions.[59] In the seventeenth century, however, political obligation moved from the office to the citizen, a designation from which women and the nonpropertied were both excluded. Yet the use of more general and abstract language of citizenship and individual rights during that century camouflaged a continuing emphasis on the citizen's holding two offices: property owner and head of household.

One of the central qualities of seventeenth-century feminism grew out of this exclusion from the political realm. Along with their arguments for intellectual-educational parity went a struggle for broader power in the area of the family rather than the state. It was in this limited political arena, they came to see, that power principally touched women and where alone they were regarded as citizens and subjects.

Although the events and writings inspired by the English Civil War did not lend themselves to expanding the rights of women, they probably provided the necessary catalyst which led some women to think about, and feminists to speak out against, the miserable education of women and their unjust position within the home. Contemporary political theories were not especially useful for the feminists because the relevant political arena for women was the family. Rather, feminists had to develop their own theories, often employing the language of the revolutionaries, about the political nature of husband-wife relationships and their negative impact on women's lives generally. Since a wife was a citizen within the domestic rather than the public commonwealth, one could hardly attack women's exclusion from public life without first attacking her subjection to her husband. A woman's husband was her lord, and if she conspired to do him bodily harm she could be convicted of petty treason.[60] Therefore, the feminists' assault on women's subordination within the home was as necessary an act as the Levellers' demand for the vote for all freeborn Englishmen. It acknowledged something feminists articulated only later, that "the personal is political" and that to deny the political aspect of familial relations was to curb those of women's rights which were external to the family.[61]

IV

New intellectual currents as well as political ones challenged traditional ways and preconceptions in the seventeenth century. While the political turmoil directed attention toward issues other than those concerning women, the rationalists and scientists began a more wholly victorious revolution in thought which was to provide the most usable framework for feminist ideology. Excluded from the institutions that drew the attention of political and academic reformers, women could hardly be excluded from the intellectual tendencies of their age, and, in these empirical and rationalist currents, feminist ideas began to coalesce.[62]

Feminists needed a system of thought which could provide them with a framework for arguing the legitimacy of women's intellectual interests and developing an ideology of the intellectual equality of the sexes. They could not use the political ideologies of the time, for these failed to confront the issue of sex relations and, conversely, stressed the importance of male independence and the integrity of the family unit constructed upon a dominant-subordinate husband-wife relationship. They could not use the arguments of legal or educational reformers which focused on changes within institutions from which women were excluded and never questioned women's general subordination within society. They could not build upon the radical religious or political groups of the revolution because the policies and organizational structures of these groups assumed the traditional social sphere of women. What these women needed was a set of ideas which, while not necessarily focused on the issue of sexual roles, would lend itself to analyzing such roles. They also required ideas that were sufficiently abstract and separate from contemporary institutions so that they could be used in new ways. Finally, these ideas had to be susceptible to formulations of fundamental principles. Science provided some limited impetus and justification for their questioning of customary beliefs and relations, and in rationalism they found the ideology that best answered their desire to assert equality and to develop a framework for questioning the status quo.

The relationship of feminist thinking to the century's scientific revolution was rather like its relationship to the political revolutions: scientific revolution provided some broad ideas and attitudes, which these women incorporated into their thought without becoming full adherents of the methodology. None of the feminists were scientists, although some showed more than a passing interest in science. Hannah Woolley wrote on medical topics in her practical handbooks for gentlewomen and governesses, as did Jane Sharp in her guide for midwives. Sarah Fyge Egerton praised Robert Boyle in a poem and employed scientific imagery in other verses. The duchess of Newcastle had the most elaborate scientific interests among the feminists, and her writings, unsystematic as they were, reveal some of the conflicting sources of enthusiasm for and reservations about science among writers concerned with women's social and intellectual opportunities.

The duchess enjoyed bringing her personal understanding to contemporary controversies and interests, including scientific topics. Unlike that of her contemporary, Anne, Viscountess Conway, her work was not serious scholarship in the area.[63] Yet it paralleled that of a large number of amateurs engaged in scientific activities during the 1600s, although the duchess's emphasis was on the intellectual aspects of science rather than the experimental or observational interests of most nonprofessionals.[64] The duchess was fascinated by science because it promised both new ways of looking at things and new answers. She was finally frustrated with it because both methods and answers varied so widely from the things that concerned her. She wrote five separate volumes of scientific interest between 1655 and 1668, beginning with *The Worlds Olio* and concluding with *The Grounds of Natural Philosophy*. Her views did not remain constant throughout these works, and, though she apologized in later works for ignorance revealed in her *Philosophical and Physical Opinions* (1663),[65] large contradictions remained unresolved.

There was a definite lack of structure or continuity in the writings of the duchess of Newcastle. The duchess insisted on the originality of her thought, and its hodgepodge nature, its bits and pieces drawn from various authors, would support that claim. She alternately took a strongly idealistic position and one that insisted, with Hobbes, on the material basis of reality, and she failed to distinguish between sense perception and the intellectual ordering of reality. Yet amid the jumble of her thought was evidence of both her contribution and the reasons for her enthusiasm and reservations about science.

Her contribution was that of many popularizers of the day, to transform abstract science into direct, commonsense language. Thus she handled the argument of "some Learned persons" who claimed against materialism that "there are Substances that are not Material Bodies." The duchess responded, "But how they can prove any sort of Substance to be no Body, I cannot tell" for "a corporeal Part cannot have an Incorporeal perception." She similarly argued that motion itself must be material: "Though Matter might be without Motion, yet Motion cannot be without Matter; for it is impossible (in my opinion) that there should be an Immaterial Motion in Nature." [66] If her explanations were often simplistic, they nonetheless reveal an attempt to translate into everyday language the issues that were most fundamental to the new science.

In her earlier writings, she showed genuine interest in the potential use of the microscope and telescope, as did many of her contemporaries. Yet this interest waned when it became clear that such experiments bore little relation to the broad social and intellectual issues she came to care about. The duchess's strong interest in science focused on its value as a tool to discover the truth, as a means of making new connections or uncovering new realities. She was disillusioned with scientific experiments and concerns that appeared to have no results other than the "success of the experiment itself." Her pragmatic reservations about science were clear in her later opinions about the microscope and telescope.

> Truly, the Art of Augury was far more beneficial than the lately invented Art of Microscopy; for I cannot perceive any great advantage this Art doth bring us, Also the Ecclipse of the Sun and Moon was not found out by Telescopes, nor the Motions of the Loadstone, nor the Art of Printing, and the like, by Microscopes; nay, if it be true, that Telescopes make appear the spots in the Sun and Moon, or discover some new Stars, what benefit is that to us? Or if Microscopes do truly represent the exterior parts and superficies of some minute Creatures, what advantages it our knowledge? For unless they could discover their interior, corporeal, figurative motions, or the courses which make such or such creatures, I see no great benefit or advantage they yield to man.[67]

Another reason for science's limited influence on feminist thought can be seen in the translation of a much more important work of popularization than those of the duchess. Bernard de Fontenelle's *Plurality of Worlds*, which popularized Copernican ideas under the guise of making it possible for women to gain a smattering of scientific knowledge without requiring them to tax their intellectual powers, was condescending to women's abilities in ways that offended seventeenth-century English feminists. Fontenelle's translator, Aphra Behn, admitted that "the author's introducing a woman as one of the speakers" attracted her to the work, but she remained unhappy with Fontenelle's description of the Marchioness, the charming young pupil to whom the wise and witty narrator-philosopher explained astronomy. Admiring Fontenelle, Behn hesitated to write "what some may understand to be a Satyr against him" but believed that it was her duty to comment on his attempt to simplify knowledge for the female sex.[68] "For this End, he introduceth a Woman of Quality as one of the Speakers in these five Discourses, whom he feigns never to have heard of any such things as philosophy before," Behn complained. "He makes her say a great many very silly things, tho' sometimes she makes observations so learned, that the greatest Philosophers in Europe could make no better." [69]

Fontenelle had made the Marchioness an unbelievable character by having her make at once both profound and ignorant comments. Behn disliked the condescension in Fontenelle's rendering ideas so that women could read them "with the same application that they do a Romance or Novel." Yet she admitted that she had not the knowledge to write an original work of astronomy where the reader would have found "the subject quite changed and made my own." [70] Her problem was that of many women. Not only did science fail to touch on questions that directly affected them, but it was increasingly pursued through societies that excluded them and in terms which required the specialized education they were denied.

Just as the duchess of Newcastle, in her final work on science, rejected or criticized scientific empiricism in favor of rationalism, so later feminists preferred reason to purely scientific research. Feminists linked their faith in reason to a distrust of custom, which perpetuated both ignorance and women's domestic status. Astell's *Serious Proposal* made explicit how reason illuminated the way custom contributed to women's enforced ignorance. "For custom has usurpt such an unaccountable Authority, that she who would endeavor to put a stop to its arbitrary sway, and reduce it to Reason, is in a fair way to render herself the Butt for all the Fops in Town to shoot their impertinent censures at. And tho' a wise woman will not value their censure, yet she cares not to be the subject of their Discourse." [71]

Not only were women scorned for suggesting seriously that they should have an education that included more than sewing, playing, and an introduction to the social graces, but custom had a deleterious effect on women themselves. "Thus ignorance and a narrow Education lay the Foundation of Vice, and Imitation, and custome rear it up." [72] Even scholarship, admired as it was by the feminists, was worthy only if it were rational and probing, rather than the customary parade of authorities that often passed for argument in male intellectual institutions. Typical was the comment in the anonymous *Defence of the Female Sex:* "These Superstitious, bigotted Idolaters of time past, are Children in their understanding all their lives; for they hang so incessantly upon the leading strings of authority, that their Judgments, like the Limbs of some Indian Penitents, become altogether crampt and motionless for want of use." [73] Women were to use their minds creatively, not simply accumulatively as in traditional scholarship.

Such attacks on custom were not unusual by the late seventeenth century, but they were not often directed against traditional sex roles. Science had justified its cry for new approaches and Bacon's concern over the customary restraints on thought had become commonplace. Yet Astell explicitly noted her debt to Descartes's method of thought in her *Serious Proposal to the Ladies, Part II,* and it would seem his rationalism provided the primary foundation for her attacks on those customs she found most objectionable. [74]

Other feminists talked of rationalism less systematically than Astell, but nonetheless glorified rational thought as justification for women's equality and as incentive to intellectual productivity or meditation. Lady Mary Chudleigh introduced her *Essays upon Several Subjects* with the contention "that the Pleasures of the Mind are infinitely preferable to those of sense" and noted that rational pursuits "have been long the dear, the favourite companions of my solitary Hours." The life of the mind could "fill up all the Spaces, all the Intervals of Time, and make my Days slide joyfully along." This work, she informed her reader, was intended for the edification of women, to make them "prefer Wisdom before Beauty, good Sense before Wealth, and the Sovereignty of their Passions before the Empire of the World," and not to be the carping, complaining wives which women with little to occupy themselves tended to become. Rational thought would leave "no room for dull insipid Trifles, debasing Impertinencies, nor any of those troublesome Reflexions, which generally proceed from narrow groveling Souls, from Souls that have not learn'd to use their Faculties aright." [75]

Faith in reason was central to the development of seventeenth-century feminism. The feminists' belief in reason's power to ferret out the truth was strong, and the use of rational thought as a tool to combat the evils of custom was a constant theme among them. Yet they used reason in a special way. To them reason not only revealed the proper use of women's minds but was also the quality which allowed them to escape the petty existence society had ordained for them. To reason meant to be serious, and this alone offered escape from women's being the simple, social fools the world demanded. Reason for feminists was both an effective tool to destroy the irrational bases for women's oppression and an uplifting activity which women could follow after they recognized the error of their lives as mere social butterflies. They were strong evangelists for intellectual pursuits.

Their evangelism was equally grounded in their bitterness at women's enforced ignorance. Lady Mary Chudleigh used pleasant, peaceful language on the topic of rational pursuits, but the passion behind this argument is clear in "To the Ladies," an attack on an antifeminist sermon:

> Wife and Servant are the same,
> But only differ in the Name:
>
>   . . . .
>
> And fear her Husband as her God:
> Him still must serve, Him still obey,
> And nothing act, and nothing say,
> But what her haughty Lord thinks fit,
> Who with the Pow'r has all the Wit.
> Then Shun, oh! shun that wretched State,
> And all the fawning Flatt'rers hate:
> Value yourselves, and Man despise,
> You must be proud, if you'll be wise.[76]

The feminists' love of reason, which they pursued with emotional intensity, grew from their understanding of women's status. Because of the primacy of their concern for women, feminists pursued reason in a unique fashion. Mary Astell accepted Cartesian dualism, but she was not really a member of the Cartesian school in the same way that another seventeenth-century follower of his might be so categorized. Feminists

generally did not accept or employ scientific or rationalist concepts in a
sophisticated or even orthodox manner but as an impetus suggesting
what women could and should do with their minds. Highly critical of
society's sexual relationships, they were indirectly encouraged in their
probing by an age in which social and intellectual questioning was
endemic. Yet their specific concerns were not those of their society, and
this reality creates ambiguities in placing them in social and intellectual
categories. They were mavericks, operating in a largely hostile environment, who employed bits and pieces of the social and intellectual criticisms they found about them to understand and to change women's lives.

NOTES

    1. Kenneth Charlton, *Education in Renaissance England* (London: Rout-
ledge and Kegan Paul, 1965), pp. 204–13. Although Charlton argues that
women's educational opportunities were enhanced by the humanists, he does
realize the very limited nature of this advancement. Henry S. Lucas, *The Renaissance and the Reformation*, 2nd ed. (New York: Harper and Brothers, 1960),
pp. 435–40. Lucas makes no distinction between Vives's educational program
for boys and for girls. Historians of Renaissance England have normally mentioned women's education only briefly, noting the period's more favorable
opinion of women's abilities than that held during the medieval period.
Medievalists such as Eileen Power argue that women may have had greater
educational opportunities during the Middle Ages because of the alternative of
the convent to marriage for those women who wished to remain single and follow
a scholarly vocation. Eileen Power, *Medieval Women*, ed. M. M. Postan (New
York: Cambridge University Press, 1976), pp. 38–43. Historians focusing on
women in sixteenth-century England have been more apt to concur in the opinion
of women's educational advance during the Tudor period. See especially Carroll
Camden's work on Elizabethan women and Pearl Hogrefe's recent works on
Tudor women. For a contrasting point of view see my comparison of male and
female education in "Feminism and the Methodology of Women's History," and
Joan Kelly-Gadol's "Did Women Have a Renaissance?"
    2. Gardiner, *English Girlhood*, pp. 170–79. For the same kind of emphasis
on a few learned Tudor ladies see also Pearl Hogrefe's chapter on classical
learning in *Tudor Women* (Ames: Iowa State University, 1975); Carroll Camden,
The Elizabethan Woman (Houston, Tex.: Elsevier Press, 1952); and the introduction to Myra Reynolds's work, *The Learned Lady in England, 1650–1760*
(Boston: Houghton-Mifflin, 1920). This discussion is not intended to undercut
the impressive abilities displayed by women such as Queen Elizabeth, Lady Jane
Grey, or Margaret Roper, but simply to place their accomplishments into a more

general picture of sixteenth-century intellectual endeavors and to make clear that they have been evaluated not as scholars but as female scholars.

3. James K. McConica, *English Humanists and Reformation Policies under Henry VIII and Edward VI* (Oxford: Oxford University Press, 1965), pp. 84–89.

4. Douglas Bush, *The Renaissance and English Humanism* (Toronto: University of Toronto Press, 1939), p. 79; Donald J. Wilcox, *In Search of God and Self: Renaissance and Reformation Thought* (Boston: Houghton Mifflin, [1975]), pp. 90–104; G. R. Elton, *Reform and Reformation: England, 1509–1558* (Cambridge, Mass.: Harvard University Press, 1977), pp. 94–97. As is illustrated most clearly by Kenneth Charlton, humanist education, especially the English version, was closely tied to the notion of the gentleman and his role in society, and thus to qualify for a humanist education one had to be able to utilize one's learning in a public and responsible position.

5. Charlton, *Education in Renaissance England*, p. 81. "whereas the medieval texts concentrated on an education expressed in terms of an ideal prince and emphasized the institutional basis of his power, those of the Renaissance widened their scope to include the education of those serving the prince, stressing the personal qualities of those who rule and showing a greater concern for the practical problems of government." See also McConica, *English Humanists*, pp. 84–89. The utilitarian nature of such an education is made clear in the following excerpt from a sixteenth-century commentator, Sir Lawrence Humphreys: "But since in a nobleman tendeth to a common weal wear he with daily and nightly study Aristotle's and other writings of civil knowledge, know he the country's ordinances, laws and manners [together] with the foreign states. . . . Read he also all writers of nobility, Erasmus *The Institution of a Christian Prince*, Sturmius's learned *Nobility* . . . and almost all Plutarch's works, in them as mirrors to see himself . . . be he also skilful in the *Chronicles* of his country . . . and both all antiquity and the law and statutes of our own realm wherein so skilful ought he to be as he dare professeth" (quoted in Charlton, *Education in Renaissance England*, pp. 84–85).

6. Ruth Kelso, *The Doctrine for the Lady of the Renaissance* (Urbana: University of Illinois Press, 1956), pp. 31, 56–60, 69–70. Kelso's work is a compendium of virtually everything printed on the subject of women in Italy, France, and England during the sixteenth century; it is, as well, the first work to postulate convincingly the significant limitation of the humanist educational program for women. Subsequent works have built on her massive evidentiary base.

7. Juan Vives, *The Instruction of a Christian Woman*, in *Vives and the Renascence Education of Women*, ed. Foster Watson (New York: Longmans, Green and Co., 1912). Further references to Vives are from this edition and will be noted by page number in the text. Watson can be criticized legitimately for overlooking Vives's serious reservations about women's advanced training; still, his work is the single most useful collection of humanist texts on women's education.

8. The focus of Vives's work was seldom on women's education. Sample

chapter headings should make clear that his main interest was the preparation of a woman for her domestic role. "What a woman ought to have in Mind when She Marrieth," "Of the Ordering of the Body of a Virgin," and "How She shall Behave Herself with her Kinsfolk and Alliance" are representative.

9. Vives understood the efficacy of religious teaching for women in developing a proper understanding of their domestic role. This understanding is made clear in the brief excerpt from the *Duty of Husbands* included in Watson's *Vives and the Renascence Education of Women* (pp. 195–210). "Religion doth make them very simple and good, and superstition very hypocrites and molestious. And . . . thereby know how she ought to love and honour her husband, whom she should take as a divine and holy thing, and obey his will as the law of God. Her house shall be unto her as a commonwealth, and she must learn what her duty and office is at home, and what is her husband's" (pp. 201–2).

10. Watson's description of the nature of Vives's work as "the first plea printed in English for the higher education of women" is simply not accurate, unless he meant "higher" in a highly restricted sense. His understanding of its significance for the sixteenth century is less open to question, however. *"The Instruction of a Christian Woman* by Vives is the leading theoretical manual on women's education of the 16th century, not only for England and the English, for whom it was primarily produced, but also for the whole of Europe."

11. Watson discusses the authors who gave some attention to the topic of women's education in his introduction.

12. Richard Hyrde, "Introduction" to *Instruction of a Christian Woman*, p. 163.

13. Ibid., p. 167.

14. Ernest Edwin Reynolds, *Margaret Roper: Eldest Daughter of St. Thomas More* (New York: P. J. Kennedy, 1960), p. 15.

15. Ibid.

16. Ibid., pp. 16–17.

17. Ibid., p. 16.

18. Thomas More, "Thomas More to his best beloved Children . . . ," letter quoted in Watson, *Vives*, p. 184.

19. Watson, *Vives*, pp. 189–90.

20. Richard Mulcaster, *The Educational Writings of Richard Mulcaster*, ed. James Oliphant (Glasgow: James Maclehose and Sons, 1903), pp. 18, 51.

21. Ibid., pp. 51–53.

22. Sir Thomas Elyot, *The Defence of Good Women* (London, 1545), n.p. This controversy over the intellectual competence of women is enclosed in a debate between Platonic and Aristotelian opponents, and the issue about women is less important for the author than his attack on Aristotle's disloyalty to his teacher's views.

23. John Aylmer, *An Harbarow for faithful and trewe Subjects* (London, 1559), p. 3. Aylmer, like the other authors defending women during the sixteenth century, was not committed to any serious defense of women's abilities. He

believed only in the exceptional abilities of a few women (such as Queen Elizabeth) and did not defend women's learning generally.

24. Kelso, *Doctrine*, p. 158.

25. Louis B. Wright, *Middle-Class Culture in Elizabethan England* (Ithaca, N.Y.; Cornell University Press, 1958), pp. 481–500; Chilton Powell, *English Domestic Relations, 1487–1653* (New York: Columbia University Press, 1916), pp. 170–78; Thompson, *Women in Stuart England and America*, pp. 228–30; Stenton, *English Woman*, pp. 141–46.

26. The literature of the early seventeenth century often appears more antiwoman than that of the previous age, and certainly there were a number of vicious attacks against women, running the gamut from approval of wife beating to denials of any responsible role for women in society. It has been argued, by Wright among others, that this is something of a revolt against the long years of Elizabeth's reign. However, there were greater numbers of tracts printed in the first two decades of the seventeenth century than in the last decades of the sixteenth century; and the tracts of this period were seldom more misogynistic than earlier writings, just expressed more often in prose and a more modern style.

27. Although in *Middle-Class Culture* Wright argues a growing negative view of women during the seventeenth century, he does recognize that guides for women were more alike than different from the late sixteenth to the mid-seventeenth century. "The literary historian who likes to trace an evolutionary development in literature will find the manuals of domestic guidance peculiarly disappointing, for there is a strange sameness in point of view and treatment in the books read by the burgher of 1558 and by his grandson in 1640" (p. 226).

28. [Edward Gosynhyll], *Scholehouse of Women* (London, 1560), n.p.

29. [Edward Gosynhyll], *The Prayse of all Women, called Mulieru pean* [1542?], n.p.

30. [Joseph Swetnam], *The Arraignment of Lewde, idle, forward, and unconstant Women:* . . . *Pleasant for Married Men, profitable for young Men, and hurtful to none* (London: Edward Allde for Thomas Archer, 1615), pp. 5–7, 64.

31. Esther Sowernam, *Ester hath hang'd Haman; or, An Answere to a lewd Pamphlet, entituled, "The Arraignment of Women"* (London, 1617), pp. 1–17.

32. James I, *King James's Instructions to his Dearest Sonne, Henry the Prince* (London: M. Flesher, 1682), pp. 54–55.

33. Ibid., pp. 60–61.

34. Ibid., p. 61.

35. William Gouge, *Of Domesticall Duties. Eight Treatises* (London: Printed by John Haviland for William Bladen, 1622), p. 272. For More's views on marriage see "Domestic Life and Character of the Utopians," in *Utopia*, with a new introduction by the Rev. T. F. Dibdin (London: William Bulmer, 1808), pp. 190–209.

36. Gouge, *Domesticall Duties*, p. 272.

37. Ibid., p. 296.

38. Ibid., pp. 303, 336–40. It is true that Vives may have had a broader meaning in mind for "instruction" than mere academic training, but it should be remembered that his work was used as the primary source for women's education by those educating their daughters in the late sixteenth and early seventeenth century, and that later commentators and historians have discussed his work as an educational treatise, not as a guide to general feminine behavior. Protestant theorists were no more willing for the wife to pursue learning to the detriment of her domestic duty than were Catholics such as Vives. Heinrich Bullinger in *The Christen State of Matrimonye* (1541) stated that the wife did not come from the head but rather the rib of man and therefore "the husband is the head and master of the wyfe." His view of marriage was securely tied to the Fall and God's commandment to Eve that her husband should rule over her; his remaining judgments flowed quite logically from the biblical arguments for marriage—the procreation of children and the training of Christians.

39. Richard Brathwait, *The English Gentleman: Containing Sundry excellent Rules or exquisite Observations . . . How to demeane or Accomodate himself in the manage of publicke or private Affaires* (London: John Haviland, 1630), p. 99.

40. Ibid., p. 155.

41. Richard Brathwait, "To the Gentlewoman Reader," *The English Gentlewoman, drawne out to the Body* (London: B. Alsop and T. Fawcet, 1631), n.p.

42. Ibid., pp. 183–84. The divisions of Brathwait's work make clear its similarity to Vives's: "Apparell, Behavior, Complement, Decency, Estimation, Fancy, Gentility and Honour." Its aim was to describe the proper social characteristics of a gentlewoman of the early seventeenth century.

43. Ibid., p. 89.

44. Ibid., p. 219.

45. Feminists drew upon revolutionary rhetoric in a negative sense, never supporting it but pointing to its failure to consider women's status within society.

46. Most female religious writers simply ignored political or feminist topics. Even Margaret Fell Fox, one of the most forceful supporters of women's being able to speak in Quaker meetings, argued in *Women's Speaking Justified* (London, 1666) that they should never speak in a way that would usurp authority over men. For the large majority of women writing religious tracts during the seventeenth century, the question of women's rights simply never arose. Women functioned as the vessels for Christ's teaching, not as speakers for themselves. Individuals such as M. Marsin and Lady Eleanor Douglas did write numerous letters to political leaders, especially Cromwell, demanding that religion be reformed and the nation cleansed. Quaker women such as Katherine Evans wrote to protest their imprisonment and the political tyranny from which it sprang. Such efforts, however, were focused on the issues of the moment and spoke most often to the question of governmental abuse of religious freedom.

47. In *The World Turned Upside Down: Radical Ideas during the English Revolution* (New York: Viking Press, 1972) Christopher Hill presents seemingly

contradictory judgments concerning the status of women and the development of radical sectarianism. Although Hill contends the Ranters, Diggers, and Quakers supported the equality of women, he provides conflicting experiences from George Fox on the issue (pp. 252–53). Further, he notes that "historians have perhaps not yet reflected sufficiently on the importance of social and physical mobility in expanding the possibilities of freedom, including sexual freedom, especially for women" in their analyses of the radicals (p. 255). However, as he makes clear in the remainder of the chapter, this social and physical mobility was primarily restricted to men and his examples of sexual freedom are from male authors. And it seems clear that Hill understands the limitations on such freedom for women, despite what he argues earlier. "Sexual freedom, in fact, tended to be freedom for men only, so long as there was no effective birth control" (p. 257).

48. Patricia Higgins, "The Reactions of Women, with Special Reference to Women Petitioners," in *Politics, Religion and the English Revolution, 1640–1649*, ed. Brian Manning (London: Edward Arnold, 1973), pp. 179–222. See esp. pp. 200–208, 215–17. For Lilburne's views see *The Leveller Tracts*, ed. William Haller and Godfrey Davies (New York: Columbia University Press, 1944), p. 6.

49. Higgins, "Reactions of Women," p. 217.

50. Richard Baxter, *The Catechizing of Families: A Teacher of Householders How to Teach Their Households* (London: T. Parkhurst, 1683). Even William Gouge, who encouraged nearly total obedience on the part of the wife, did not ask her to obey her husband against God's will (*Domesticall Duties*, pp. 326–27). Members of the Quaker sect argued most strongly for the religious equality of men and women, but even here their support of women's active role within the congregation was restricted. Women were not to speak within the church as women, but as spiritual vessels carrying the word of Christ. This blunted any conflict the Quakers might have had with Paul's restrictions against women's speaking in public. See Richard Farworth's *A Woman forbidden to Speak in the Church, The grounds examined, the mystery opened, the Truth cleared, and the ignorance both of Priests, and People discovered* (London: Giles Calvert, 1654). Females must not speak in church, but neither should males in their fleshly state "for that nature is adulterated from God, and nothing must speak in the Temple, either in male or female, nothing must speak in the church, but the Spirit of Truth, whom the World and carnal minded ones know not, God is a Spirit, and they that know him, and know him to be so, and none know him but they are spiritual . . ." (p. 3). *Minute Book of the Men's Meeting of the Society of Friends in Bristol, 1667–1686*, Bristol Record Society's Publications, 25, ed. Russel Mortimer (Bristol: Bristol Record Society, 1971). The men's meeting was jealous of its prerogative in questions of discipline and complained that a women's monthly meeting took up the issue. They invited women to explain this unprecedented act and when Margaret Heale, speaking for the women, noted that a letter by George Fox was read at the women's gathering, the minutes from the men's meeting recorded the following reaction: "Friends generally doe conclude that that letter of George's (which was directed only to men Friends and not

to women friends) was not the letter intended by the men's meeting to be sent to
and read at the women's meeting, but that the paper recommended by the men's
meeting was a paper against vanity and excess." The editor speaks of the
dominance of the men's meetings: "In theory the Men's and Women's meetings
for discipline and government in the Society were equal in status, but they tended
to have different spheres of activity, and where these coincided the Men's meeting
always gained control" (pp. x–xl).

51. C. B. MacPherson, *The Political Theory of Possessive Individualism:
Hobbes to Locke* (Oxford: Clarendon Press, 1962), P. 296. In interpreting a
comment Lilburne made in his *Freemans Freedome Vindicated* (London, 1646),
that "all and every particular and individual man and woman" were "by nature
all equal and alike in power, dignity, authority, and majesty, none of them having
by nature any authority, domination or magisterial power one over or above
another" except "by mutual agreement or consent," MacPherson argues that this
did not signify political rights for women. Such is the case, he argues, because one
can assume such a "transfer of authority from women to their husbands." Thus
women freely give up their political rights upon marriage and therefore do not fall
under the Leveller program. J. C. Davis takes exception to MacPherson's interpretation of the Levellers' political ideology, noting that they sometimes supported servant and copyhold suffrage, depending upon the politically wise stand
for the moment. He is, however, referring only to a "manhood suffrage," even
though he concludes with the following summary. "What I hope to have suggested here is that it is still possible to conceive of the Levellers as having at times,
a radical concept of 'the people' akin to our own." J. C. Davis, "The Levellers and
Democracy," *Past and Present* 40 (July 1968): 174–80. Gerard Winstanley, in
*The True Levellers Standard Advanced: or, The State of Community opened, and
Presented to the Sons of Men* (London, 1649), appears at times to be including
women in his program when he says of the individual: "every single man, Male
and Female, is a perfect Creature of himself," but women were ignored when he
spoke of political rights or officeholding and the supporters who signed the
frontispiece of this work were men. Christopher Hill, *Milton and the English
Revolution* (New York: Viking Press, 1977), pp. 117–19. Hill notes that no
groups supported the political rights of women, and that even the radical sects
had a limited view of women's religious rights. He quotes from a local Baptist
tract from Abingdon which argued that "they [women] may not so speak as that
their speaking shall show a not acknowledging of the inferiority of their sex and
so be an usurping authority over the man." Alan MacFarlane's *The Origins of
English Individualism: The Family, Property and Social Transition* (New York:
Cambridge University Press, 1979) does comment on women's omission from the
development of English political rights but focuses on the interaction between
alteration in inheritance customs and the political rights of men.

52. J. G. A. Pocock, *The Ancient Constitution and the Feudal Law* (Cambridge: At the University Press, 1957); and Gordon Schochet, *Patriarchalism in
Political Thought: The Authoritarian Family and Political Speculation and Attitudes Especially in Seventeenth-Century England* (Oxford: Basil Blackwell,

1975). Much has been written on the essentially conservative nature of the revolutionary arguments put forth by the parliamentary party during the English Civil War, but perhaps Pocock's is the definitive work in the area. Schochet builds on Pocock's thesis but focuses on the family, especially the authority of the father, to document the conservative nature of mid-seventeenth-century political theory.

53. The term "free-born Englishwomen" is first used in a feminist work by Elizabeth Johnson, a friend of Elizabeth Rowe, in an introductory essay to Rowe's collection of poetry. See Ch. V.

54. For the best discussion of the importance of patriarchal ideas in seventeenth-century political theory see Schochet's *Patriarchalism in Political Thought*.

55. Thomas Hobbes, *The English Works of Thomas Hobbes of Malmesbury*, ed. Sir William Molesworth, vol. 2 of *Philosophial Rudiments concerning Government and Society* (1841; reprint ed., Aalen: Scientia Verlag, 1962), pp. 116–17.

56. Ibid., pp. 6, 121.

57. John Locke, *First Treatise*, in *Two Treatises of Government*, ed. Peter Laslett, 2d ed. (Cambridge: Cambridge University Press, 1963), p. 204. Melissa A. Butler, "Early Liberal Roots of Feminism: John Locke and the Attack on Patriarchy," *American Political Science Review* 72 (Mar. 1978): 135–50. The author argues that Locke's criticism of Filmer necessitated a critique of women's political subordination and this formed a basis for later feminist views. Yet Locke's citizenship was clearly not open to women in fact or theory, nor did he envision an equal relationship between husband and wife.

58. Locke, *Second Treatise*, in *Two Treatises*, pp. 368–69.

59. Power, *Medieval Women*, pp. 38–43.

60. A thorough discussion of women's legal status during the seventeenth century can be found in Glanz's dissertation. For a discussion of the punishment for petty treason committed by wives see William Holdsworth, *History of English Law*, vol. 5 (London: Methuen and Company, 1924), pp. 311–15.

61. For the most influential arguments about the personal as political among contemporary feminist writers see Kate Millett's *Sexual Politics* (New York: Doubleday and Co., 1970), pp. 23–58.

62. In the ancient-modern controversy of the seventeenth century, as outlined by Richard F. Jones, the feminists certainly came down on the side of the moderns, but they were less interested in Baconian concern with empirical knowledge or the general efforts to overhaul the classical curriculum than they were in the scientists' use of a rationalist perspective. Richard F. Jones, *Ancients and Moderns* (St. Louis: Washington University Press, 1962). Numerous works have appeared devoted wholly or in part to explaining the origins and nature of the scientific revolution in seventeenth-century England: for example, Herbert Butterfield's *Origins of Modern Science, 1300–1800* (London: G. Bell, 1949); and Thomas Kuhn's *Structure of Scientific Revolutions* (Chicago: University of Chicago Press, 1962). Other works have analyzed English science during this period primarily in institutional terms, linking it especially to the founding of the

Royal Society in the 1660s. See esp. Margery Purver, *The Royal Society* (Cambridge, Mass.: MIT Press, 1967). More recent works have argued that the scientific revolution cannot easily be isolated from the other revolutionary changes of seventeenth-century England. For such treatments see J. R. Jacob, *Robert Boyle and the English Revolution* (New York: Burt Franklin and Co., 1977); and Margaret C. Jacob, *The Newtonians and the English Revolution, 1689–1720* (Ithaca, N.Y.: Cornell University Press, 1976). One can discover similar viewpoints among the scientists and the feminists but any such link has been of little interest, understandably so, to those focusing on the development of scientific thought. An older work such as Jones's *Ancients and Moderns* is useful because he is more concerned with the activities of amateur scientists and with the kind of popular scientific ideas that were afloat in the mid-seventeenth century.

63. For a discussion of Anne's intellectual interests and a brief biography see Marjorie Nicolson, ed., *Conway Letters: The Correspondence of Anne, Vis-Countess Conway, Henry More, and Their Friends, 1642–1684* (New Haven, Conn.: Yale University Press, 1930).

64. Jones, *Ancients and Moderns*, pp. 148–80.

65. Margaret Cavendish, Duchess of Newcastle, "The Preface to the Ensuing Treatise," *Observations upon Experimental Philosophy* (London: A Maxwell, 1666), n.p.

66. Gerald Dennis Meyer, *The Scientific Lady in England, 1650–1760* (Berkeley: University of California Press, 1955), p. 29. He notes that by 1666 the duchess of Newcastle had become disenchanted with scientific instruments, especially the telescope, and "during 1666 she published her most important scientific treatise, *Observations upon Experimental Philosophy*, a kind of summary of contemporary science containing a rationalistic criticism of the empirical method." Margaret Cavendish, Duchess of Newcastle, *The Grounds of Natural Philosophy* (London, 1668), pp. 1–2.

67. Newcastle, "Preface," *Observations upon Experimental Philosophy*.

68. Aphra Behn, Translator's Preface to *A Discovery of New Worlds*, by Bernard de Fontenelle (London, 1688).

69. Ibid.

70. Ibid.

71. [Astell], *Serious Proposal*, p. 75.

72. Ibid., p. 32.

73. *An Essay in Defence of the Female Sex*. Written by a Lady, 2d ed. (London: Printed for A. Roper and E. Wilkerson, 1696), p. 29.

74. [Mary Astell], *A Serious Proposal to the Ladies, Part II*, (London: Printed for Richard Wilkin, 1697), pp. 135, 145–57.

75. Lady Mary Chudleigh, "To the Reader," *Essays upon Several Subjects in Prose and Verse* (London: T. H. for R. Bonwicke, W. Freeman, T. Goodwin, 1710), n.p.

76. Chudleigh, *Poems on Several Occasions*, p. 40.

CHAPTER III

"Daughters Are but Branches"
English Feminists, 1650–80

Between 1650 and 1680, isolated English women began exploring for the first time various social and intellectual questions specifically in relation to their bearing on women as a social group. Often their feminist concerns were restricted to particular fields of interest or expertise: Bathsua Makin and Hannah Woolley on education, Margaret Fell Fox on religion, and Jane Sharp and Elizabeth Cellier on midwifery. Another woman, however, Margaret Cavendish, Duchess of Newcastle, offered a very wide-ranging and penetrating, if inchoate, survey of the way sexual stereotypes infiltrated and influenced society. Both tentative and contradictory elements often characterized these women's feminist gropings—unsurprising in the first group of English writers to explore sex-related injustices—but yet their topics and their emphases were to be those that later feminists pursued. In these writings, and particularly in the duchess's sharp observations on a broad range of issues, one can see new perceptions emerging from the cocoon of traditional preconceptions.

I

No work of a seventeenth-century feminist poses so many interpretive problems as the writings of the first of their number, the duchess of Newcastle. Her views were at once the most radical and far-reaching and the most contradictory. She appears to have understood, better than any of her sisters, the multifaceted nature of women's oppression. She noted

75

their poor education, exclusion from public institutions, political subordination within the home, physiological dictates of childbirth, and society's pervasive vision of women as incompetent, irresponsible, unintelligent, and irrational. Yet she often suggested that society's perception was correct; women had made few contributions to past civilization, not because they were ill educated but because they had less ability than men. She could denounce the unjust treatment accorded to women as vehemently as anyone, but she could also be as critical of her sisters as the staunchest misogynist. None of the feminists considered sex roles more broadly than the duchess and none proved so reluctant to offer unambiguous conclusions.

In 1653, at around the age of twenty-eight, the duchess of Newcastle began publishing works in various fields of scholarship. Her writing career had begun earlier, for she had been composing manuscript works, both poetry and prose, from the age of thirteen. By 1668, when her last book was published, she had written fourteen works in fifteen years. These volumes included plays, poetry, fantasies, biography, autobiography, letters, "orations," and works on experimental and physical science. The production of five scientific treatises, five collections of poetry and works of fantasy, two groups of essays and letters, and two volumes of plays was a feat unequalled, in scope at least, by any other seventeenth-century woman and rarely matched by later English women.[1]

Rambling and showing little sense of the dramatic, the works of the duchess of Newcastle were a conglomeration of her untutored views on every imaginable subject. Often insightful, they also revealed a woman whose scant education did not prevent her from arguing about the scientific and social questions of the day. Frequently she included an idea of an imaginary phenomenon followed by a description based on current knowledge in natural philosophy, without clearly segregating the fantasy from the fact. In other works, she piled example upon example of what she considered truth, friendship, justice, or fame. Many of her poems, devoted to natural descriptions, prove the extreme difficulty of maintaining a poetic tone while describing the various sorts of atoms. The worst of these are works such as "Nature calls a Council, which is Motion, Figure, Matter and Life, to advise about making the World," "The four Principal Figured Atomes Make the four Elements," or "Of Contracting and Dilating, whereby Vacuum must needs follow." Such titles make clear the truth of her claim that she did not really desire to write poetry at all.

"The Reason why I write it in Verse, is," she explained in one of her many oddly straightforward apologies, "because I thought Errours might better pass there, than in Prose, since Poets write most Fiction, and Fiction is not given for Truth, but Pastime." [2]

As such passages illustrate, there is arrogance in the duchess's work, but only in the sense that she presumed to speak about many things concerning which her knowledge was meager. Often tedious, her writings are nonetheless interspersed with particularly telling points, amusing comments, and an impressive honesty which keeps them from being boring or pompous. Certainly her work was better when she recognized the limitations of her education and did not write obscurely about subjects in which she had little training. These books are the products of a writer painfully aware of her lack of education and of the prejudices against a woman's thinking publicly, but a writer nonetheless determined to use and to speak her mind. None of her books has fewer than five prefatory remarks explaining her defects in particular areas of scholarship. A few have more than a dozen such prefaces, surely a record even in a century much given to this form of apologia. With each new work she tried to defend herself against the attacks lodged against previous ones. Seldom has an ambitious author devoted so much effort to excusing faults or fending off expected criticism. Yet some of her best writing appears in these introductory materials, where she discussed most directly herself, other women, or various social groups. In one of her innumerable excuses for the poor quality of her writings she asserted: "I wish heartily my Braine had been Richer, to make you a fine Entertainment . . . and though I cannot serve you on Agget Tables, and Persian Carpets, with Golden Dishes, or Chrystall Glasses, nor feast you with Ambrosia, and Nector, yet perchance my Rye Loafe and new Butter may tast more savoury, then those that are sweet, and delicious." [3]

Whatever her literary shortcomings, the duchess and her rye bread and butter remain likeable. No individual could have worked harder to please or impress, and no one could follow contradictory paths with more spontaneous honesty. This is evident, for instance, in her treatment of scholarship and of scholars, who represented the world to which she aspired but to which, as a woman, she had little access. At times she applauded wisdom and those who possessed it, and lavished fulsome praise on university dons. At other times she called their learning "artificial" and praised those who, like herself, had natural rather than artificial wit. But the most difficult choice for her to make was whether to support other women, accepting her sisterhood with them and writing of the general restraints on their lives, or to ally herself with men, criticizing women and praising male genius.[4]

Tragically, the overriding force which molded the life and writings of the duchess of Newcastle was her desperate desire for fame in an age when women had little chance for action, acclaim, or preeminence. She wanted to be read, to be popular, to be remembered. Her social position brought her attention, but the duchess wanted the world to admire her for her own talents and works, not because she married well. This desire for personal recognition inspired her repetitious defense of the originality of her work. Her writings, she reiterated, came not from her husband nor others, but solely from her own rational powers.[5] This self-conscious ambition contributed to the overreaching in her works, but it also gave impetus to her most important theme.

Her greatest contribution to feminist thought was the degree to which questions of sex division dominated her work. No matter what her subject, no matter what the context of a particular piece, the duchess introduced the fact that she was a woman and explained how this influenced her work. She made an exception to this rule in her purely descriptive pieces devoted to the physical sciences, but even here she handled the issue in her introductory materials. This focus on sex distinction, repeated in all subsequent works, was prominent in her very first publication. "Spinning with the Fingers is more proper to our Sexe," she wrote "then studying or writing Poetry, which is the spinning with the braine," but "Having no skill" in weaving made her "endeavour to Spin a Garment of Memory, to lapp up my Name, that it might grow to after Ages." [6] Yet she expected the "smile of scorne" from men hostile toward women's encroaching on their territory, "for they hold Books as their crowne . . . by which they rule and governe." [7] This work, *Poems and Fancies*, had a further introductory note "To All Noble, and Worthy Ladies," in which she called upon the ladies to support her effort. "Condemne me not as a *dishonour* of your *Sex*, for setting forth this *Work*, for it is *harmlesse* and *free* from all *dishonesty*." Since men would probably scorn her work, she often asked women's support on a basic tenet of feminism—a common sisterhood among them. In making her appeal she referred to a contemporary play, *The Wife*, in which the leading lady was aided by her female acquaintances who "help [ed] her, to keep her *Right,* and *Priviledges,* making it their owne Case." She called upon women particularly to use their sharp tongues to defend her: "So shall I get *Honours,* and *Reputation* by your *Favours*; otherwise I may chance to be cast into the *Fire.* But if I burn, I desire to die your *martyr.*" [8]

Although these introductory remarks reveal a strong feminist perspective, they also show the ambivalence evident in so many of the duchess's works. She defended the writing of poetry by saying that poetry conformed to the fanciful and emotional nature of women and was therefore an acceptable form of expression. Then, when calling on her sisters for support, she noted that women's particular power lay in sharp and vicious tongues. Asking women's help, at the same time she satirized them in the commonplace antifeminist judgments of her day. Such a conflict appeared again and again in her work. Still, whatever her criticisms of women, she presented one of the earliest and most inclusive catalogues of women's subordinate role in society. No one expressed women's exclusion from citizenship more vigorously than the duchess of Newcastle in her *Sociable Letters*: "And as for the matter of Governments, we Women understand them not; yet if we did, we are excluded from intermeddling therewith, and almost from being subject thereto; we are not tied, nor bound to State or Crown; we are free, not sworn to Allegiance, nor do we take the Oath of Supremacy! We hold no offices, nor bear we any Authority therein; we are accounted neither Useful in Peace nor Servicable in War, and if we be no Citizens in the Commonwealth, I know no reason we should be subjects to the Commonwealth. And the truth is, we are no Subjects, unless it be to our Husbands." [9] Yet here, as well, she undercut her feminist analysis with the conventional idea that women were actually more powerful than men because they ruled them secretly in the home with "beauty, and other good Graces, to help us to insinuate our selves into men's Affections." Without such advantages, the duchess concluded, "we should have been more inslaved than any other of Nature's Creatures she hath made." [10]

Despite her inconsistencies of perspective, the significance of the duchess's writings lay in the fact that she raised such major issues so intelligently. Her introductory comments to one of her scientific works, *The Worlds Olio,* made clear the vitality and the limitations of her feminist perspective. The work, written in 1650 when the duchess was twenty-five years old but published five years later, began with her usual apologies for its numerous failures. "It cannot be expected I should write so wisely or wittily as Men," she allowed, "being of the Effeminate Sex, whose Brains nature hath mix'd with the coldest and softest Elements." [11] There followed an argument that men were more clever, inventive, strong, and just than women. But she concluded this paean to men with an analysis that was to become a standard feminist historical interpretation of how "men from their first Creation usurped a supremacy to themselves, although we were made equal by Nature." This "Tyrannical Government they have kept ever since," began her feminist litany of grievances against men, "using us either like Children, Fools, or Subjects, that is, to flatter us to obey, and . . . not let us divide the World equally with them." This process had led women into a "slavery" which "hath so dejected our spirits, as we are become stupid . . . whereas in Nature we have as clear an understanding as Men, if we were bred in Schools to mature our Brains, and to manure our Understandings, that we might bring forth the Fruits of Knowledge." [12]

Seventeenth-century feminist writers sketched this picture again and again, linking men's tyranny over women to prohibitions against women holding public office or gaining a decent education. But having made the feminist case with such vigor, the duchess reverted to detailing the great literary works, scientific inventions, and military exploits of men. Nor did she limit masculine accomplishments to the gentle classes; she spoke as well of manual labor. [13] Precious metals, she contended, would not have been drawn from "the Bowells of the Earth if there were none but Effeminate hands to use the Pick-axe and Spade." Nor could the ore be made into goods "if none but Women were to Melt and Hammer them out whose weak spirits would suffocate and so faint with the heat, and their small arms would sooner break than lift up such a weight." [14]

Such seeming contradictions were embedded in the duchess's peculiar intellectual and historical role: her intelligence led her to develop probing feminist explanations, but without abandoning truisms about women. There are innumerable instances in her works where she clearly described the social controls which had prevented women's accomplishments, but almost equally numerous are the times when she argued that women's failing came from inherent physiological weakness. It is difficult to imagine any individual thinking more often about how being a woman influenced her life or how being male determined the life of men.

The theme was as constant in her works as her conclusions were inconsistent.

The duchess of Newcastle was often more expansive about women's unlimited capabilities in her works of fiction. Her plays were consciously centered upon the exploits of a daring heroine or the intellectual accomplishments of a female scholar. Often it was she herself who personified such accomplishments. One of her lengthiest fantasies, *The Description of a new World called The Blazing-World*, described the life of a woman who became shipwrecked in the South Seas, along with a number of corpses on board the vessel. She was rescued by natives, then transported to paradise, where she was married to the local emperor. The remainder of the tale, obviously representing the scientific interests of the duchess, described the new empress asking the natives questions about their religious customs (specifically why they excluded women) and at greater length about their scientific beliefs. She used this questioning to reveal her advanced scientific knowledge and to expose their limited understanding of scientific concepts. A spirit then appeared to the empress and directed her to call upon the duchess of Newcastle to become her scribe because the duchess wrote with such reason and sense. The empress was most impressed with her skills, and they formed a close attachment, although the duchess did eventually return to England. Yet her soul continued to commune with the empress and "they became Platonick Lovers, although they were both Females." In this fantastical manner the duchess was able to gain the position of influence denied her in the real world and to move toward the goal stated in her preface to *Blazing-World*, "though I cannot be Henry the Fifth, or Charles the 2nd; yet, I will endeavour to be, Margaret the First." [15]

The duchess's longest sections of feminist commentary occur in the "Female Orations" section in *Orations of Divers Sorts*.[16] This book was primarily a work in moral philosophy which included orations on topics like truth, friendship, and pride. Brief sections on the roles of peasants, merchants, and scholars were included so that the debate over women's place was similar to arguments about other groups. The "Female Orations" are curious short essays (written as dialogues) ranging from brief paragraphs to almost two pages. It is often difficult to decide when the views are those of the duchess, perhaps because the opponents represent some of her own divided consciousness. One group of speakers argued that women had been oppressed by and for the benefit of men, while the other side contended that women were naturally irresponsible creatures who had been able to survive only through the efforts and generosity of male protectors. Although the dialogue closed with the antifeminist side, the feminist side presented the more lengthy, numerous, and convincing arguments—at least to the extent that they went unanswered by their opponents. The orations also illustrate a continual problem in judging the duchess's writings—namely, their imaginative nature. She so often made her points through stories and fantasy that it is hard to be sure when she was being serious and when merely argumentative.[17]

The "Female Orations" began with the feminist argument which set the tone for the remainder of the debate:

> Ladies, Gentlewomen, and other Inferior Women, but not less Worthy: I have been industrious to Assemble you together, and wish I were so Fortunate, as to persuade you to make frequent Assemblies, Associations, and Combinations amongst Our Sex, that we may unite in Prudent Counsels, to make ourselves as Free, Happy and Famous as Men: whereas now we Live and Dye, as if we were produced from Beasts, rather than from Men; for, Men are happy, and we Women are miserable; they possess all the Ease, Rest, Pleasure, Wealth, Power, and Fame; whereas Women are Restless with Labour, Easeless with Pain, Melancholy for want of Pleasures, Helpless for want of Fame. Nevertheless, Men are so unconscionable and Cruel against us, that they endeavour to bar us of all sorts of Liberty, and will fain bury us in their houses or Beds, as in a Grave. The truth is we live like Batts, or Owls, labour like Beasts, and dye like Worms (pp. 238–40).

This strongest criticism of women's position in society yet written by an English woman was obviously a broad social indictment, not a personal lament. In this speech the duchess presented a picture of women in abject misery which was alien to her own life. By her own admission her life and marriage were most happy, and she never suffered the pain of childbirth. Rather than being buried in her house, she encouraged the duke to avoid the court after the Restoration and to live with her in isolation at Welbeck. The passage was an exaggerated outline of her observations on women's general status and not a plaint about her particular situation.[18]

The next oration attacked men even more vigorously as women's devils as well as their tyrants. This speaker argued that the first orator "hath spoken wisely and eloquently, in expressing our Unhappiness," but complained that she failed to declare "a Remedy, or shew . . . us a way to come out of our miseries" (p. 240). The previous speaker, she assured her hearers, would be regarded as a goddess if she could help women escape from the labyrinth men had built for them.

The third orator defended men, who were not the enemy but women's friends and protectors, "our Admirers and Lovers." Men both worked and fought for women, doing "all which we could not do ourselves." To complain about men was "as ungrateful as inconsistent," for all sexual differences came from nature "who hath made Men more Ingenious, Witty and Wise, than Women; more Strong, Industrious, and Laborious, than Women." This orator concluded that women were "Witless and Strengthless, and Unprofitable Creatures, did they not bear Children" (pp. 241–42).

Whatever her distance from the orations' initial feminist arguments, the duchess's personal image must have been further from this picture of female incompetence. She was far from "witless" or "strengthless." Not only did she publish many works, contrary to social custom, but while her husband remained exiled in Holland she spent much time in England attempting to raise funds for his support. She also admired the ability of her mother to manage the family estate following the death of her father. This speaker's oration was suspect not only because it went beyond anything the duchess believed, but because it far exceeded even the conventional arguments about women's limitations.

The next speaker attacked the last views by arguing that, if women had no wit and no strength, "it is that we neglect the one, and make not use of the other" (p. 242). A common feminist argument followed, that before society criticized women it must open up its institutions to determine if they could do as well as men. To insist on natural inferiority without changing those institutions that caused or at least encouraged it was obviously unjust.

An antifeminist replied that women who imitated men would become natural defectives, hermaphrodites who were neither good men nor good women. She glorified women who were "Modest, Chaste, Temperate, Humble, Patient, and Pious" as possessing those qualities surest to produce happiness (p. 243). The remaining arguments in this dialogue stressed chivalry and its relevance to the question of whether men or women had the better lot in society. An orator supporting change argued that women should imitate men "so that, by our Industry, we may come, at last, to Equal Men, both in Perfection and Power" (p. 244). This moderate stance, premised nonetheless on women's inherent equality, perhaps came closest to the duchess's own views, but she let the anti-feminists have the last word. Women were superior creatures because they lived more comfortable and safe existences, and because, an orator exclaimed, their beauty and grace made them men's "Saints . . . Tyrants, Destinies, and Goddesses" (p. 246). That this view was not the duchess's again seems underlined by her own life and writing, which showed little evidence of the pursuit of the safe, the comfortable, or the conventional.

Those works which portray most vividly what the duchess conceived as women's sorry state were funeral orations also included in *Orations*, proposed for delivery following the deaths of two young women. In "A Funeral Oration for a Woman dead in Childbed," the duchess of Newcastle related the death of one woman to the tribulations of all and to men's dismissal of these tribulations. She contended that "although all Women are tender Creatures, yet they endure more than Men," in facing both suffering and dangers. Even so, "Men think all Women meer Cowards, although they do not only venture and endanger their lives more than they do, but endure greater Pains, with greater Patience, than Men usually do." Women suffered pain in childbirth and all the problems involved with bringing up children and caring for them during times of sickness, while men avoided these trials. Therefore "Nature hath made her Male Creatures, especially Mankind, only for Pleasure; and her Female Creatures for Misery." Women remained slaves to their troubles while men "are made for Liberty." Nor was this slavery restricted to the troubles associated with children, because women are "Slaves to Men's Humours, nay, to their Vices and Wickednesses; so that they are more enslaved than any other Female Creatures" (pp. 194–95).

This oration condemned a broad spectrum of women's existence. She insisted that females suffered in a way that men did not, and then underwent the further humiliation of being damned as weak and cowardly despite the heavy dangers and duties they bore. In another oration, she made a similarly wide-sweeping attack on both women's sufferings and the unrealistic and unsympathetic view men held of them. Yet the bitter vividness of such passages raises questions about their intent. Her reference to male pleasure and female misery seems particularly exaggerated in view of its neglect of the sufferings of men, especially those of the lower class. Was she being serious in creating such a dichotomy between the sexes, or was she speaking only of her class, or only of matters like childbirth and child-care? The duchess observed and thought tellingly about sex-related issues, but her comments were too fragmentary to lead to a sustained analysis of the relationship between the sexes. They contained a kernel of truth, but that kernel was never nourished to fruition.

Yet the duchess's tone should not make her views seem more of an anomaly than they actually were. For instance, the death of a newly married woman inspired an oration that argued somewhat extremely that "Death is far the happier condition than Marriage." In "A Funeral Oration for a Young New-Married Wife," she argued that even though marriage may be pleasant early "yet, after a time, it is displeasing; like Meat which is sweet in the Mouth, but proves bitter in the Stomack." Marriage cannot survive those day-to-day realities which include "Neglects, Disrespect, Absence, Dissembling, Adultery . . . Cross Answers, Peevishness, Forwardness" or "Frowns" (p. 181). Although Mary Astell, during a later period, wrote in much more restrained language, she still viewed marriage as a private tyranny, and Hannah Woolley, writing at the same time as the duchess, spoke of women in revolt. The duchess may have enjoyed writing shocking things, or simply following a single idea or observation beyond the bounds of the wholly reasonable. But the occasional extremity of statement does not contradict a quality of emotional sincerity in these passages. Others professed comparable views, but simply couched them in more acceptable terms or used less one-sided arguments.

The life of the duchess of Newcastle offers some clue as to why the issue of sexual distinction in structuring society should have formed, very haphazardly and intermittently, the core of her work. Her autobiography (appended to the famous *Life* of her husband) revealed a telling dichotomy between domestic peace and external distress. She had a most happy childhood and, by all accounts, an equally successful marriage. However, when she ventured outside the confines of home and family she often experienced acute embarrassment and a sense of being an outsider. She knew, particularly later in her life, that her intellectual interests and strange appearance—she often designed her own unconventional costume—made her the butt of numerous jokes in polite society. She avoided this society, but her apologetic prefaces make clear that she could not be indifferent to those who mocked her intellectual aspirations. The autobiography shows throughout this mixture of pleasure in her work and in her family and unhappiness with the social scorn that perhaps lay at the heart of her incipient feminism. Surrounded as she was by warmth and encouragement in her home both as a child and an adult, her talents and aspirations took root. But there was thin soil for them to grow in, she was well aware, in a society that provided women with little education and even less opportunity for public use or display of intellect.

Her autobiography, a mere forty-three pages written with delightful frankness and simplicity, began with the assertion that her father, who died while she was still an infant, "was a gentleman, which title is grounded and given by merit, not by princes." As wealthy and well-situated as many of those holding titles, her father refused to purchase nobility, as he was urged to do, because he "did not esteem titles unless they were gained by heroic actions." [19] This emphasis on her family status may have grown from her resentment toward those who cautioned the duke against marrying beneath himself. Yet the emphasis was similar to that which she was to pursue in her own life and writings; socially granted status mattered little compared to that which was awarded for intellectual contribution or personal merit. Her literary labors and her desire for fame grew out of a belief that merited worth, of the kind she believed her parent possessed, mattered more than the titled position her marriage brought her.

With her father's early death, her mother was left to manage a large estate, supervising much of the field work as well as the domestic. As a woman who inherited an important practical role, her mother became an important model of female competence. The perceptive daughter recognized her mother's skills and her enjoyment of practical duties. "She was very skillful in leases, and setting of lands, and court keeping, ordering of stewards, and the like affairs," her daughter noted. "And though she would often complain that her family was too great for her weak management . . . , yet I observe she took a pleasure and some little pride, in the governing thereof" (p. 294). Practical accomplishment, which her mother inherited with widowhood, the daughter pursued in a less socially accepted form during the life of her husband.

She was the youngest girl in a large and prosperous family, and it cost a great deal to train her and her sisters to be proper young ladies.

Still, her mother developed generous natures within all her children by treating them "tenderly" and trying to "please and delight" them, "not to cross or torment them, terrifying them with threats" (p. 278). Reason rather than force was the means of discipline, but the girls got very little in the way of serious intellectual instruction. Their tutors concentrated on teaching them "singing, dancing, playing on music, reading, writing, working and the like" (p. 280). It was an education that varied sharply from her brothers', who were taught in a "different manner of ways from those of women" (pp. 280–81).

She praised her brothers for their martial abilities and love of honor—two of them had died during the Civil War. Although three of the brothers had married while she was yet a young girl, they, like her married sisters, lived one-half of the year with their mother. This indicates exceptionally close parental ties and relationships among the brothers and sisters, and the duchess certainly suggested that this was so. The closeness of the family, upon whose approval she felt she depended too much, made her uneasy in her external relations. Her brothers and sisters opposed her becoming an attendant to Queen Henrietta Maria because they feared she might behave improperly away from their guidance: "Which indeed I did, for I was so bashful when I was out of my mother's, brothers' and sisters' sight, whose presence used to give me confidence—thinking I could not do amiss whilst any of them were by, for I knew they would gently reform me if I did . . . I was like one that had no foundation to stand, or guide to direct me, which made me afraid, lest I should wander with ignorance out of the ways of honour, so that I knew not how to behave myself" (pp. 286–87). This pattern of close support in the family and insecurity outside it was to remain throughout the duchess's life.

Her shyness led her to believe the court judged her "a natural fool," but her mother opposed her giving up the position once she had committed herself. She followed her mother's advice and, after two years at court, she met the duke of Newcastle, who "wooed me for his wife . . . though I did dread marriage, and shunned men's company as much as I could." There is no clue as to why she dreaded men or marriage other than out of shyness. Nor did this keep her long from accepting him "by reason my affections were fixed on him, and he was the only person I ever was in love with" (p. 288).

Theirs must have been a strange union in many ways. He was thirty years her senior and the father of a large family, while she was not only young but had been brought up in a sheltered environment. She insisted that her feeling for the duke "was not an amorous love," which she knew only "by relation, not by experience" (p. 288), but presumably his attraction to the twenty-year-old girl was less dispassionate. His fifty years and his social standing must have placed early strains on their romance. There are hints of difficulties in the duke's love poems to his future wife and in her letters of reply. The duke's poems reveal a passionate love framed in an amateurish but enthusiastic poetic style. He believed a gentleman should write poetry to his lady fair, and he did so at the rate of about one poem a day—seventy in all. The duke argued for the ardor of an older love in a charmingly risqué manner. He asked that she not be cruel to his love because of his age, for seasoned wood was "love's best of fuel":

> No man can love more, or love higher;
> Old and dry wood makes the best fier,
> Burnes cleerest, and is still the same,
> Turn'd all into a living flame.
> It lasts not long, is that your doubt,
> When am to ashes all burnt out?
> A short and lively heate that's pure,
> Will warme one best, though not indure.
> When young, wett wood makes but a smoake,
> And never warmes but doth you Choake;
> Though with your panting Bellows trie,
> That little fier seemes to die;
> Smother'd in Vapours, dimly lies;
> Pleasant, not Usefull, Spoyles your Eyes.[20]

Perhaps this promise that his seasoned love would keep her "both warme and heated" meant less to the future duchess than his assurances that his love was not like that of a young "self lover" who "Bridles no Passion but is loose to Sinne, Takes lust for love, runnes over Woman kinde." [21]

The letters of the young Margaret Lucas reveal a wary wisdom over the duke's professions of love. Friends had warned her that she should be cautious because the duke had "ashured your selfe to many and was constant to non." [22] She worried about court gossip and spent much of her correspondence warning the duke what could happen to her reputation if they were seen too often together. She also feared that the duke might interpret improperly her correspondence and admitted, "I am a lettell a shamed of my last leter . . . not that my affection can be to larg but I fear I discover it to much . . . for women must love silently." [23] Her other major concern was to thwart any possible opposition by the queen, who she felt might be influenced by those who opposed the marriage. On the whole she appears a most competent twenty-year-old, who was able to secure the duke's affection without becoming subordinate to him, even refusing to pass notes from him to the queen. Her letters reveal shrewdness, but also a real affection for the duke.

The duke's poetry suggests he was overcome by her beauty, wit, and charm, but the duchess, when she wrote the *Life* of her husband, claimed that he "having but two sons" wanted to marry her to "increase his posterity by a masculine offspring. . . . He was so desirous of male-issue, that I have heard him say, he cared not, (so God would be pleased to give him many sons) although they came to be persons of the meanest fortunes; but God frustrated his designs, by making me barren" (pp. 87–88). Whatever the duke's desire for issue, disappointment did not "lessen his Love and Affection" for his wife. All the evidence points to his pride in his wife's literary efforts. His encouragement is made clear in one of the duchess's many prefaces in praise of him. It might have been expected, she wrote, that her husband would chide "Work, Lady, Work, let writing Books alone, for surely Wiser Women ne'r Writ one," but such was not the case: "your Lordship never bid me to Work nor leave Writing, except when you would perswade me to spare so much time from my Study as to take the Air for my Health." She appreciated such consideration because she felt her incompetence at needlework and "such works as Ladies use to pass their Time" and that "the materials of such Works would cost more than the Work should be worth, besides all the time and Pains bestow'd upon it." [24] There was recognition here of the emptiness of women's work, but also some latent suggestion of embarrassment at her unsuitability for housewifely pastimes.

The duchess may have also felt some self-consciousness about being childless, and her single personal reference to the duke's desire for more heirs may have derived as much from her uneasiness at diverging from the accepted wifely pattern as from his wishes. Her *Sociable Letters* condemned a second wife for wanting children when her husband already had heirs to carry on his name: "I know no reason why she should be troubled for having no Children, for though it be the part of every good Wife to desire Children to keep alive the Memory of their husband's name and Family by Posterity, yet a Woman hath no such Reason to desire Children for her own Sake." She proceeded to justify this negative view of motherhood by pointing to all the social injustices involved. The woman had no family name to pass on once she married, and no estate "according to the laws and customs of this countrey." After undergoing the risk of bearing children and the burden of raising them, mothers could not "assure themselves of Comfort or Happiness by them" for sons continued the male line "whereas Daughters are but Branches which by Marriage are broken off from . . . whence they Sprang, & Ingrafted into the Stock of an other Family, so that Daughters are to be accounted but as Moveable Goods or Furnitures that wear out." [25] Whether the duchess intended this as a self-defense, the argument against motherhood—seldom voiced in the seventeenth century—was made solely from the woman's interest. Nor did she neglect the foolish motives that often led women to want children: "but many times Married Women desire Children as Maids do Husbands, more for Honour than for Comfort or Happiness." Pregnancy too was often an excuse for self-indulgence, for spending fortunes on special foods and linens.[26]

However strong her argument that "a Woman hath no such Reason to desire Children for her own Sake," the duchess surely knew that few married women in the seventeenth century had the choice of when or whether to have children. The passage would suggest some ambiguous feelings about and need to justify her own barrenness by attacking other women's sentimental glorification of motherhood. There is also some sense of personal inadequacy in fulfilling an accepted female role in her attack on "breeding women" who "are so Coyly Amorous" to their husbands or "so Amorously Fond and so Troublesome Kind, as it would make the Spectators Sick." [27] Certainly the picture here is the mirror opposite of her self-portrait in the autobiography. "I love extraordinarily and constantly, yet not fondly" (pp. 311–13).

As seen in her *Life* of the duke and appended autobiography, the duchess's life during the troubled years of the Civil War was a hard one. In their seventeen years of exile and relative poverty, the duchess endured moves from Paris to Rotterdam to Antwerp—each determined by the need to find more willing creditors—and the deaths of her mother, two brothers, and a sister. Fortunately the duchess had her mother's example to guide her, for in all these difficulties it fell to her to placate creditors, borrow funds, and keep the family afloat financially. Even the Restoration did not completely undo the financial damage, for although some of the duke's former estates were restored to him, both he and the duchess believed he was never fairly compensated for his sacrifices for Charles I (pp. 289–98).

Yet the years after their return to England seem to have been comfortable. They had been married for thirty years when the duchess died, and their relationship appears to have grown from the stereotypical May-September affair to one based on mutual admiration, if one believes the biography the duchess wrote and the verses the duke wrote for her works, especially lyric poems for her plays. He encouraged her in all her intellectual pursuits and spent great sums on books for her to read and on the costs of her publications. And he certainly did not stint praise, writing of her *Orations:* "Were all the Graecian Orators alive, / and swarms of Latines" who could write each "word so soft and gentle," even their wisdom would be dimmed by hers. All that was required to lessen the ancients' reputations was to "look / On this admired Ladies witty Book! / All Europ's Universities, no doubt, / Will study English now, the rest put out." [28]

The duke's most touching tribute to his wife was the inscription he placed on what was to be their joint tombstone:

> Here lyes the Loyall Duke of Newcastle, and his Dutches, his second wife, by whom he had noe issue; Her name was Margaret Lucas, youngest sister to the Ld. Lucas of Colchester, a noble familie; for all the Brothers were Valiant, and all the Sisters virtuous. This Dutches was a wise, wittie, and Learned Lady which her many Bookes do well testifie; she was a most Virtuous and a Loveing and carefull wife, and was with her Lord all the time of his banishment and miseries, and when he came home, never parted from him in his solitary retirements.[29]

The duke's flattery in verse and eulogy suggests the need to convince a largely hostile world of the worth of her activity. But society remained scornful of the duchess's work and personality. Upon meeting her for the first time, the wife of John Evelyn criticized the duchess's style of dress, while admitting it suited her figure, disapproved of her attempts to hide her age, and singled out "her gracious bows, seasonable nods, courteous stretching out of her hands, twinking of her eyes, and various gestures of approbation." She also characterized her conversation as "airy, empty, whimsical and rambling . . . terminating commonly in non-sense oaths, and obscenity!" [30]

Perhaps this description simply reflects prejudice against a woman who dared to be different, as did Dorothy Osborne's glib opinion: "Sure the poor woman is a little distracted, she could never be so ridiculous else as to venture at writing books and in verse too." [31] Certainly Evelyn's picture contrasts sharply with the honest and naive self-portrait with which the duchess concluded her autobiography. She believed herself to be "more inclining to be melancholy than merry, but not crabbed or peevishly melancholy, but soft, melting, solitary, and contemplating melancholy" (pp. 311–13). Yet the two personality sketches are possibly compatible. The duchess described her character within the confines of her supportive family life, while Evelyn reported something of the social loudness with which the duchess hid her shyness and her haunting knowledge that society did not sanction the role she'd chosen.

Probably the duchess cared more for the opinions of the learned, but here too the reactions ranged from condescending to glaringly obsequious. Joseph Glanvill's praise of her scientific work must have pleased the duchess, although he made clear he considered it an extraordinary achievement for a woman. He wrote, "I am, Madam an admirer of rarities, and your Grace is really so great an one" that he wished to offer "some testimony of a proportioned respect and wonder" to her. Her work had convinced all "by a great instance, that women may be philosophers, and, to a degree, fit for the ambitious emulation of the most improved masculine spirits." His comments had the ring of a self-serving and condescending tribute of dubious integrity. [32]

Scholars alternately praised and ridiculed the duchess of Newcastle's work, with much of the praise coming from groups who had something to gain from her. For instance, Cambridge University officials were particularly obsequious in a letter to her because they expected a large bequest from the duchess, whose husband, two brothers, and father had attended the school. The Master and Fellows of Trinity wrote in 1663 to call her "both a Minerva and an Athens to yourself, the Muses as well as Helicon, Aristotle as well as his Lyceum." [33] But even they were outdone by a letter of thanks the Vice Chancellor and Senate dispatched. Their obligation was not only for the recently received *Life* of her husband, they assured the duchess, "for whensoever we find ourselves nonplussed in our studies we repair to you, as to our oracle; if we be to speak you dictate to us; . . . if we compose an history, you are the remembrancer; if we be confounded and puzzled among the philosophers, you disentangle us and assoil all our difficulties." [34] Probably the duchess was too hungry for approval not to enjoy such fulsome praise, and too intelligent not to detect its patent insincerity.

Her many prefaces suggest that her own doubts about her suitability for the intellectual work she loved were as great, and perhaps more nagging, than those of the public. Her early education had been that of a girl, and its nonintellectual character is suggested well in an early letter to the duke, who had been advised not to marry beneath himself. "Me lord, me lord Widdrington in his advies has don as a nobell and a true affectshoinit fri[e]nd would doe," she admitted, "yet I find I am infinninghtly obleged to you whose afectshoins are above so powerfull a parswashon." [35] Even given the vagaries of seventeenth-century spelling, the passage demonstrates that women of her class received inadequate training. The duchess was simply not trained to do what she wanted to do most—write—and this she both recognized and resented.

She understood well the connection between her sex and not only her lack of acclaim but also her sense of her work's imperfections. In a second edition of her *Philosophical and Physical Opinions*, she began by thanking her husband again for supporting her work, and went on to say that she had little hope that her views would become generally known: "and I being a Woman Cannot, or if I could, it were not Fit for me Publickly to Preach, Teach, Declare or Explane them by Words of Mouth, as most of the most Famous Philosophers have done, who thereby have made their Philosophical Opinions more Famous, than I fear Mine will ever be." [36] What she obviously missed here was the community of scholars to which only men had access, where her ideas could have been brought to others' attention and been argued, tested, and perhaps sharpened. A letter to a friend, to whom she had recently sent a present for her daughter, reveals touchingly the duchess's longing for women with similar interests. The toys were sent not "for Bribes, to corrupt her from Edifying Learning and Wise Instruction, for I would not have her Bred to Delight in Toyes, and Childish Pleasures." Her wish was that the gifts might "allure her to that which is most Profitable, and Happiest for her Life . . . to Listen to Wise Instruction, to study Profitable Arts or Sciences." Her notion that "Tinsell-Toyes" are more persuasive to children than "Terrifying Threats and Cruel Blows" makes sense, but there is an element of pathos in this strategy to lure one girl toward intellectual interests.[37]

Lacking any intellectual community to which she could belong, the duchess was sharply aware of the limitations of the scholarly groups from which she was excluded. She attacked pedantry and argued forcefully against the popularity of rhetorical flourishes and a too great dependence on ancient sources. Those men who excluded her from the inner sanctums of learning were not keeping so much to themselves after all, she argued, for much of their scholarship was simply squabbling over given formulas or echoing age-old discoveries. Despite her limitations—indeed in part because of them—at least her work was original and based on experience. She saw some worth in her academic failings by noting that because "I was not Bred in an University or Free-school, to Learn the Art of Words," she did not concern herself with "Forms, Terms, Words, Numbers or Rymes." Rather, she assured her readers, "I leave the Formal, or Worditive part to Fools, and the material or Sensitive part to Wise men." [38]

Yet the "wise men" seldom responded enthusiastically and the duchess was left to ponder why. This lack of response created the obsession with fame that dominated her thought and, along with her feminism, provided a constant theme in her massive and disorganized collection of writings. The idea troubled her "like a conscience" that it was honorable "to aspire towards a Fame." Surely it was good to "run after Glory, to love Perfection, to desire Praise," and even if she was unworthy of fame, she felt "some Satisfaction in Desiring it." [39]

And did she deserve it? Cursed with the limited education that was women's lot and the inability of society to take seriously women's ideas except as a "rarity," how could she know? Perhaps women were less competent than men; perhaps they were made inferior by a social and educational system run by and for men. Would her works be more acceptable if she explained her flaws as natural to woman or inevitable in an unjustly sexist society? Whatever her answers to these questions, they related to the central fact of her life, in society's eyes and her own, that she was a woman determined to act in what was considered a male sphere. She did the best she could with what opportunity she had, and her work was most impressive in the profound if inconclusive thoughtfulness she brought to her social role of a publicly thinking woman. In defending herself and her work she was often defending all women in ways that had never been used before.

II

The lives of the other women raising feminist issues between 1650 and 1680 were more obscure than that of the duchess, and their writings were much more limited to specific social interests. Yet those interests spilled over at times toward general areas of women's status and centered on questions of vast importance to women, many of which were basic to the concerns of later feminists. Margaret Fell Fox, a Quaker, stressed the practical implementation of the idea of sexual equality within the meetinghouse, marking the culmination of the limited raising of women's role among English religious dissidents. The other early writers concentrated on questions of more importance to later feminists. Jane Sharp and Elizabeth Cellier were concerned with maintaining women's position in the one quasi-profession females had traditionally dominated, midwifery. Most important, two governesses, Bathsua Makin and Hannah Woolley, called attention to the issue that was to be a central concern of later feminists—the need for women to have greater educational opportunity.

Fell, much like Cellier and Sharp, limited her feminism to a single issue but based her argument squarely on the propriety, indeed the desirability, of women's holding responsible positions in the area that mattered most to her and her coreligionists. In a pamphlet on women's preaching, in her personal efforts to encourage women to become Quaker ministers, and in her involvement in the women's meeting of the Society of Friends, Fell argued straightforwardly for the equality of women before Christ and in religious activities. Her pamphlet, quite similar to George Fox's writings on the subject, stressed the mutual duties of men and women in their allegiance to Christ and denied women's subservience in areas of religious activity, but without raising the issue of women's role in the household or in society more generally.[40]

Margaret Fell Fox's case was largely biblical. That male and female were created as one by God, with both inextricably united under Christ, provided the basis for her religious egalitarianism: "God created Man in his owne Image; in the Image of God created he them, Male and Female." She interpreted this verse to mean that "Here God joyns them together in his own Image, and makes no such distinctions and differences as men do." Because distinctions did not come from God, she claimed that those who criticized women's speaking in the church were in league with the devil and spoke "out of the enmity of the old Serpents Seed." Because Christ was always one, the same "in the Male and Female," he obviously could and would speak and act through both.[41]

She also stressed that the church was feminine and those who would silence women would silence the church, that Christ honored women and that they were the group kindest toward him, and that Paul was referring to one specific instance of the Corinthians speaking in unknown tongues when he issued his statement about women's silence in church.[42] It was strictly a scripturally based argument and did not touch upon women's social status. She asked merely that the Christian woman be allowed to practice her religion as fully and variously as a man. This was far from a small demand, even if it did not include a questioning of other aspects of sexual hierarchy.

Fell's religion made no sex distinction—either in terms of duties or of rewards. She labored long as a minister and dissenter whose determination to speak out led to conflict with the authorities and to arrest. She also put in ˑ practice her belief that women should have a role in the meetings by supporting the organization of the women's meeting on an equal footing with the men's within the Society of Friends. She organized the monthly meeting for women at Swarthmore—the Lancashire estate of her first husband—and attended its gatherings until she was eighty-four. By the time the women's meetings were solidly established, she was older and took a lesser role than her daughters in their organization, but she was an active member until her death.[43]

The women's meetings, although they met monthly and quarterly with the men's, had separate functions, including visiting the sick and prisoners, looking after the poor, the widowed, and the orphaned, being in charge of the moral care of women Friends, and finding places for Quaker servants. Yet such duties, despite their connection with women's traditional sphere, regularly took them away from their homes, and Margaret Fell Fox was often separated from George Fox for long periods to carry on preaching or prison visitations. Her focus was a limited, spiritual one, but her words and deeds made clear how taking equality before God seriously could lead women to take on religious and philanthropic functions commonly regarded as male prerogatives and to carry out these new duties most competently.[44]

In the late seventeenth century, male infringements on the realm of midwifery, which had been women's one area of quasi-professional dominance, engaged Jane Sharp and Elizabeth Cellier in women's issues. Jane Sharp wrote the *Complete Midwife's Companion; or, The Art of Midwifery Improved* in 1671; it had gone through four editions by the 1725 printing, which was signed "Mrs. Jane Sharp, Practitioner in the Art of Midwifery above 40 years." She dedicated her work to her "sisters," the "Celebrated Midwives of Great Britain and Ireland," and wrote because she had "often sat down sad in the Consideration of the many miseries Women endure in the Hands of unskilled Midwives." Since much of this suffering grew from inadequate knowledge of anatomy, Sharp explained that she had "been at a large Expence in Translating of Books, either French, Dutch or Italian of this kind," which she combined with "my own experience" to create a book that would aid all midwives "in this Great Work." [45] Her printer verified Sharp's skills and noted that the great popularity of her work had caused him to reissue it.

Her guide for midwives was organized like other gynecological texts of the period. The topics of the six books followed the general pattern of seventeenth-century guides for women, advancing from a description of male and female genital organs to advice on the conception and bearing of children and their care immediately following birth.[46]

Her feminist views appeared in her introductory defense of midwifery, "the most useful and necessary of all Arts, for the Being and Well-Being of Mankind." For this reason a midwife had to be both God-fearing and "exceeding well Experienced in that Profession." [47] Following a discussion of the historical importance of midwives, which even the "Holy Scriptures" had recorded, she defended women's "Natural Propriety" to the calling. In primitive societies, women handled the task effectively, and even in England among "poor Country People"— except for the starving who had "more need of meat than midwives"— with only female assistance "the Women are as fruitful, and as safe and well delivered, if not much more fruitful, and better commonly in Childbed, than the greatest Ladies of the Land." Most women could only expect other women to attend them in their labor, and these often fared better than wealthy ladies with physicians in attendance. Sharp's was very much a sex-based argument. Men could "employ their Spare time in some things of deeper Speculation than is required of the Female Sex; but the Art of Midwifery chiefly concerns us." [48]

Sharp recognized only one legitimate argument against women's dominating the profession. It was hard for them to gain "Knowledge of Things as Men may, who are bred up in Universities . . . where Anatomy Lectures being frequently read, the situation of the Parts of both Men and Women, and other things of great Consequence are often made plain to them." Her book was intended to rectify this deficiency by supplying the theoretical knowledge which was essential, but no more so than the practical understanding that midwives possessed more abundantly than most physicians. [49]

The view of midwife incompetence came, Sharp thought, from those who had little experience in deliveries and who imposed irrelevant demands such as the knowledge of Greek on such competence. To have anatomical and medical terms "in our Mother tongue," she tartly observed, "would save us a great deal of needless labor." Midwives had the experience, as well as the empathy with their patients, that made them more skillful in their trade than any possible male replacements, if simply given some chance to acquire anatomical knowledge. In arguing for the primacy of women as midwives, she defended the abilities of women as a whole, urged the need for greater female educational opportunities, and pointed out the empty pretensions of male claims to superiority in the field. [50]

Elizabeth Cellier argued for the qualities of women as midwives along similar lines, and worked more actively to organize them. In several short tracts defending her proposal for a corporation of midwives, she presented her case at a time when the question of who would license midwives was being debated. The possible candidates were the Bishop of London (or some other church official), the College of Physicians, a combination of midwives under the control of Dr. Peter Chamberlen, or a college of midwives which would act both as a body of instruction and as an arbiter of standards. In the first three options men would act as outside experts to establish standards of professional competence for the midwives. Although Chamberlen was himself a male midwife, he was also a member of the College of Physicians and nominated himself to be head of the midwives because of his supposed higher qualifications. [51]

During the sixteenth century the most significant criterion for acceptance as a midwife had been religious orthodoxy. Church examiners of that period had tried to discover possible Catholics, witches, or heretics among the midwives and to prevent them from practicing their trade. As the seventeenth century progressed there was a greater emphasis placed on the medical competence and scientific knowledge of the midwife, and often members of the College of Physicians would work with the church investigators to remove any medically unsound midwives. The college, determined to extend its authority to all realms of medicine, opposed Chamberlen's plan to license midwives himself and saw him as arrogantly insubordinate to its will. The midwives opposed Chamberlen for the same reason, but thought that control by the college was no more acceptable.[52] Cellier's proposal for a corporation of midwives insisted practitioners had sufficient medical knowledge and practical skills to act as a self-governing body.

Cellier noted that her written proposal developed from an oral presentation to James II in June 1687. Her idea included a royal hospital for foundling children and a corporation of midwives which would act as overseers for the children and teach skills and establish standards for others of their profession. Cellier's plan was modeled on practices in France, where midwifery was more highly organized and respected during the seventeenth century than its English counterpart. Married to a Frenchman, Cellier had lived in that country for a portion of her life and hoped to upgrade her profession in England along the lines she had observed abroad.[53]

In response to the College of Physicians' assumptions that all professional wrongs were attributable to the ignorance of individual midwives, Cellier argued that such questions must be judged by the numbers dying as a result of childbirth. Drawing attention from educational abstractions to pragmatic results in terms of female suffering, she insisted that the numbers of maternal deaths increased while the College of Physicians was licensing midwives. In the last twenty years, she claimed, 6,000 women had died in childbirth and 18,000 children had been stillborn, "above 2/3 of which . . . have in all probability perished, for want of due skill and care in those women who practice the art of midwifery" (p. 142). Her proposal, she felt confident, would lessen the frequency of such deaths by uniting "the whole number of skillful midwives . . . into a corporation, under the government of a certain number of the most able and matron-like women among them." This group of women, properly organized and subject to visitation by a Royal appointee, could then control what would be in effect a midwives' guild (p. 142).

Cellier suggested that the number of midwives admitted be no more than 1,000 and that they be charged fifty shillings for joining and fifty more per annum for dues. Money from the first sum should be used to purchase "one good, large, and convenient house, or hospital" to take needy children and to pay "one governess, one female secretary, and twelve matron-assistants" to care for the foundlings and to train them "in proper learning, arts, and mysteries, according to their several capacities" (p. 143). In addition to midwives' fees, she proposed that the king should guarantee that "one fifth part of the voluntary charity" collected in the participating parishes be devoted to the hospital and that contributions for it also be solicited in church boxes and from private bequests. She also urged the establishment of twelve smaller houses to take in expectant mothers whose children, if wards of the parish, would be placed in the charge of a matron and assistants from the corporation of midwives (pp. 143–45).

Cellier stipulated that the governess would have final say over the operation of the hospital and the appointment of personnel, but she envisioned male midwives and surgeons associated with the institutions. Boys would come under the supervision of the principal chaplain when the children were segregated by sex at age five. The male midwives and physicians in attendance would conduct classes for the midwives and present commentary on any unusual cases which might arise. There would be a principal male midwife in charge of the other men associated with the hospital, but his election would fall to the women with the governess having three votes, the secretary two, and the twenty-six female assistants one each (p. 145). Cellier's plans, particularly in regard to the care of the children, were highly detailed. First, the children would be given place names as surnames, which would make them "capable, by such names of any honour or employment, without being liable to reproach for their innocent misfortune." They would be treated as apprentices to the corporation and taught skills they could use in later life; such employment would also bring funds to the hospital. They were free to leave the hospital at age twenty-one, but could, if they wished, remain for their entire life as long as they abided by its regulations

(p. 145). Such a system would surely have aided illegitimate or exposed children considerably more than the charities which were taking care of them at the time. Finally, she included one of the earliest demands for child-care funds for midwives who appeared before the college's experts to describe any difficulties recently faced in their deliveries. "In the first years before the charge of the said hospital can be great," she urged that, "out of the annual dues," money "be paid to the proposer to enable her to provide for her children" while she presented her information to the college (p. 144).

Cellier's well-organized program would have provided care for the unwed mother, shelter for exposed children, and training for those children who were charges upon the parishes. In addition, her hospital would have upgraded the training of midwives, by allowing them to be supervised and licensed by experienced midwives. It would also have given administrative responsibility for all these tasks to one group of skilled women.

As might be expected, there was opposition to her proposal, which Cellier answered in a tract entitled *To Dr. . . . An Answer to his Queres, concerning the College of Midwives.* She hit first at those who argued that such an organization of midwives had never existed before by pointing out that associations of midwives existed hundreds of years before any such were heard of among physicians. She also listed authorities for her idea: the first chapter of Exodus, Paul's writings and Origen's "11th Homily upon Exodus." She further noted Hippocrates' praise of the goddess as well as the god of physic, and his sage advice, apparently forgotten by her physician detractors, that any special skills should be left to those "skilful in that Practice." Yet this difficult medical art "which ought to be kept as a Secret amongst Women as much as is possible" was now to be taken over by men who "understand nothing of it." [54]

Medicine, Cellier continued, was originally divided among the arts of midwifery, surgery, and the concocting of drugs. Unfortunately the mixing and prescribing of medicines, "the servile part, hath now usurp'd upon the other two; but we pretend only to the first, as being the 'most antient, Honourable and useful Part' " which had been practiced since the time of the Druids and Gaels by "wise women." [55] Her use of quotations around the honorable phrase is interesting in that it was very close to the language of Jane Sharp and could easily have been taken from her work. Only in the modern period had outside bodies of men examined and licensed midwives, and with no good results. In England in the sixteenth century bishops began licensing, and in 1642 surgeons took over and set up "three Examinations, before six skilful Midwives, and as many Chirurgions, expert in the Art of Midwivery." The Act of Uniformity sent the midwives "back to Doctors Commons, where [now they pay their fee to] take an Oath which is impossible for them to keep and return home as skilful as they went hither." [56]

Cellier ended her argument on a note of optimism by assuring her adversaries that James II had agreed to support both the establishment of a corporation for midwives and the hospital for exposed children which she had proposed. She also noted that her prediction of the queen's ability to have a child had been vindicated, an ironic triumph since this birth led to the ouster of James and the end of her proposals. Yet Cellier had made her case well, using arguments centered around the superior abilities of midwives and women to perform these tasks without outside interference. The proposed organization of her hospital, as well as her defense of midwives, had a decidedly feminist cast. [57]

Sharp's and Cellier's concern that midwives be better trained was similar to the more broadly aimed educational pleas for women that Bathsua Makin and Hannah Woolley voiced. Bathsua Makin, the sister of a mathematician, was governess to Charles I's children and ran a school for young gentlewomen at one point in her life. Woolley, also a governess, married and had children, but other details of her life have been lost. Both women were concerned with education, seemingly on levels that reflected their own class background. Makin, sister of an academic and governess to the king, wanted to educate young gentlewomen, particularly those gifted in foreign languages and philosophy, while Hannah Woolley was concerned with giving women, not necessarily wealthy ones, a practical guide to use in operating their households, educating their children, and caring for the sick. Despite these differences each woman argued for a higher education for women than was currently their lot and suggested that men kept them ignorant to enhance male prerogatives.

Bathsua Makin dedicated her work to all "Ingenius and vertuous Ladies," particularly Princess Mary, daughter of the future James II. In urging better education for young gentlewomen, Makin insisted that the prevailing view that women were intellectually incompetent had evil results for society. Makin wrote anonymously and in the persona of a man, which gave a conservative tone to much of her essay. When she spoke most explicitly as a male the work was most conservative: one man who tried to convince his brothers that their position would not be threatened if they allowed their wives or daughters to become educated. This masculine mask seemingly tempered her work, for the introductory materials, before she assumed a male perspective, were more feminist in tone: "Custom, when it is inveterate, hath a mighty influence: it hath the force of Nature itself. The Barbarous custom to breed Women low, is grown general amongst us, and hath prevailed so far, that it is verily believed (especially amongst a sort of debauched Sots) that Women are not endued with such Reason, as Men; nor capable of improvement by Education, as they are." [58] Such foolish views led foolish men to fear learned women as a "comet, that bodes Mischief, whenever it appears." Liberal female education, they feared, would "make Women so high, and men so low, like Fire in the Housetop, it will set the whole World in a Flame" (p. 3).

Even though Makin ridiculed antifeminist views, there was more appeal than denunciation or demand in this work. Women must be educated to make a better world, but such education must recognize the natural subordination of women. Everyone, she argued, would gain from women's education: "Women would have Honour and Pleasure, their Relations Profit, and the whole nation advantage" (p. 3).

She idealized the Renaissance education of women because it led to the intellectual greatness of Queen Elizabeth and Lady Jane Grey and provided a model for the type of education she supported. Throughout she insisted that she did not advocate "Female Preeminence" or familial equality—in part, one presumes, because she believed that "To ask too much is the way to be denied all." [59] Women's education was to recognize that "God hath made the man the head," so that husbands would be wise to consult educated wives but the latter should accept "that your Husbands have the casting Voice, in whose determinations you will acquiesce." She then directed a comment to women alone in which she expressed the hope that she would have no difficulty in getting the ladies to read her work "because it is your Cause I plead against an ill custom, prejudicial to you, which Men will not willingly suffer to be broken" (pp. 4–5).

In her pose as a man, Makin assured her readers that she had no desire to threaten masculine control, only to spur men on to greater accomplishments. If women could excel men in learning, it would "make us Court Minerva more heartily, lest they should be more in Her favour."

Even in male guise, however, Makin was sharp-tongued toward anti-feminists. While still assuming her masculine identity, she wrote, "It is an easie matter to quibble and droll upon a subject of this nature, to scoff at Women kept ignorant on purpose to be made slaves." It was hardly manly "to trample upon those that are down" (p. 5).

In answering the foes of women's education, especially those who argued that women were incapable of certain studies, Makin presented long lists of accomplished women. Her knowledge of both past and present women scholars was extensive, and she listed many more contemporary women than did most authors of such works. She had special praise for the duchess of Newcastle, who, "by her own Genius, rather than any timely Instruction, over-tops many grave 'Gown-Men' " (p. 10). In substantiating women's competence, she divided female scholars into groups of linguists, orators, logicians, philosophers, and mathematicians, all fields in which she wanted women educated. This new training was needed because conventional emphases were not only limited but really pernicious. "Meerly to teach Gentlewomen to Frisk and Dance, to paint their faces, to curl their hair, to put on a whisk, to wear gay clothes, is not truly to adorn," she asserted, "but to adulterate their bodies; yea (what is worse) to defile their souls." (p. 22).

Her *Essay* contained a postscript which outlined the plan for a school to be opened at Tottenham-High-Cross. The course schedule included conventional topics: "works of all sorts," which referred to needlework, "Dancing, Music, Singing, Writing, and keeping Accounts." The remainder of the time was to be spent on learning French and Latin, and for those who wished, Greek, Hebrew, Italian, and Spanish, "in all which (this Gentlewoman) hath a competent knowledge." She began with girls of eight or nine who could read well, instructing them in French and Latin. Not only could they learn languages, but they were to be given instruction in names, natures, values, and use of "Herbs, Shrubs, Trees, Mineral-Juices, Metals and Stones." At an advanced level students might study astronomy, geography, and especially arithmetic and history. If their parents were opposed to their learning a language, they could limit their advanced study to experimental philosophy (pp. 41–43).

The tuition was to be £20 per annum, and the charges increased as the student became accomplished in the various languages. This plan for her school ended on a practical note which provides insight into how teachers of girls' schools recruited their students in the seventeenth century. "Those that think these things Improbable or Impracticable" were invited to get further information "every Tuesday at Mr. Masons Coffee-House in Cornhill, near the Royal Exchange; and Thursdays at the Bolt and Tun in Fleet Street, between the hours of three and six in the Afternoons" from one of Makin's assistants (p. 43).

Bathsua Makin, because she loved scholarship, deplored the fact that it was denied to women. "There is in all an innate desire of knowing, and the satisfying of this is the greatest pleasure. Men are very cruel that give them leave to look at a distance, only to know they do not know" (p. 25). To make women aware of learning without giving them chance to participate fully was "torment." Her feminism centered almost exclusively on this desire to upgrade gentlewomen's education and overcome such exclusion.

Hannah Woolley's concern for women's education was more general and practical than Makin's and couched in blunter and less circumspect language. Most of her feminist opinions were contained in *The Gentlewoman's Companion*, although she also published, among other works, *The Ladies Directory* and *The Cooks Guide*. Woolley's writings were more utilitarian and less scholarly than Makin's, which made them seem applicable to more women. She intended her book as "a Universal Companion and Guide to the Female Sex, in all Relations, Companies, Conditions, and State of Life, even from Childhood down to Old-age; and from the Lady at the Court, to the Cook-maid in the Country." She thought there was no single book covering her range of topics, some of which she claimed were solely "the Product of my Thirty years Observations and Experience." [60] She acknowledged the need to be a Solomon in order to be competent in such a wide range of fields, but said that she convinced her bookseller of the basis of her knowledge and experience "lest any should think I am able to speak more than I perform." A glance at the "Table of Contents" for *The Gentlewoman's Companion* confirms broad experience indeed:

The duty and qualification of a Governess to Gentlewomens Children

Good Instructions for a young Gentlewoman, from the age of Six to Sixteen

Of the Gait or Gesture

Of Speech and Complement
Rules to be observed in walking with persons of honour, and how
    you ought to behave your self in congratulating and condoling
    them
Artichoaks Fried
Beef A-la-Mode
Jellies of several Colours, for all Sorts of Souc'd Meats, and to be
    eaten alone
An introduction to Physick and Chyrurgery
An approved Medicine to London-Midwives to break and heal
    womens sore breasts
Against a stinking Breath
To Nursery-Maids in London or elsewhere
Scullery-Maids
A method of Courtship on fair and honourable terms.

In her "Epistle Dedicatory," Woolley noted that she made use of
recent women's guides in French and Italian, but the focus on her work
was distinctly less scholarly than Makin's; she did not praise learning and
scholarship as an end in itself: "I look upon the end of Life to be
Usefulness." Usefulness in women she associated particularly with "having a competent skill in Physick and Chyrurgery," in part because of a
long medical tradition in her family which encouraged her to support
women's role in the field. In pursuing her interest in women's practical
needs, she confessed to ignoring the "airy and leight" writings done to
praise women, but which ignored their real needs.

Yet Woolley's pragmatism led her to emphasize, much as Makin
had, the need for upgrading women's instruction. "The right Education
of the Female Sex, as it is in a manner every where neglected, so it ought
to be generally lamented," she asserted in the opening sentence of her
"Introduction." "Most in this depraved later Age think a Woman
learned and wise enough if she can distinguish her Husbands Bed from
another."

Her language in the "Introduction" tags Woolley as either a woman
who believed one should say exactly what one meant or one whose
upbringing did not strongly stress feminine delicacy. She was refreshingly
blunt and vigorous, especially when she dealt with male prejudices
against female abilities. "Vain man is apt to think we were meerly

intended for the Worlds propagation, and to keep its humane inhabitants sweet and clean," she noted sharply "but, by their leaves, had we the same Literature, he would find our brains as fruitful as our bodies." She was not only sure of women's capacity but was certain that men kept women from learning "lest our pregnant Wits should rival the towring conceits of our insulting Lords and Masters." She asked pardon for such severe language, not really wishing "to infuse bitter rebellion into the sweet blood of Females." Women ought "to be loyal and loving Subjects to their lawful (though lording) Husbands," and perhaps parents more than simply men were at fault "in letting the fertile ground of their Daughters lie Fallow."

Unlike many sixteenth-century authors on women's education, Hannah Woolley did not envision female students simply memorizing moral and religious homilies and Scripture. She encouraged governesses to teach children with kindness, to find tasks appropriate for their particular ages, and to accommodate teaching to the needs of each individual child. Her sensitivity as a teacher and her desire to make girls think seriously were continued threads. If the child liked reading, Woolley suggested, the teacher should draw out "what she thinks of such a book." If the child liked to converse, encourage her to define why she liked "such a great Gentlewoman or Gentleman whose virtues she hath a great esteem for." From such casual interrogations the teacher could "make the Scholar cautious of what she delivers," and also gain "a great insight both into her disposition and understanding" (p. 6). The kind of sensitive practicality of such advice was the strongest trait in Woolley's treatise.

In a section entitled "A Short account of the life and abilities of the Authoress of this Book," Woolley gave her opinions on women in general and herself in particular. She showed a reluctance to appear as an author seeking fame, but little modesty in asserting her skills. She wrote not from any "ambitious design of gaining a name in print (a thing as rare for a Woman to endeavour, as obtain)," but out of sympathy for her readers who "have not received the benefits of the tythe of the ensuing Accomplishments" (p. 10). She then proceeded to list her accomplishments, ranging from needlework and crafts to medicine, from cooking to arithmetic.

Her chronicle of the life during which she had developed such broad-ranged abilities suggested extraordinary competence. At age fourteen she started to plan what she should do with her life, and before the age of fifteen became the sole mistress of a school. A gentlewoman (whom she does not identify) was impressed with Woolley's teaching skills and employed her as a governess, and from this lady she learned the arts of preserving and cookery. Following the death of this employer, she worked as a governess for another lady for seven years. In this position she advanced from governess to become "her Woman, her Stewardess and her Scribe or Secretary." As such she "kept an exact account of what was spent in the house" (p. 12) and greatly improved her knowledge of French through reading plays to her mistress. During this period she perfected the courtly graces and mingled with persons of high social standing, by her own account always with great success. She reported that she "gained so great an esteem among the Nobility and Gentry of two Counties, that I was necessitated to yield to the importunity of one I dearly lov'd, that I might free myself from the tedious caresses of a many more" (p. 13).

After her marriage, Woolley used her skills within her own household for a short time. After her husband's death, Woolley returned to her employments as a governess. Obviously Woolley was continually in need of a position, and was not born to association with the gentry. Her abilities made hers a productive life but one in which all her competence did not make achieving "an honest livelihood" easy. "The Almighty hath exercised me in all manner of Afflictions," she reported "by death of Parents when very young, by loss of Husband, Children, Friends, Estate, very much sicknes, by which I was disenabled from my Employment" (p. 14).

It is less surprising that most feminist writing was done by upper-class women than that a few ambitious middle-class females like Woolley got their ideas into print. In the general text of her works there was less material specifically about women, but there were sections of advice for young girls on how to order their futures. Only about one-eighth of her work was devoted to proper social behavior, while the remainder included recipes and medical advice, material comparable to that found in innumerable seventeenth-century household guides. Woolley, influenced by her own life and perhaps that of the early employer who had taught her to cook and can, steadily criticized giddy or pretentious behavior and praised industry and piety. "Incline not to sloth, and love not to laze in bed, but rise early having drest yourself with decency and cleanliness," she urged girls in one of her many bourgeois sermons. She then suggested that, cleanliness having been attended to, the ideal girl would "prostrate yourself in all humility upon your bended knees before God Almighty" (p. 17).

Along with these went stress on the need for girls to think seriously and not just follow forms. In reading, for instance, pupils must not just repeat words "but strive to understand what you read" (p. 18). Amidst a wealth of practical tips, there was also substantial discussion of proper marriage relationships. Here, Woolley's position, as might be expected in a book intended to prepare women for life in society, was conventional. She accepted male domination and taught women to be patient and forgiving of their husband's failings. Marriage, she argued, could be the most beautiful and comfortable relationship between people, but these were unions "not of hot tempered love, but endeared affection." In her utopian marriage of well-ordered affection, the husband ruled and the wife obeyed because "Superiority and Inferiority" were essential in marriage. "Undoubtedly the Husband hath power over the Wife, and the Wife ought to be subject to the Husband in all things," Woolley concluded (p. 104). She stressed that the husband should use his power wisely and kindly, but she never questioned its existence. Woolley was aware that women had to be prepared to accept the heavy costs of this reality: she concluded her work with examples of numerous women of past times who had sacrificed for husband and children. Woolley did, indeed, "not infuse the hot blood of rebellion" in women, but she surely made them more conscious of the costs of adaptation and of the need to cling to serious education as the best protection against those costs.

An increased respect and independence for women, based on their improved education but within the patriarchal structure, was at the heart of the earlier feminist writings of the seventeenth century. There were occasional outbursts of anger and general condemnation of the status quo throughout these writings, but they were offset by specific support of a hierarchical structure within marriage. The authors were unhappy with women's lot, but these early feminists hesitated to attack the institution of marriage or the reality of male dominance. Their work was to reflect on and create a deeper consciousness of sex-related prejudices and injustices that later feminists would more clearly probe and protest.

NOTES

1. For a biography and discussion of the writings of Margaret Cavendish, Duchess of Newcastle, see Douglas Grant, *Margaret the First: A Biography of Margaret Cavendish, Duchess of Newcastle, 1623–1673* (London: Ruper Hart-Davis, 1957).

2. Margaret Cavendish, Duchess of Newcastle, "To Natural Philosophers," *Poems and Fancies* (1653; facs., London: Scolar Press, 1972), n.p.

3. Ibid, p. 49.

4. Her numerous prefaces, often totaling ten for a single work, shifted from defenses of her writings based on the fact that she was a woman and that this limited the sophistication of her work to uncompromising arguments of the inherent worth of her work and society's unwillingness to give it or her proper recognition.

5. Margaret Cavendish, Marchioness [later Duchess] of Newcastle, "The Preface," *CCXI Sociable Letters* (London: Printed by W. Wilson, 1664).

6. Newcastle, "To Sir Charles Cavendish, my Noble Brother-in-Law," *Poems and Fancies*, n.p.

7. Newcastle, "To All Noble, and Worthy Ladies," *Poems and Fancies*, n.p.

8. Ibid. One questions the sincerity of the duchess in a comment such as this; it is doubtful that she truly wished to be women's martyr.

9. Newcastle, *Sociable Letters*, 16, p. 27.

10. Ibid.

11. Margaret Cavendish, Duchess of Newcastle, "The Preface to the Reader," *The Worlds Olio* (London: Printed for J. Martin and J. Allestree, 1655), n.p. Here the duchess was repeating seventeenth-century gynecological views (based on ancient texts) of the differing levels of temperature and moisture in males and females. For a more thorough discussion of these views see my "Ideology and Gynecology in Seventeenth-Century England," in *Liberating Women's History: Theoretical and Critical Essays*, ed. Berenice A. Carroll (Urbana: University of Illinois Press, 1976), pp. 369–84.

12. Newcastle, "Preface to the Reader," *Worlds Olio*, n.p.

13. Although the duchess wrote about manual labor and the lives of the peasantry in generally greater detail than did contemporaries of her class, that life was so foreign to her that she never connected it to women. When she spoke of lower-class exertion she spoke almost exclusively of male labor.

14. Newcastle, "Preface to the Reader," *Worlds Olio*, n.p. In this comparison of male and female talents the duchess made clear that she understood the controls placed on women's lives but believed such controls were not totally effective in limiting women's potential. She stated: "Thoughts are free, those can never be inslaved, for we are not hindered from studying . . . but may as well read in our Closets, as men in their Colleges . . . and though most of our Sex are bred up to the Needle and Spindle, yet some are bred in the public Theaters of the World." Thus, although women have lacked the advantages of men, still

some have been able to excel outside of the domestic sphere, and all could learn in private.

15. Margaret Cavendish, Duchess of Newcastle, *The Description of a new World called The Blazing-World* (London: Printed by A. Maxwell, 1668). Later scholars have linked this work to the origins of science fiction and, in particular, to Coleridge's *Rime of the Ancient Mariner*.

16. Margaret Cavendish, Duchess of Newcastle, "Female Orations," *Orations of Diverse Sorts*, 2d ed. (London: Ptd. by A. Maxwell, 1668). Further references to the *Orations* are from this edition and are cited by page number in the text.

17. This was especially true for her fantasies such as *Blazing-World* or her two volumes of plays, in which she developed female characters of intelligence and power who acted independently of men. Her plays revolve around a continual war between the sexes, such as in *The Comedy named the Several Wits*, in *Playes* (London: Ptd. by A. Warren for John Martyn, 1662). A male character asked a Madam Volante whether marriage did not equal friendship, and she replied that it was "a common-wealth, which is a contract of bodyes, or rather a contract of industry" where there are "oftner Civil Wars" than in "publick common-wealths" (p. 107). Two of her other plays, *The Female Academy* and *The Convent of Pleasure*, describe women's schools similar to Mary Astell's later plan for a women's college and portray male opposition to an isolated community of female scholars. One male observer of the academy notes, "it's a dangerous example for all the rest of their Sex; for if all women should take a toy in their heads to incloyster themselves there would be none left out to breed on" (p. 678). Her works were replete with strong women, comments about the destructiveness of marriage to women's power, and even a seemingly lesbian relationship in *The Convent of Pleasure*, but the degree to which these themes represented her own views or were simply fictional accounts is less clear.

18. Henry T. E. Perry, Introduction to *The First Duchess of Newcastle and Her Husband as Figures in Literary History* (Cambridge, Mass.: Harvard University Press, 1919). Elizabeth Bassett, the duke's first wife, is described as follows by Perry: "This lady, of whom little is known, seems to have led a very troubled life until her death in 1643. We find occasional allusions to her ill health and once an extensive list of remedies to ease her labor in childbirth; the fact that she was the mother of ten children, five of whom died in infancy, may explain this, and indeed she seems to have been a poor harmless drudge, destined to be worn out by the highest function of woman."

19. Margaret Cavendish, Duchess of Newcastle, *The Life of William Cavendish, Duke of Newcastle, to which is added the true relation of my birth, breeding, and Life*, ed. C. H. Firth (London, 1886), p. 155. Further references to the *Life* are from this edition and will be noted by page number in the text.

20. William Cavendish, Marquis of Newcastle, *The Phanseys of William Cavendish, Marquis of Newcastle, addressed to Margaret Lucas and her Letters in Reply*, ed. Douglas Grant (London: Nonesuch Press, 1956), p. 95.

21. Ibid., p. 47.

22. Ibid., p. 97.

23. Ibid., p. 107.

24. Newcastle, "To His Excellency The Lord Marquess of Newcastle," *Sociable Letters*.

25. Newcastle, *Sociable Letters*, pp. 183–84.

26. Ibid., pp. 184–86.

27. Ibid.

28. Newcastle, "To the Lady Marchioness of Newcastle on her Book of Orations," *Orations*, n.p.

29. Firth, Introduction to Newcastle, *Life of William Cavendish*, p. xli.

30. Grant, *Margaret the First*, p. 17.

31. Ibid., p. 111. The statement comes from a letter of Osborne's which was reprinted in her *Letters*, ed. G. C. Moore Smith (Oxford: Clarendon Press, 1928), p. 37.

32. Grant, *Margaret the First*, p. 212.

33. Ibid., pp. 219–20.

34. Ibid., p. 220.

35. Newcastle, *Phanseys*, p. 82.

36. Margaret Cavendish, Marchioness [later Duchess] of Newcastle, "An Epistle to the Reader," *Philosophical and Physical Opinions* (London: Ptd. by William Wilson, 1663).

37. Newcastle, *Sociable Letters*, p. 317.

38. Newcastle, "Preface," *Sociable Letters*, n.p.

39. Newcastle, "An Epistle to Mistris Top," *Poems and Fancies*, n.p.

40. George and Margaret Fell Fox present their central ideas about the proper role of Quaker women in the following tracts. George Fox, *The Woman learning in silence; or, The misterie of the Womans subjection to her husband: as also, the daughter prophesying* . . . (London, 1656). Margaret Fell Fox, *Women's Speaking Justified*.

41. Fell Fox, *Women's Speaking Justified*, pp. 3–5.

42. Ibid., pp. 5–8.

43. Isabel Ross, *Margaret Fell, Mother of Quakerism* (London: Longman's, Green, 1949), pp. 283–301. For a brief autobiography as well as evaluations of her by friends and acquaintances see Margaret Fell Fox, *A Brief Collection of Remarkable Passages . . . Relating to the Birth, Education, Life . . . of . . . Margaret Fell . . . Fox* (London: Printed and Sold by J. Sowle, 1710).

44. Ross, *Margaret Fell*, pp. 283–301; Fell Fox, *Women's Speaking Justified*, p. 17. There were limitations not only on the kinds of duties women performed but also on the kinds of women encouraged to speak in meetings: "the Apostle permits not Tatlers, busie-bodies, and such as usurp authority over the man. . . ." Only those who speak "neither in the Male or Female" were permitted to voice their opinions in meetings. See Ch. II for a more complete discussion of Quaker attitudes toward women.

45. Jane Sharp, *Complete Midwife's Companion; or, The Art of Midwifery Improved* (London, 1725). The 1671 edition was entitled *The Midwives Book. Or the whole Art of Midwifery* (London: Printed for Simon Miller, 1671).

46. For a more complete discussion of the nature of these works see Smith, "Ideology and Gynecology," pp. 369–84.

47. Sharp, "Of the Necessity and Usefulness of the Art of Midwifery," *Complete Midwife's Companion*, p. 1.

48. Ibid., pp. 5–8.

49. Ibid.

50. Herbert R. Spencer, *The History of British Midwifery from 1650–1800* (London: John Bale, Sons, 1927), p. iii. For discussion of the training and skills available among those who provided medical treatment for women in seventeenth-century France and England see Richard L. Petrelli, "The Regulation of French Midwifery in the *Ancien Regime*," *Journal of the History of Medicine and Allied Sciences* 26 (1971): 276–92; Thomas R. Forbes, "The Regulation of English Midwives in the Sixteenth and Seventeenth Centuries," *Medical History* 8 (1964): 235–43; and a two-part article by R. S. Roberts, "The Personnel and Practice of Medicine in Tudor and Stuart England," Pts. I and II, *Medical History* 6 (1962): 363–82, 8 (1964): 217–34. The latter provides a thorough discussion of the treatment available in seventeenth-century England, but fails to devote any significant attention to women or midwives.

51. Spencer, *British Midwifery*, pp. i–xxiii.

52. For a specific discussion of the development of obstetrical forceps and the enhanced role of the Chamberlen family in midwifery see J. H. Aveling, *The Chamberlens and the Midwifery Forceps* (London: J. & A. Churchill, 1882), pp. 30–59.

53. Elizabeth Cellier, "A Scheme for the Foundation of a Royal Hospital and Raising a Revenue of Five or Six Thousand Pounds a year, by and for the Maintenance of a Corporation of skilful Midwives, of such Foundlings, or Exposed Children, as shall be admitted therein," in *Harleian Miscellany* IV: 142–46 (London: White and Company, 1809). Further references to this work are noted by page number in the text.

54. Elizabeth Cellier, *To Dr. . . . . An Answer to his Queres, concerning the College of Midwives* (London, 1687/8), p. 5.

55. Ibid., pp. 5–6.

56. Ibid., p. 6.

57. See Smith, "Ideology and Gynecology" for a general discussion of the feminist implications of the professional rivalries between midwives and physicians.

58. Bathsua Makin, *An Essay to Revive the Antient Education of Gentlewomen, in Religion, Maners, Art, and Tongues* (London: Printed by J. D. to be sold by Tho. Parkhurst, 1674), p. 3. Further references to this work are noted by page number in the text.

59. Her reference to female preeminence and against those who desired too much was most likely directed toward Agrippa's treatise on female preeminence,

which appeared first in the sixteenth century but was reprinted in England during the mid-seventeenth century.

60. Hannah Woolley, "Epistle Dedicatory," *The Gentlewoman's Companion; or A Guide to the Female Sex* (London: Printed by A. Maxwell for Dorman Newman, 1673), n.p. Further references to this work are to this edition and are noted by page number in the text.

CHAPTER IV

"A New Path to Honor"
English Feminists, 1690–1710

Later seventeenth-century feminists were to build on the ideas which earlier ones had given currency. They both created more fully coherent structures for feminist thought and increased the rigor of their attacks on marriage. Mary Astell, whose full-length feminist book *A Serious Proposal to the Ladies* advocated a women's college—an idea that drew wide if controversial attention—set the tone for the later feminist writings. The preface to the period's most serious scholarship by a feminist, Elizabeth Elstob's *English-Saxon Homily on the Birth-day of St. Gregory*, also pressed the feminist case for women's intellectual potential and educational needs. And the anonymous *Defence of the Female Sex* presented the growing feminist argument with a much more polemical, antimale tone. That these ideas were widely shared is clear from the frequent use of feminist themes by the large group of women poets writing around the turn of the century.

These later feminists wanted what the earlier writers had sought—a greater respect for women which explicitly included recognition of their equal intellectual capacity, their need for education, and the desirability of marriage based on companionship, not domination. They made their arguments in more systematic presentations than the earlier feminists and, while not demanding total sexual equality, they focused more clearly on the oppression of women than Makin or Woolley, while their views were less self-contradictory than those of the duchess of Newcastle. They were less passive and often assumed the role of women's advocate, making a point of arguing with those who would misrepresent women.

These later feminists gained strength from building on the earlier writings; ideas that had seemed strange or transitory could now be developed because, if still controversial, they were much better known. Many women were now ready to argue their case with men and to make practical proposals for changing their status. In doing the latter, they were more and more compelled to attack aspects of the institution of marriage and often to accept or glorify the superiority of spinsterhood. Their stance became pronouncedly antimale at times, and more questioning of that institution where male domination was most direct. "Women are subject to no one—unless it be their husbands," the duchess of Newcastle had shrewdly observed; the later feminists were to enlarge upon the implications of this subjugation.

There were at least two other examples of feminist expression which were influential during the second half of the seventeenth century. Those were the works of Henry Cornelius Agrippa (originally written during the mid-sixteenth century), which appeared under two separate titles in mid-seventeenth-century editions, *The Glory of Women* (1652) and *Female Pre-eminence* (1670), and of Francois Poulain de la Barre, *The Woman as Good as the Man* (1677), published originally in French during the same decade.[1]

Agrippa's work was typical of works by a few men praising women in overly laudatory terms. In addition to influencing Nahun Tate's work later in the century, Agrippa was the model for a number of anonymous or obscure writings which argued that women were superior to men. This superiority derived from a number of sources: creation, where Eve was created as the last and most perfect of God's creatures; beauty, where women obviously excelled men; linguistically, where Eve meant soul while Adam meant lowly earth. Agrippa's work was not a serious analysis of the relations between the sexes, simply a listing of women's glories based on ancient and biblical examples and language.

Poulain's work, on the other hand, was one of the earliest and best historical and Cartesian analyses of the differing positions of men and women in society. He undercut the customary arguments for women's inferior social role, saying they were not based on reason but rather on prejudice. The status of women, he contended, was an excellent test for

Descartes's method because it was so clearly a product of traditional and irrational values. To support this contention, he traced the history of women's exclusion from society's institutions and determined that it was based on male jealousy rather than on logical dictates. For instance, at the establishment of academies in ancient Egypt, he contended, women were not excluded for reasons of intellectual incapacity but because their husbands did not approve of their contact with male instructors. Poulain continued his analysis by noting similar irrational reasons for women's being excluded from government and the military, and argued that force, not reason, dictated over the course of history that men would come to dominate society. Both as a Cartesian and as a thinker fundamentally interested in sexual division, his work was similar to that of the English feminists. We do not, however, have exact information that Astell read him, but there are strong similarities between his work and the anonymous *In Defence of the Female Sex*.

I

Mary Astell was the most systematic feminist theorist of the later seventeenth century. In 1694, at the age of twenty-six, she wrote her first essay on women, *A Serious Proposal to the Ladies*, one of the earliest and most impressive books to concentrate on women's position within society. The work discussed the powerful and negative impact of culture on women's lives, especially in the area of education. Here Astell took up the arguments that Bathsua Makin had presented twenty years earlier, enlarged upon them, and made them more philosophically sound. She suggested a practical solution to at least a few of women's educational dilemmas: a private women's college.

Each of the seventeenth-century feminists was inconsistent in her own way. The conflict within Astell's feminism revolved around the axis of church, state, and women's subordinate status. She was a particularly strong Anglican who espoused high-church principles in a number of writings on the Occasional Conformity Act and in more general essays defending the theology and structure of the Anglican establishment.[2] She professed an unquestioning acceptance of both godly and episcopal authority and saw no conflict between such faith and her unhappiness with women's status in seventeenth-century England. Her fundamental opposition to revolution or disobedience to the state or to those in positions of authority also created inconsistencies in her attack on the subordinate position of married women.[3]

Rather than confronting these conflicts directly, Astell circumvented them in a number of ways. She would emphasize women's subordinate role while discussing marriage as a religious institution ordained by God, but would ignore or downplay that subordination when discussing marriage as it actually functioned in seventeenth-century England. Or she would claim—in a very abstract and general way—that women's rational abilities and unlimited potential had been given to them by God and that to curtail their fulfillment was to thwart God's will. On rare occasions, she argued against the accepted interpretations of Pauline doctrine opposing women's active religious involvement, by contending that Paul was speaking of the particular circumstances of the early church at Corinth, not establishing principles for all women for all time. On political issues, she maintained royalist and Tory attitudes, while encouraging women to fight unjust marital and public restraints. She could most comfortably integrate her conservative politics and her feminism in jests and barbs at Puritans or parliamentarians who rebelled against the king while ruling their homes with an iron hand. Sharply aware of the sexist elements in theories of the rights of Englishmen, Astell mocked their inconsistencies but generally ignored her own.

In an appendix to the 1730 edition of her book on marriage she, speaking of herself in the third person, made a typical jibe at her political-sexual adversaries: "Far be it from her to stir up Sedition of any sort: none can abhor it more; and she heartily wishes, that our Masters would pay their Civil and Ecclesiastical Governours the same Submission, which they themselves exact from their Domestick Subjects." [4] Her point is well taken, but no better than if it were reversed: if questioning a king's actions or power were seditious immorality, was not the same true of attacks on husbandly behavior and authority? For good reason, her political apologetics of 1704–5 largely excluded her feminist concerns.

Her Anglican-Tory scorn for Whig dissenter theorists gave particular intensity to her devotion to Cartesian rationalism. Her feminism required an attack on custom, which she saw as both the chief cause and the central defense of women's inferior position. No one could try to improve female status while arguing that whatever is, is right. "That the

Custom of the World, has put Women, generally speaking, into a State of Subjection, is not denied," Astell noted in *Some Reflections upon Marriage*, "but the Right can no more be prov'd from the Fact, than the Predominancy of Vice can justify it" (p. 139). To attack custom within the English revolutionary framework was impossible for a devout Anglican and royalist who opposed raising questions about the English social and political hierarchy; to attack custom from a Cartesian perspective accorded precisely with Astell's religious proclivities.

Her writings reveal that Astell was a dedicated Cartesian, but one of a particularly religious bent. She began with a philosophical doubt about all knowledge, and, working from the assumption that we know there is a God because we can imagine perfection in our minds, she, like Descartes, reasoned toward the truth of our existence and on to a surety that God created us and that we are obliged to follow his plan. Her works combined Christian faith with a sophisticated rationalist constuction in a system that paralleled Descartes's "Discourse on Method." [5] Because her arguments that women were treated unjustly were based primarily on rational dictates rather than historical evidence, she spent little time tracing the history of women's subjugation. What mattered was that Reason and reasoning proved the necessity of freeing women from the customary controls which limited the full use of their rational powers and God-given abilities.

The strength of her commitment to a Cartesian thought process was evident in her defense of Anglican theology, *The Christian Religion, As Profess'd by a Daughter of the Church of England* (1705), where Astell documented why she believed a woman should follow the same path to salvation as a man and why the proper path lay through the teachings of the Church of England. The work was a response to a current work, *A Lady's Religion*, which encouraged female religiosity without combining it with rational understanding of the Scriptures. Astell argued that the mystical and unintelligible exhortations so often used to encourage women's beliefs were ridiculous and destructive. Women's spiritual development demanded that they must know, as well as men, why they believed in a particular form of Christianity. To love God "with all her Heart and Strength" was not enough; the female Christian must also "love Him with all her Mind and Soul." Women could not rely on others for their salvation. "God never requires us," she assured her readers, "to submit our Judgments to our Fellow-Creatures, except in cases wherein

He makes them, and not us, answerable for the Error and all its evil Consequences" (p. 5).

Her religion was not inherited, she claimed. She did not become a member of the Church of England because it had been the faith of her parents, "but because I have according to the best of my Understanding, and with some application and industry, examin'd the Doctrine and Precept of Christianity, the Reasons and Authority on which it is built" (pp. 6–7). On this foundation of women's need to study the Scriptures intelligently and independently, she constructed a Cartesian train of thought to establish her own being—"I am only because He is"—and that of God's other creatures. Her existence required the existence of some prior being who must be "Absolute and Infinite Perfection" and therefore God, "since God is by the supposition the most Perfect Being." No matter where she lived, she reasoned, she would have posed the question "What am I? and from whence had I my Being?" and been led toward the same conclusions and the next question, "What Obligations am I under? What Acknowledgments am I to make to that Being from whom I hold my All?" To love God and to serve his creatures was the purpose and the joy of life, "for surely the only way to be happy is, by conforming my self to his Will" (pp. 8–11).

This religious argument ended, as did so much of her writing, with a call for the serious education of women, which would be good for society in general, not merely for women. "I make no question but great Improvements might be made in the Sciences, were not Women enviously excluded from their proper Business" (p. 296). The strongly Christian bias in her feminism caused her to offer somewhat narrow options for the educated woman, but also stimulated her intense concern that women's opportunities be widened.[6]

Astell's conservative politics, religious intensity, and feminist views clearly have roots in her familial background and life experiences, although the only information about her family comes from parish records, guild accounts, and tombstone inscriptions, and none exists regarding Mary's childhood or education. From these we know that she was born to Mary Errington and Peter Astell, a member of the guild of hostmen whose duty it was to entertain "merchant strangers" and to supervise "their peaceable conduct" and "their sales,"[7] and was baptized at St. John's at Newcastle-on-Tyne on November 12, 1666. Peter Astell was not admitted to the company of hostmen until 1674, although he had acted as clerk of the company for several years before, but the family was solidly middle class. Both the Astells and the Erringtons were prominent in the affairs of Newcastle. Furthermore, there was a strong royalist tradition, at least among the Astells; her grandfather, undersheriff at Newcastle, was a noted supporter of the king in that region. Although later admirers and biographers argued that Mary Astell knew classical languages, her own lament suggested no education in the ancient tongues: "My Ignorance in the Sacred Languages, besides all other disadvantages makes me incapable of expounding Scriptures with the Learned." [8] Astell's brother, Peter, doubtless had much better training, because he became a lawyer, a profession he practiced in Newcastle until his death in 1711. Such were the common educational discrepancies between boys and girls in English society, but in this case it may have fostered Astell's devoting much of her life to urging better educational opportunities for women. Upon her father's death in 1678, the company voted "3£6s 8d dureing the companies pleasure to old Mrs. Astell," and half that amount was paid out the following year. Following her mother's death in 1684 and the resultant breakup of the family, Mary Astell, aged eighteen, left for London.[9]

By the early 1690s, Astell was living in Chelsea, where a circle of women with similar intellectual interests had grouped about her. She dedicated a work to one of them, Lady Catherine Jones, in 1695.[10] Astell probably lived with Lady Catherine, the daughter of the earl of Ranelagh, after 1715, and through her became familiar with the ways of the court. Other close friends included the duchess of Mazarine, whose unhappy marriage inspired Astell's strongest feminist book, Lady Elizabeth Hastings, and Lady Mary Wortley Montagu. Florence Smith, Astell's biographer, suggests that she also became intimate with Elizabeth Elstob, the Anglo-Saxon scholar, who live in London between 1709 and 1715.[11]

Unmarried and without strong family ties, Astell obviously found in this circle of women the affection and mental stimulation that gave her both the support needed for her work and a sharpened awareness of how little society encouraged the intellectual potential and interests she and her friends shared. Her proposed college seemingly would have institutionalized this informal network of mutually supported, sisterly intellectual development. In addition, the marital troubles of her friend and neighbor, the duchess of Mazarine, as well as Astell's own spinsterhood, certainly encouraged the jaundiced eye Astell cast on marriage's relation to female subjugation.

Astell was also on good terms with a number of Anglican divines and philosophers such as John Norris. She does not appear to have led an isolated or lonely life as an adult, and her work received general attention, with each of her volumes on women going through four editions. In a gesture suggesting the general respect in which Astell was held, Queen Anne offered her a pension in her later years. The note of bitterness in her later writings seemingly owed less to personal unhappiness than to her disappointed aspirations for her sex and their education.

The strong relation between Astell's personal friendships, her feminism, and her religion was clear in her *Letters concerning the love of God*, exchanged between Astell and John Norris. Norris, a Platonist most noted for introducing Malebranche's work to England, was a member of the Athenian Society and jointly edited the *Athenian Mercury*, a 1690s publication which encouraged women's readership. Norris's printing these letters revealed not only his favorable impression of Astell but a sufficiently wide distribution of her work of the previous year to make it worthwhile to note on the title page that the letters were "Between the Author of the Proposal to the Ladies and Mr. John Norris." [12]

Astell began the correspondence in 1693, showing a refreshing and uninhibited intellect willing to question the opinions of a scholar of Norris's stature. The letters demonstrated that the twenty-seven-year-old Astell was groping toward an understanding of both her duties to God and her duties toward her sex; the interactions between these were highlighted in her doubts about the degree of devotion required by Norris's God. In these eleven letters, Astell questioned and Norris defended his doctrine that not only must we love God above all things, but that any other kind of love or earthly passion interfered with this primary obligation to divine adoration.

Astell began the correspondence by noting that a problem arose while she was reading the third volume of Norris's discourses, which she always read "with great pleasure and no less Advantage." Still, as with all her reading, Astell tried "to raise all the Objections that ever I can, and to make them undergo the severest Test my Thoughts can put 'em to," and came across a problem that bothered and interested her (p. 3). She wondered why Norris shifted from the truths that God was the only "efficient Cause of all our Sensations" and the "sole Object of our Love," to the premise that mankind loves God because he "is the only efficient Cause of our Pleasure." Could the latter be the case, she asked, since God was the source of both pleasure and pain, and Norris implied that we loved him only when he gave us pleasure (pp. 4–5).

Norris, a little taken aback that such a response came from a woman, asked forgiveness for the tardiness of his reply because he needed "some time to recover my self out of that wonder I was cast into, to see such a letter from a Woman, besides that was necessary to consider the great and surprising Contents of it" (p. 8). Norris's substantive reply was inadequate and really only addressed her question in the postscript where he argued that God inflicted pain only as a good, and out of kindness rather than malice. Pain was, therefore, really a form of pleasure, although not perceived as such by people suffering it.

This opinion reflected his belief in a Platonic unity that saw God as the source of all things, and therefore the only proper object of human love. "And why then should it be thought such a Stretch of the Love of God to make it intire and exclusive of all other Lovers?" he asked. Not only was God the sole proper recipient of our love, but this love was the best path to truth. "An affectionate Sense of GOD will discover mor of him to us, than all the dry study and speculation of Scholastick Heads," Norris insisted. "The Fire in our Hearts will give the best and truest Light to our Eyes." [13]

In her answer Mary Astell told Norris that she accepted the primacy of God's love and of our duty to him, and believed that everything except sin (but including pain) emanated from God. But she raised another question closer to Norris's major point—that our whole being must be directed toward a love of God that excluded other love. Astell thought "that I need not cut off all Desire from the Creature, provided it were in Subordination to, and for the sake of the Creator." Despite Norris's effort to teach her better, it remained her "weakness" to love with "something of Desire," and her desire centered on her projects to improve women's lot: "Now I am loath to abandon all Thoughts of Friendship, both because it is one of the brightest Vertues, and because I have the noblests Designs in it. Fain wou'd I rescue my Sex, or at least as many of them as come within my little sphere, from that meaness of Spirit into which the Generality of 'em are sunk" (pp. 48–49).

Her love of God did not subsume but encouraged her love for her sex, which was never wholly disinterested but which, when responded to, created "an agreeable Movement in my Soul towards her I love," surely an "Indication of somewhat more than pure Benevolence" (p. 50). Here and elsewhere in these letters one senses the bases in personal affection of her feminist concerns, which caused her to question Norris's notion of love of God divorced from passionate and human direction. In other works, she alluded to passions and offered an almost sensual description of the joys of study.

Her insistence that Norris dedicate the work to Lady Catherine Jones seems significant. In the dedication itself she praised Lady Catherine in a rhetorical question that capped her argument with Norris: "And where can a Discourse of the love of GOD be more appositely presented than to a Soul that constantly and brightly shines with these Celestial flames?" Love of God did not war with devotion to this friend because "I love her with the greatest Tenderness," as "all must love her who have any Esteem for unfeigned Goodness, who value an early Piety and eminent Vertue." [14] This dedication highlighted how Lady Catherine provided Astell with a model "free from the least Tincture of Vanity," and yet filled with "such a serious, reverent and unaffected Devotion . . . so equally composed of Heat and Light . . . as gave me a lively Idea of Apostolical Piety, and made me every time I prayed by her, fancy my self in the Neighborhood of Seraphick Flames!" [15]

Seventeenth-century writers often wrote passionately about religious fervor, but the rapturous description here appears both peculiarly personal and passionate. Certainly Astell suggested the excitement of a young woman in discovering a special individual who combined all the qualities she believed to be paramount, but the image of the two women praying together was not wholly spiritual. There was emotional excitement welding together Astell's love for her friend, her sex, her religion, and the newly discovered wonders of scholarship that does much to explain her early feminist thought and plans. A female college would combine all these things, where learning would become "a Joy whose perpetual Current always affords a fresh Delight, and yet every Drop of it so entertaining, that we might live upon it to all Eternity." Such study in such company would more than adequately substitute for all other satisfactions that people sought in life. "Whilst our Souls are inebriated with its Pleasures, our very Bodies partake of its Sweetness; for it excites a grateful and easie Motion in the animal Spirits, and causes such an agreeable Movement of the Passions as comprehends all that Delight" (p. 29).

This passion for learning as the preferable alternative to the more commonly pursued of life's satisfactions obviously infiltrated Astell's first and best-known work, *A Serious Proposal to the Ladies,* which she published in 1694. It was an amazingly ambitious scheme, yet its tone was determinedly unemotional, moderate, and conciliatory, which probably contributed to the attention it attracted. Her *Proposal* was an appeal to society to provide some opportunity for women's higher education, and to upper-class women to give up lives of leisure and petty pleasure to combine serious study and Christian service. She hoped to convince women that her design was "to improve your Charms and heighten your value by suffering you no longer to be Cheap and contemptible." Redirecting interest from the looking glass to the library, "from a corruptible Body to an immortal Mind" would allow women to "be wits, or what is better Wise." Women need not be "like Tulips in a Garden, to make a fine show and be good for nothing," if only they would avoid "such a degrading thought of our own worth" that their goal became "to attract the eyes of men." She assured women that "my design is not to expose, but to rectify your Failures" because they grew not from women's nature or desires but because the world trained them to be preposterously humble in their aspirations. Astell never doubted, as did the duchess of Newcastle, that women's limitations stemmed solely from socially defined sex roles.[16]

The idea that an evil education lay at the heart of women's ignorance permeated all of her writings, and she established it early in her *Proposal.* She asked rhetorically whether men would not "sink into the greatest stupidity and brutality if they were neglected, in regards to their talent, as are women?" Women's defects "if not wholly, yet at least in the first place" all grew out of faulty education, which then spread "its ill influence thro' all our Lives" (p. 25).

Her women's college was to combat this systematic miseducation. She perceived a vicious circle; women were brought up in ignorance, and then that ignorance was used to prove their incapacity for better training. "Women are from their very infancy debar'd those advantages, with the want of which, they are afterwards reproached, and nursed up in those Vices which will hereafter be upbraided to them" (p. 26). To reverse this pattern women needed training beyond the meager offering of the dame

school or the governess, needed to escape irrational customs to realize
that their real worth was not a matter of personal beauty. Without such
an education a woman valued what her admirers praised. She would "be
proud of her Beauty, or Money, and what that can purchase," and in
addition "think her self mightily oblig'd to him" who offered the praise
(pp. 34–35). Women, she insisted, never made decisions freely, for they
were not taught their true interest, but "Tyrant Custom" dictated "all
those irrational choices which we daily see made in the World." Only
reason operating in women's lives could free them from the false judgments of men, and only an education of their own making that removed
society's artificial barriers could inculcate reasonable standards. A truly
religious and intellectual education for women would destroy the chains
of custom that bound them. But the strong religious orientation of her
proposed curriculum would not, of course, allow for a genuinely liberating education (p. 46).

The college was to be a retreat for women from the vanities of the
world as well as an advance into intellectual training. Away from the
distractions of society, women could develop true friendship and focus
their attention on learning. Wealthy fathers should support it because
"heiresses and Persons of Fortune" might here "be kept secure, from the
rude attempts of designing Men" (p. 146). In addition young women
whose consciences needed support would find it here. The school would
also be a haven for those, Astell wrote with some thoughts to her own
situation, who were "quite terrified with the dreadful name of Old Maid,
which yet none but Fools will reproach her with, nor any wise Woman be
afraid of" (p. 160). Not marrying was certainly preferable to making a
dishonorable or unhappy match, and Astell's college would provide an
alternative that would give productive social roles to women who would
or could not wed.

The school was, of course, for women who planned to marry as well
as those who did not. Men would come to see the advantages of marrying
wives with such intellectual backgrounds, for they could expect interesting and serious companions and educated mothers for their children. For
all students, the school would provide opportunity to contemplate
seriously the direction of their lives, something women did not generally
have in a society which provided "no opportunities for thoughtfulness
and recollection" but instead forced "an unthinking mechanical way of
living" on women. "Like Machines we are condemn'd every day to

repeat the impertinencies of the day before," Astell complained, a process which inevitably shortens "our Views, contracts our Minds, exposes us to a 1,000 practical Errors, and renders Improvement impossible" (p. 120). At her college there would be time and encouragement to think, the lack of which in the outer world rendered women's lives so futile and empty.

This training was to take place in an atmosphere of sisterly affection and mutuality between faculty and students; one senses a kind of institutionalization of the bonds Astell felt with her Chelsea friends. She downplayed any strict regulations and stipulated voluntary attendance, without "vows or irrevocable Obligations." Students would be encouraged to follow harmless diversions and not asked to assume "an affected severity and waspish sourness" (pp. 93–94). Love would be the dominant force, developing a general affection among the students, "for tho' there may be particular Friendships, they must by no means prejudice the general Amity." The administration of the school would be correspondingly lenient, with failings handled "by friendly Admonitions, not magisterial Reproofs." She envisioned a deep affection and "the most refin'd and disinteress'd Benevolence" binding students and faculty. Surely few regulations and little discipline would be needed where one found "a love that thinks nothing within the bounds of Power and Duty, too much to do or suffer for its Beloved: And makes no distinction betwixt its Friend and its self, except that in Temporals it prefers her interest" (pp. 137–38). Hers was to be a female paradise in which good, intelligent women would happily come to care for each other and grow both spiritually and intellectually through an expansive education based on rational instruction.

The love which should permeate the school was modeled on Astell's version of Christian principles, which her college was to inculcate along with scholarly interests. There would be perfect harmony between a rational, informed religion and the wisdom based on solid training which would undergird the affectionate atmosphere of the college. This religious sensibility would also flow outward to the community as students actively engaged in works of charity and conversion which would at once insure their social purpose and better their society.

There was an aura of naiveté in this scheme that went beyond doubts about its probable funding. Had the idea gained support from wealthy young women and from families concerned that they be well educated or

convinced that they were unmarriageable, there would have remained a
certain utopian quality in the college's organization. The idea that
pettiness and conflicts would end with the exclusion of the world in
general and men in particular hardly seemed realistic. Astell too easily
transposed the structure of her circle of personal, highborn friends in
Chelsea to an institutional structure. This analogy also probably informed the college's aristocratic cast. It was a school designed for people
like Astell's closest friends, women with sufficient leisure and interest to
pursue a life of religious contemplation and serious scholarship.

In the second part of her *Proposal* (1697), Astell sketched much
more fully the intellectual and religious curricula for the school, but not
before prefatory remarks which repeated her faith in women's capacity,
though in a tone of growing irritation at women's limited enthusiasm for
the new directions she wished them to take. "Can you be in love with
servitude and folly? Can you dote on a mean, ignorant and ignoble life?"
she impatiently asked, before stressing again the untapped potential in
her sex. "An Ingenious Woman is no Prodigy to be star'd on, for you
have it in your power to inform the World, that you can every one of you
be so, if you please your selves." [17] And surely much of this potential
would develop in a situation where "your Friendships are not cemented
by Intrigues nor spent in Vain Diversions, but in the search of Knowledge, and acquisition of vertuous Habits," all cemented by "a mutual
love" (p. 12).

In this volume Astell contrasted even more strongly the female
degradation common in society with the flowering that would come if
women learned to love books and contemplation. Parents and guardians
had "barbarously us'd" women by showing no concern for women's
minds so long as "their Purse was full and their outside plausible." If
women were taught "their Catechism and a few good Sentences, to read a
Chapter and say their Prayers, tho perhaps with as little Understanding
as a Parrot," that was judged enough "to secure them against the tempta-
tions of the present world and to waft them to a better" (pp. 16–17). All
women must fight against the ignorance and sloth the world encouraged
and refuse to accept such "Employments as the generality of Women
have in all Ages been engaged in." Yet Astell suggested growing fears that
women would not slough off these things. "What did we come into the
World for?" she chided with some bitterness. "To Eat and to Drink and
to pursue the little Impertinencies of this Life?" (pp. 36–39).

The gist of the second part of the *Proposal* was a description of the intellectual training, which would use the thought of Descartes to lay the foundation for both religion and scholarship. It was primarily an elaboration of Astell's Cartesian epistemology, but she also mentioned Locke's view of knowledge and praised Boyle as well. Without initially mentioning the French philosopher, Astell nonetheless suggested a concern similar to his in demanding thought from first principles: "Reason wills that we shou'd think again, and not form our Conclusions or fix our foot till we can honestly say, that we have without Prejudice or Prepossession view'd the matter in Debate on all sides, seen it in every light, have no bias to encline us either way, but are only determin'd by Truth itself, shining brightly in our eyes, and not permitting us to resist the force and Evidence it carries" (p. 44). Much like Descartes, she applied this questioning of all authority "no farther than to matters purely Philosophical, to mere Humane Truths," and would not let philosophic doubt cast "any Prejudice to the Authority of the Church which is of different consideration" (pp. 51–52). One simply had different requirements for religious truths than for the truths of science or society. It was necessary to demonstrate the latter, but, since the former permitted no such proofs, it was folly to search for them.

Astell was not explicit about the sorts of books a student should use to guide her to truth, because logic, rather than information gleaned from books or tutors, was the key to developing proper understanding. Her reliance on Descartes was again clear in her defense of "that *Natural Logic* I wou'd propose." It was natural because it existed in one's own mind. Some knowledge might be helpful "but a good Natural Reason, after all, is the best Director." Without reason, "the Choicest Books and Tutors" would be of no substantial use (p. 119).

She quoted directly Descartes's notion that the operations of the mind proceeded more from nature than from formal training in logic. This was an individualistic and rationalistic approach to knowledge, which allowed great freedom for women to develop their personal conception of truth. Astell's view, which contrasted strongly with those of earlier writers whose faith in women's abilities led to lists of proper books for them to read, negated the need for an explicit curriculum. Astell suggested that the kind of books apt to improve women's mental capacities were to be "not loosly writ, but require an Attent and Awakened Mind to apprehend, and to take in the whole force of 'em."

Books that stretched the mind were those "writ with Order and Connexion, the Strength of whose Arguments can't be sufficiently felt unless we remember and compare the whole System." Within these general rules, there was to be much freedom to use what fit the individual's needs and interests for "every one may easily find what Authors are most apt to stay their Attention, and shou'd apply to them" (pp. 108–9).

Astell argued, again after Descartes, that one must proceed from the sure and simple to the doubtful and more complex. In the search for truth, the student must move from two ideas of which she had a "Clear and Distinct Conception" toward a third idea to judge comparatively the validity of all. Here, as was often the case, Astell moved from reason to religion by tying the Trinity to this tripartite process of testing. She protested that knowledge of the Trinity was an object of faith rather than science, though both reason and revelation supported it. "We are certain," Astell said, "both because GOD who cannot lie has Reveal'd 'em, and because we have as Clear an Idea of 'em as it is possible a Finite Mind shou'd have of an Infinite Nature" (pp. 72–73).

Mary Astell stressed the necessity for clarity and precision in scholarship and human knowledge. One must use language skillfully and carefully, for often "our Ideas are thought false when the fault is really in our Language." She invoked "a celebrated Author" again in defining clarity as that "which is Present and Manifest to an attentive Mind" (p. 135).[18] There was as "much difference between Artificial and natural eloquence as there is between Paint and True Beauty," which had caused Descartes to warn about "avoiding certain evil ways of Writing and Speaking, and above all an Artificial and Rhetorical Stile compos'd of false Thoughts, Hyperboles and forc'd Figures which is the greatest fault in Rhetoric" (p. 175). Her stylistic views here closely resembled those of the duchess of Newcastle.

Developing Descartes's epistemology, she cautioned the prospective student to acquaint herself thoroughly with the question at hand, to establish a sure knowledge and grasp of the terms involved, and, finally, to cut out all that was not inevitably connected to the subject. Astell made it clear that these general educational precepts, though principally directed to the woman student, were equally at the base of human learning for men.

After establishing the general rules of learning for students, Astell returned to the special educational needs of women. Wives and mothers needed strong intellectual training, but Astell especially praised what a trained intellect might do for single women. "Nor will Knowledge lie dead upon their hands who have no children to instruct," she insisted, for "the whole World is a single Ladys Family." The opportunities for good open to the educated spinster were so limitless that Astell suggested that "the Glory of Reforming this Prophane and Profligate Age is reserv'd for you Ladies," and she assured her readers that "Sentiments of your minds being handsomly express'd, may carry a more strong conviction than the Elaborate Arguments of the Learned" (pp. 211–12).

Perhaps it was because Mary Astell accepted, at least in principle, the Christian view of the subordinate wife, that she moved beyond the domestic sphere to establish a school for women who were either permanently or temporarily separated from men. Here she did not have to be concerned with the delicate question of just how much energy a wife could legitimately devote to learning. The single woman, for whom the home set no limits, could freely pursue learning and Christian benevolence. There is little doubt that Astell was a woman concerned with the welfare of her sex. She encouraged women to test their abilities and to expand their horizons, and only when this expansion impinged upon Christian dogma did she hesitate. Yet, in concluding this work on women's scholarship, she ended with a judgment aimed squarely at the conventional Christian view of women's proper nature: "But we are not so forward in aspiring after Poverty, tho nothing shows a Braver Mind than the bearing it Nobly and Contentedly; we care not to be the Oppressed Person, that we might exercise Meekness and Forgiveness, Patience and Submission" (p. 272). Surely the last four words reflect Christian duty and make this statement a clear conflict between the values of Christian humility and those of feminist pride.

Astell grounded this association of oppression with the traditional wifely virtues outlined above—"Meekness and Forgiveness, Patience and Submission"—in a skepticism about marriage that she broached even in the first part of her *Proposal*. Here her defense of spinsterhood and her expectation that this state, if enhanced by education, could be as rewarding personally and socially as marriage was tied to a realistic vision of what marriage often meant. "When the Passion of a Lover is evaporated in the cool temper of a husband," Astell observed, the wife often retained "no more than such a formal respect as decency and good breeding will require, and perhaps hardly that" (p. 170).

This theme, lightly raised in the *Proposal* so as not to deflect attention or support from its educational goals, was central in *Some Reflections upon Marriage* (1700), where her Christian values and her feminist sensibility came into sharpest conflict. One of the most striking aspects of this work was its progression from spiritual to political imagery and language. In the first portion she discussed marriage abstractly and theologically, as a sacred institution instituted by God for the propagation of the race and the good of mankind. But when she discussed the relationship between the sexes within marriage, her imagery changed, and she spoke not in religious but in political terms of the power and advantage the husband had over his wife. "If absolute sovereignty be not necessary in a state, how comes it to be so in a family?" she asked in a 1706 preface to a new edition of the book. "If all men are born free, how is it that all women are born slaves?"

It was not easy both to accept the sanctity of marriage and to present the institution as fundamentally unfair to women, so tension steadily grew between her theological abstractions and the evidence and arguments she compiled about the unequal role women had in the home. Without openly arguing for equality between husband and wife, by the end of her essay Astell had criticized masculine dominance so thoroughly that there were virtually no areas left in which the husband's superiority could legitimately operate. One gets from Astell the feeling that, although the husband was formally the God-ordained head of the family, he should not exercise this power. Or, if he chose to exercise his will, Christian doctrine, respect for women's equal capacities, and basic responsibility for the ills of the relationship would make him a thoroughly constitutional and strictly limited ruler. There is a strong impression that, whatever husbandly power Astell supported in principle, in practice she would have made it as difficult as possible for a man to implement. Though she would not have appreciated the analogy, the power she tolerated in the husband was finally rather like what many Whig theorists allowed the monarch: a good deal so long as it was not much used.

Because of her theological commitment to traditional marriage, Astell might not have written on the institution extensively had not a friend's particular case directed her toward public treatment of the subject. The duchess of Mazarine had left France and moved for a divorce because of her husband's well-known and often outrageous liaisons with other women. She, however, was criticized for living alone and for possible romantic engagements, while her husband's more noto-rious actions were often ignored. This classic example of the sexual double standard led Astell to defend Mazarine's case in *Some Reflections upon Marriage*, even though she did not totally approve of her friend's conduct. As always Astell moved from the specifics of this case to the generalities of women's social reality, so that this one instance of a bad marriage propelled her from the particular evil to an understanding of a system that put all the power of both law and custom in male hands, where it was likely to be abused, sometimes most grossly so. Her failure to attack marriage frontally did not detract from the breadth or the vigor of her criticism of the commonplace realities related to its essential power structure (pp. 56–58, 70).

Marriage, she began, was ordained by "the great Author of our Being, who does nothing in vain," for the good of mankind. Yet what ought to have been a blessing frequently became a curse, what "was appointed for mutual Comfort and Assistance" often took a "contrary Effect through our Folly and Perverseness" (p. 17). Part of the reason for this transformation lay in the way "modern pretenders to wit" cast scorn on the institution rather than recognizing that it was "too sacred to be treated with Disrespect, too venerable to be the Subject of Raillery and Buffoonery." People who indulged in this "loose Talk of the Town" impiously undercut "a Divine Institution," and, as with so many other aspects of marriage, women were the main targets and sufferers from such drivel. It was these shallow wits who spread the idea that "a Wife is nothing better than a Domestick Devil" (pp. 17–18).

Astell recognized that the serious considerations in marriage mat-tered more than the light jokes about it in explaining why, given the divine status of the institution, "there are so few happy Marriages." The responsibility lay primarily with the men for their desires in marrying so commonly neglected the real values in marriage and in women. "For pray, what do Men propose to themselves in Marriage? What Qualifica-tions do they look after in a Spouse?" Astell asked, and answered "What will she bring? is the first Enquiry: How many Acres? Or how much ready Coin?" (pp. 23–24). When men married with such worldly mo-tives, "with an Indifferency, to please their Friends or increase their Fortune," Astell astutely noted, such indifference commonly "proceeds to an aversion, and perhaps even the Kindness and Complaisance of the poor abus'd Wife, shall only serve to increase it" (p. 25).

Nor did other things that attracted men, such as beauty or wit, provide a much more lasting basis for affection when the excitement of courtship gave way to the familiarity of marriage. "Beauty, with all the Helps of Art, is of no long Date," Astell pointed out. Since "the more it is help'd, the sooner it decays," the man who weds out of physical attraction "will in a little time find the same Reason for another Choice." Wit also soon rang hollow against the day-to-day realities of marriage. The situation was little better with those men who married "for Love, as they call it" and who hurried into marriages where they soon found "Time enough to repent their rash folly" and whose wives learned "that whatever fine speeches might be made in the Heat of Passion, there could be no *real Kindness* between those who can agree to make each other miserable" (pp. 34, 24).

The list of bad influences on marriage included parents who forced children to marry for reasons of family politics "without ever consulting the Young one's Inclinations," upon the possible penalty of forfeiting their estate. When one added to all these unfortunate impetuses to union the inclination to "marry without any Thought at all, further than it is the Custom of the World, what others have done before them, that the Family must be kept up, the antient Race preserv'd," obviously very few men were left to marry "out of better Considerations" of steady affection and respect. And "amongst the Few that do, not one in a Hundred" acted to earn the happiness that wise choice permitted (p. 36). Hers was a dismal picture of male competence in either choosing or cherishing a wife.

Men, with chief initiative in these situations, were chiefly responsible, but, Astell asked, "do the Women never choose amiss? Are the Men only at Fault?" Admitting "that neither Sex are always in the right," she also pointed out that women had little opportunity to be at fault here. "A woman indeed cannot be properly said to choose," she argued; "all that is allow'd her, is to Refuse to Accept what is offer'd." Astell would not allow the misdeeds of some women to override the basic truth that only men possessed any real power before or after marriage, so that whatever a woman's mistakes, "a generous spirit will find more Occasion to Pity, than to reprove" (pp. 36–37).

The bulk of Astell's work was devoted to the abuses found in marriage, which fell hardest on women because of man's unlimited power within the marital union. If the marriage went sour the woman was left with very little protection, and "she must make Court to him for a little sorry Alimony out of her own Estate" (p. 26). An institution established for the glory of God quickly degenerated into one in which the man was allowed to misuse both his wife and her possessions. Although the code of chivalry, which discouraged both verbal and physical abuse of women, mitigated male power, Astell was aware of the limitations of such protection. "Nor is there a Man of Honour amongst the whole Tribe, that would not venture his Life, nay, and his Salvation too in their Defence," Astell noted, before going on to her point, "if any but himself attempts to injure them." She argued that some vestiges of chivalry toward women should be retained "since a little Ceremony and outside Respect is all their Guard, all the privilege that's allow'd." As poor protection as chivalry was for women, it was barbarous to deprive them of it when there was nothing to take its place (pp. 37–38). Yet it was easier for a man to show kindness than respect, for "how can a Man respect his Wife when he has a Contemptible Opinion of her and her Sex?" True to the feminist underpinnings of her thought, Astell did not view marriage as an isolated phenomenon between two individuals but as an integral part of the general subordination of women to men in seventeenth-century England, as her choice of words such as "monarch" and "slave" revealed.

The difficulties women faced in marriage could not be totally laid at the feet of their husbands. One source of distress was women's unwillingness to view their role as wives realistically. Instead parents taught the girl "to think Marriage her only preferment, the sum total of her Endeavours, the Completion of all her hopes, that which must settle and make her Happy in this World." Given this kind of buildup, any woman would "find a terrible disappointment when the Hurry is over, and when she comes calmly to consider her condition . . . as it truly is." When wives did learn the true meaning of being united to cruel, wasteful, or philandering husbands, they often reacted strongly (pp. 78–79). Some, like the duchess of Mazarine, even attempted to follow the example set by their husbands, and, although Astell disapproved of such philandering, she condemned the double standard, not the wife. She asked about husbands, "with what Face can he blame her for following his Example, and being as extravagant on the one Hand, as he is on the other?" A wayward wife perhaps could "not justify her Excesses to God, to the World, nor to her Self," but she could be exonerated in relation to the husband who added "to all the rest of his Absurdities" the expectation of "Vertue from another which he won't practice himself" (p. 30).

Although she never encouraged a woman to leave an unfaithful husband to follow an independent life, she did argue that a woman should be aware of her own interests and endeavor to protect them. Matrimony, if it were to develop into a just and happy relationship, must be taken as a serious business by both parties, especially by women, who had "by much the harder bargain." Men should choose their wives more rationally than they did, and treat them with respect following the wedding. Women had to be better informed about what the marriage actually meant for them and be able to handle "the business . . . as Prudently as it can be on the Woman's side." Calculation was essential before marriage because, once wed, the wife was put "entirely into her Husband's Power, and if the Matrimonial Yoke be grievous, neither Law nor Custom affords her that redress which a Man obtains" (p. 44). Women should think realistically about their position as wives, not to revolt against it but to gain as much as they could from the relationship and to protect themselves as much as possible from the vicissitudes bound to occur.

Everything about Astell's work created the impression that she did not believe man's authority was justified, at least as it was commonly exercised, but her religious convictions would not allow her to encourage revolt on the part of the wife. To abandon marriage as ordained by God would surely be a sacrilege. Yet, although she accepted the wife's duties as "humility and Self-denial, Patience and Resignation," she questioned the positive effects of women's passive responses: "their Timorousness does them this one, and perhaps this only Piece of Service, it keeps them from breaking through these Restraints, and following their Masters and Guides in many of their daring and masculine Crimes. As the World goes, your Witty Men are usually distinguish'd by the Liberty they take with Religion, good Manners, or their Neighbours Reputation: But, GOD be thank'd, it is not so bad, as that Women should form Cabals to propogate Atheism and Irreligion" (pp. 33–34). Significantly, she worried about female independence primarily in connection with irreligious thoughts. This tension between a Christianity which taught female subordination and a feminism that wanted to end this situation was evident throughout Mary Astell's writings, and this contradiction, which she could not squarely face, was most apparent in her dealing with marriage, where traditional religious sanction of male hegemony, she well knew, created greatest costs for women.

Astell's essay on marriage was, in many ways, the most modern of her feminist writings and the one most clearly relevant to later feminism, but it was the *Serious Proposal* which attracted the greatest attention during her lifetime. Although it sounds today like a rather quaint solution for the problems of women, her *Proposal* evoked broad discussion and wide debate. The book was sufficiently newsworthy for a relative of Bishop Burnet's to write to the Electress Sophia about the furor it was creating and the general amazement people felt at this young woman who was suggesting women should be educated.[19] Perhaps it was her practical appeal for a workable institution rather than her views on women's education that attracted unique attention to her work.

John Evelyn suggested in his *Numismata* (1697) that Astell in her *Proposal* tried "to show by her own Example what great things and Excellencies" her sex was capable of. Evelyn not only described the *Proposal*, but supported it as well because he had never seen any "solid reasons" advanced against it.[20] Bishop Burnet also praised the book, if not the project, and George Hickes suggested it should be read by all serious young women. Daniel Defoe specified Astell's work as the inspiration for his "Academy of Women" and in a lesser-known tract, *A Protestant Monastery* (1698), George Wheler noted his debt to Mary Astell.[21]

Still, most of the comment seems to have been negative. The attacks came from two separate directions and two distinct perspectives. Men such as Bishop Burnet opposed the idea and influenced Queen Anne against it by arguing that the college sounded too much like a convent, and Protestants might accuse the crown of supporting a papist project. More scurrilous and less serious attacks came from those who wrote about the college in sexual terms, describing in play and pamphlet how male visitors would seduce the students and teachers. Such criticism especially angered Astell, who seemed to have anticipated it in the very adjective she attached to her *Proposal*, "serious." Astell was a serious person, strongly committed to deeply held religious values and to well-thought-out and consistent intellectual principles in an age and society that stressed wit more than wisdom and gracefulness more than conviction.[22]

This tension with her age contributed to an underlying tone of sarcasm and sometimes bitterness in each of her works, a tone that became sharper as the years passed. She directed this anger against men, against falsely erudite scholars, against dissenters, and against the modern, witty pamphleteers of her age. In her numerous prefaces to later editions of *Some Reflections upon Marriage* she attacked her opponents in increasingly severe language. By the time the *Reflections* had gone through a reprinting of the fourth edition in 1730, she was particularly incensed at those who could joke about women's domestic restraints or their desire for education. Her preface, by this edition, had become sufficiently long that the printer now included it as a lengthy appendix rather than retaining it as a preface.

This appendix made clear the length to which Astell was willing to carry her arguments and clarified, as well, the ways in which her heightened feminism came from a growing reaction to the negative reception her earlier suggestions had received. Years of unresponsiveness to her moderate pleas, and of flip jokes about her serious proposals, had pushed her toward an angrier stance. This heightened feminism was revealed in her sarcastic answers to those who argued that she was trying to instill rebellion into the hearts of women.

In a third-person reply to one facetious gentleman who actually claimed that he had written the *Reflections*, Astell maintained that she was responsible for the work, "which is unfortunately accus'd of being so destructive to the Government, (of the Men, I mean)." How could she, she continued, subvert the "Masculine Empire?" She could hardly try to convince women their husband's rule was truly just—a statement they would ultimately discover to be erroneous—since such arguments "required a Flight of Wit and Sense much above her poor Ability, and proper only to Masculine Understandings" (pp. 133–35).

After a rather lengthy argument against those who said the Scriptures, especially St. Paul, denied women rights separate from those of their husbands, Astell ended this appendix with a sarcastic commentary on dependent women. "I do not propose this to prevent a Rebellion," she noted with some bitterness "for Women are not so well united as to form an Insurrection." Women, merely "wise enough to lower their chains, and to discern how very becomingly they fit," thought "as humbly of themselves as their masters can wish, with regard to the other Sex, but in regard to their own they have a Spice of Masculine Ambition; everyone would Lead, and none would Follow" (p. 175). Her bitterness against women who seemed "to find themselves born for slavery" was perhaps the saddest part of this appendix. Instead of responding to their potential and to her desire to unleash their abilities, most women acted with a "tame, submissive and depending temper" and seemed to "glory in this wonderful Humility" (pp. 175–76).

This sarcasm contrasted glaringly with the hopes of sisterhood embodied in her proposed college and in her preface to a work by Lady Mary Wortley Montagu, where she begged: "Let her own sex at least, do her justice, lay aside diabolical Envy, and its Brother Malice, with all their accursed company, sly whispering, cruel backbiting, spiteful detraction, and the rest of that hideous crew, which I hope are very falsely said to attend the Tea Table." [23] Men might jealously malign one another, but let all women be "pleased that a *woman* [her italics] triumphs, and proud to follow in her train."

That so few women followed in Astell's train saddened her later years, but sharpened rather than blunted her feminism. Her concluding sentence in the 1730 appendix stressed the broad nature of her goals, and her depth of bitterness revealed that those goals seemed more distant than they had three decades earlier. Her work had been dedicated "To the Women's tracing a new Path to Honour, in which none shall walk but scorn to Cringe in order to Rise" and "to those Halycon, or if you will, Millennium Days, in which the Wolf and the Lamb shall feed together, and a Tyrannous Dominion, which Nature never meant, shall no longer render useless, if not hurtful, the Industry and Understandings of half of Mankind" (pp. 179–80).[24]

Her tart pen and logical mind probably angered her male opponents, but they failed to touch most of that "half of mankind" about which she was most concerned. Although she was a devout Christian and a solid royalist who opposed those raising questions about the social and political hierarchy of England, she could still make stinging barbs against those who would deny women their rightful place in God's universe. Despite her disappointments, Astell remained, as she had signed her original *Proposal*, "A lover of her Sex." Many had listened to her arguments, perhaps more had responded than Astell knew, but her "Millennium Days" were, as she suspected, still far off.

II

Perhaps one person Astell influenced was Elizabeth Elstob, a scholar who included feminist comments in her work on Anglo-Saxon grammar.

Although she had ample reason to dislike the limitations placed on women's educational aspirations, why Elstob espoused feminism is not self-evident. In all likelihood, a guardian who prevented her from studying foreign languages did not endear to her the general attitudes men held about women's intellectual needs. Association with her brother and his Oxford colleagues, who shared her interest in Anglo-Saxon studies, alerted her to the difficulties a woman scholar faced in pursuing academic interests. However, such awareness came to many women who did not go on to develop a feminist critique of society. Elstob's friendship with Mary Astell is perhaps the best explanation for her feminist thought.

Elizabeth Elstob was the one "pure" scholar among the seventeenth-century feminists. Although she was unable to participate fully in the late-seventeenth-century revival of Anglo-Saxon studies at Oxford, she provided some of the earliest guides to Anglo-Saxon grammar and was included in discussions of many of the projects that were implemented at that time. A mondern scholar, E. O. James, credited this "highly original writer" and "unique and neglected figure in literary history" with "the first Anglo-Saxon English grammar," as well as the first critical edition of Ælfric's sermons and homilies, an edition which became a major source of Anglo-Saxon criticism. Her translations he judged remarkably good because of their clarity and accuracy.[25]

Elstob's life and career illustrated the difficulties women faced in gaining education and pursuing learning cut off from all institutional support. She had to overcome disapproval of her activities during much of her life, though her contribution would probably never have been made had she not been afforded some rare opportunities as a child. The details of her life were published by George Ballard in 1740, from a brief third-person account written by Elstob herself. In her account, she attributed her love of scholarship to her mother, "a great admirer of Learning, especially in her own sex." The mother encouraged her precocious daughter's love of books, and "there was nothing wanting for her improvement so long as her Mother liv'd."[26] When she was eight years old her mother's death brought her education to an abrupt halt for some time. She was put under the guardianship of a relation, Dr. Charles Elstob, canon of Canterbury, "who was no Friend to women's Learning, so that she was not suffer'd to proceed notwithstanding repeated requests that she might." Dr. Elstob deemed foreign languages unnecessary for a woman, but after much struggle he reluctantly allowed her to learn French and read books in that language as well as in English. When she was permitted to live with her brother things took a turn for the better, for the brother "very joyfully and readily assisted and encourag'd her, in her studies, with whom she labour'd very hard as long as he liv'd."[27] This unusual support, intellectual and financial, again vanished with her brother's death in 1715. Then began a forty-year struggle against poverty in pursuit of her scholarly interests.

Elstob translated Madeline de Scudery's *An Essay of Glory*, later published her translation, and "had several other designs," in which she "was unhappily hinder'd, by a necessity of getting her Bread, which with much difficulty, labour, and ill health, she has endeavour'd to do for many years." The "indifferent success" of all these efforts was apparent in her first attempt to set up a dame's school at Evesham, which failed because of her ignorance of "the two accomplishments of spinning and knitting." She didn't consider herself "above doing any commendable work proper to my sex," and her years of struggle caused her to develop such skills. "The gown I had on when you gave me the favour of a visit was part of my own spinning," she wrote to Ballard, "and I wear no other stocking but what I knit myself." But as a young teacher she did not spin and knit, and all her other accomplishments were not compensation for these essentials of female education.[28]

Nearer to the time the sketch was written, her life had been easier because of her position as governess to the children of the duke and duchess of Portland, whom she identified only as "good and general friends" near the point the autobiography ended. In a letter to Ballard she also spoke highly of the treatment afforded her by the duke and duchess, whose daughters she especially enjoyed teaching. "I think my self the happiest creature in the World," she wrote. These final years were obviously ones of some economic security and personal respect.[29]

Her comments on the outlook for women's learning were less contented. The great achievements she saw as being in the past, and she chided Ballard—though with some pleasure in the parallel—for comparing her to Margaret Roper, "a Lady to whose least perfection, it will be impossible for me ever to attain." She also agreed with him about Katherine Philips's "charming performances" in poetry in the mid-seventeenth century. Elstob appreciated the literary accomplishments of some of the women of her age, but was pessimistic about the future of women's scholarship.[30] In one letter commenting on hostility toward Ballard's proposed work on women, she elaborated her view that "this is not an age to hope for any encouragement to Learning of any kind." It was special folly to try to interest people in serious accounts of women's accomplishments when "you can come into no company of Ladies or Gentlemen, where you shall not hear an open and Vehement exclamation against Learned Women."[31] Paradoxically, near the end of her life and at the beginning of the great age of the bluestocking, Elizabeth Elstob argued that the times were particularly inhospitable to women's learning. Some of this pessimism grew from the hostility with which her scholarship was received. To one contemporary, for example, she was "a northern lady of an ancient family and a genteel fortune" who had "pursued too much the drug called learning and in that pursuit failed of being careful of any one thing necessary."[32] But Elstob never segregated her personal struggles from those of women in general who cared for learning.

The introductory remarks to *An English-Saxon Homily on the Birth-day of St. Gregory* contained the major part of Elstob's published feminist thought. In this book, dedicated in 1709 to Queen Anne, Elstob, addressing the queen, noted the prominent role women played in furthering the cause of Christianity in England, first by "the ever glorious" Helena's introducing the faith into the Roman Empire and then by "the Endeavours of the first English Christian Queen Bertha" to promote Christianity in the British Isles.[33] This "noble Instance of two Royal Ladies, promoting the Advancement of the Christian Faith" was obviously intended to encourage one female ruler and one impoverished female scholar to help advance Anglo-Saxon learning.

In her preface Elstob confronted her would-be critics, whose opposition, she assured the reader, came from "ignorance on one Hand, or an affectation of Wit and Knowledge on the other." Those who were ignorant found all learning useless, and those who affected learning declared all worthless that they did not know themselves. But such criticisms, endemic to all scholarship, were compounded when a woman undertook it. "What has a Woman to do with Learning?" was the question asked by some men, "with an Envy unbecoming that greatness of Soul, which is said to dignify their sex." If a woman had a soul, Elstob argued, surely it deserved "greatest Care for its Improvement," and "if good Learning be one of the Soul's greatest Improvements," surely women's pursuit of knowledge was desirable.

She then attacked the common ideas that women's learning made females impertinent or caused them to neglect their household affairs. Such faults never derived from learning, which refined human nature and gave structure and guidance in fulfilling life's tasks. She insisted that most women's following household pursuits was no reason for "those few among us, who are Lovers of Learning" being denied the joy of scholarship. Those who criticized learning were probably less concerned about time taken from practical duties than about the loss of empty pastimes "or tedious Dressings, and visiting Days, and other Diversions, which steal away more time than are spent at Study." Elstob felt "more surpriz'd and even asham'd, to find many of the Ladies even more violent than they [men], in carrying on the same charge." These women seemed so "despairing" of gaining any "laudable degree of Knowledge" that they totally "abandon themselves to Ignorance . . . as if they either had not Reason, or it were not capable by being rightly cultivated." Men who deplored women's scholarship or women who scorned their sisters who pursued learning both seemed simply people who "would declare openly they hated any Woman who knew more than themselves."

She connected her defense of women scholars to her support of the study of Anglo-Saxon literature. Those who viewed such study as useless were comparable to those who denounced all learning as empty merely because they did not understand it. Elstob personally respected any kind of learning "be it in any Person, of any Sex" and would never blindly conclude that some knowledge was worthless simply because it was of no interest to her. Her defense of her field and of her sex went hand in hand; in the words of E. O. James, her intellectual efforts led her "to proceed from a defense of Old English literature to a general claim for women's share in scholarship." [34] The foolish questions always raised could not be separated really: "Admit a Woman may have Learning," Elstob said in her preface to *English-Saxon Homily*, "is there no other kind of Learning to employ her time? What is this Saxon? What has she to do with this barbarous antiquated stuff? so useless, so altogether out of the way." She went on to argue that the modern barbarians were those familiar with foreign cultures who knew nothing of "the Faith, Religion, and Laws and Customs, and Language of their Ancestors." Scholars such as George

Hickes, also a seventeenth-century Anglo-Saxon specialist, who supported her attempt to study were "imitating the Practice of the Primitive Fathers, who were very zealous to encourage good Learning amongst the Ladies."

Elizabeth Elstob was able to use her interest in Anglo-Saxon scholarship to further the cause of women's education. While her feminist interests were limited primarily to the area of learning, her argument and her example made clear what women had to offer and what they sometimes could manage to contribute even with little financial and intellectual support and no institutional encouragement. Along with only the duchess of Newcastle among these feminists, Elstob signed her name to her books. This may have been in part because of the respectable scholarly nature of her work, but one suspects it also resulted from a conviction that women should not hide what they could do under traditional anonymity.

III

One of the most vigorous feminist writings of the late 1600s was *An Essay in Defence of the Female Sex* (1696) "written by a lady." Who this lady was remains unknown; the work has been attributed, wrongly it would seem, to Mary Astell. The British Library attributed the authorship to a Mrs. Barker, and others have speculated the writer might have been Judith Drake. Whoever its author, the work was an intelligent polemic for women and against their age-old mistreatment by men.

The tone of this attack on the commonplace antiwomen tracts was certainly more irreverent than the *Serious Proposal*, in many ways closer to Poulain's *The Woman as Good as the Man*. The author apologized for her limitations as defender of her sex, in that she knew only French and English, but showed her ability to use her native tongue effectively in her sex's cause. Hers was not the systematic and practical plea of Astell or Elstob's scholarly defense of women's scholarly potential, but a vigorous presentation of ideas that now needed less to be justified or proved than to be driven home. The arguments which the early feminists broached and Astell and Poulain unified were here treated as self-evident.

The book's steady point of attack was "the Usurpation of Men; and the Tyranny of Custom (here in England especially)" which ensured that few women were well enough educated to defend themselves intellectually and that no "Man of Wit should arise so generous as to engage in our Quarrel, and be the Champion of our Sex against the Injuries and Oppressions of his own." [35] Men were the enemy "by Interest or Inclination," and even those unlikely to engage in antiwomen diatribes were not willing to endanger their power and prerogatives by defending women's general character and competence. Because women were naturally equal, men had found it necessary to establish institutions to enforce social injustices that contributed to male power and comfort.

What Astell found in Descartes, this author found in Locke, who had given the world "a treatise on the art of Reasoning" and her a foundation for her belief in equality of the sexes. Learned men had always said that all souls were equal and alike, and now it was clear "that there are no innate Idea's, but that all the Notions we have, are deriv'd from our External Senses, either immediately, or by Reflection" (pp. 11–12). Thus one was compelled to look at nature to discover any supposed sexual differences. In the animal world, she contended, females of the species were not inferior. In humans, sexual inequality was more obvious among the wealthy than the poor, which proved that social rather than natural barriers accounted for differences. In nations, differences in women's activities showed how society determined roles; Dutch women, for example, who were allowed to take greater part in financial and business duties, showed skill in them (pp. 15–17). There were some natural distinctions in the physical strength between the sexes, but if these suggested anything it was that weaker women, in a clever reversal of the usual conclusion, "were chiefly intended for Thought and Exercise of the Mind" (p. 18). The author accepted that some physical differences endowed the man with greater strength to gather the necessities of life and his wife with superior prudence to manage his stores and care for his children. What differences did exist, however, tended to prove the greater suitability of women for mental realms.

To anyone who inspected the situation fairly, it was obvious that women's intellectual inferiority had nothing to do with native intelligence and everything to do with education. Boys and girls might be given similar schooling up to age six or seven, but then boys began their serious learning in grammar schools, while girls went—if it fitted "the Humour and the Ability of the Parents"—to boarding schools "to learn Needle

Work, Dancing, Singing, Musick, Drawing, Painting, and other Accomplishments." To learn to be graceful and ornamental rather than thoughtful was the education society decreed for girls (p. 37).

Men also plotted to keep subordinate those few women who somehow managed to develop a taste for serious books and ideas, making sure they could read only French and English rather than Latin and Greek—the learned tongues. The author had no doubt "that Gentlemen have just inverted" the proper meaning of "learned" to become "the knowledge of words," which they alone were privy to, rather than the property of understanding, where women might compete (pp. 46–48). Her views were reminiscent of the duchess of Newcastle's contention that her age had confused shadow with substance and of Sharp's and Cellier's attack on men's assumption of medical superiority on the basis of linguistic rather than curative skills. Since most of the classics were now translated, the *Defence* contended, women who read them should be considered as learned as men. After all, Locke and other English writers currently produced much of the world's wisdom (pp. 48–54).

Despite men's vastly superior educational chances, they often squandered their greater opportunities, the author asserted. Scholars might be at home with dusty tomes, but they were worth little in social conversation or practical matters. One could expect as much from them on contemporary affairs as "from an animated Egyptian Mummy" (p. 28). Riveted to ancient tomes and manuscripts, they had few ideas of their own. If scholars were deadly bores, the "educated" gentleman was even worse. Following a short and intermittent stay at the university, this fellow's "Conversation for some years succeeding is wholly taken up by his Horses, Dogs and Hawks" and "his Groom, Huntsman and Falconer are his Tutors" (pp. 29–31). He next became a Justice of the Peace and was a terror to all the poachers in the neighborhood. Such was one feminist's view of the intellectual history of most of the increasing numbers of men then gaining a higher training.

Men did not make much use of their own educational opportunities, but they had good reason to be afraid of decently trained women, the *Defence* contended. Men knew in their heart of hearts "the Abilities of Mind in our Sex" and secretly feared "that we, who in the Infancy of the World were their Equal and Partners in Dominion might in process of Time, by Subtlety and Stratagem, become their Superiours." For this reason women were "born slaves, and live Prisoners all their lives," in eastern countries, while in western ones subtler enslavement occurred. Even in France, where there was more general respect for women, the Salic law prevented them from becoming monarchs. And the historical record of women's ascendency had been tampered with, "for if any Histories were anciently written by Women, Time, and the Malice of Men, have effectually conspir'd to suppress 'em" (pp. 19–25). The *Defence* has some of the spice of exaggeration and conspiracy that marks a radical movement's march toward more popular dissemination.

The author had no doubt why men, in discussing sex roles, liked to concentrate on alleged natural distinctions rather than the more obvious variations in educational chances: "there is no Honour to be gain'd by it." For man's pride in mental superiority, "if he owe his Advantage to a better Education, or greater means of Information," was as ludicrous as boasting about "his Courage, for beating a Man, when his Hands were bound" (p. 20). Talking about "natural" sexual distinctions was simply making the best camouflage and the best justification for real social oppression.

Men did all they could to make women vain, frivolous, and fickle, and then proceeded to blame them for such traits. But, despite all their social disadvantages, women managed to be no worse in these ways than men. Surely no woman was sillier than many a beau who "has more learning in his Heels than his Head." Men liked to talk about women's fickleness, but it was obvious to all that "Men are less constant in their Affections." Beauty, usually the object of male passion, inevitably faded, and hence men's love commonly "abated by Familiarity" (pp. 68, 128–29). Her examples of men's folly and flaws more than matched the opposing lists in misogynistic tracts.

Finally, men limited women's sphere to the home and then interpreted the interest women took in it as proof of their trifling natures. "When they hear us talking to, and advising one another about the Order, Distribution and Contrivance of Household Affairs, about the Regulation of the Family, and Government of Children and Servants, the provident Management of a Kitchin, and the decent ordering of a Table, the suitable matching and convenient disposition of Furniture and the like, they presently condemn us for impertinence" (p. 85). The author of the *Defence* wanted women to have an opportunity to expand their education and activities, but she argued that women's household work was of more practical and human importance than anything men did— and proved women's greater general competence as well.

The *Defence* provided the perfect counterpart to Astell's *Proposal*, the emotional opposites of a single argument. If these two books of 1694 and 1696 are taken together, Descartes and Locke, logic and polemic, the conciliatory and the aggressive joined to argue more vigorously and unambiguously than ever before that women were men's natural equals but social victims, who would continue to be so until society's attitudes, institutions, and especially its educational patterns radically altered.

NOTES

1. For a specific study of Poulain de la Barre see Marie L. Stock's "Poullain de la Barre: A Seventeenth-Century Feminist" (Ph.D. dissertation, Columbia University, 1961.) To place Poulain into the general context of seventeenth-century French feminism see Carolyn Lougee's *Paradis des Femmes*, esp. pp. 18–21 and 53–54. I take exception, though, to Lougee's viewing his thought as little different from those other seventeenth-century writers who favored women's public activities. For a discussion of the English translation of his work see Michael A. Seidel's "Poulain de la Barre's *The Woman as Good as the Man*," *Journal of the History of Ideas* 35 (1974): 499–508. For seventeenth-century editions of Agrippa and Poulain see Henry Cornelius Agrippa, *The Glory of Women; or, A Looking-glasse for ladies* (London, 1652); *Female Pre-eminence; or, The Dignity and excellency of that Sex, above the male* (London, 1670); and [Francois Poulain de la Barre] *The Woman as Good as the Man; or, The Equality of Both Sexes*, trans. A. L. (London, 1677).

2. Her most complete defense of Christianity, both generally and with specific reference to women, was presented in *The Christian Religion, As Profess'd by a Daughter of the Church of England* (London: Printed by S. H. for R. Wilkin, 1705). Further references to *Christian Religion* are from this edition and are noted by page number in the text. A representative tract on her views on the Occasional Conformity Act was *The Case of Moderation and Occasional Communion, Represented by way of Caution to the True Sons of the Church of England* (London: Printed for R. Wilkin, 1705); her opposition to the principles of the Civil War (and the sincerity of their professors) was outlined in *An Impartial Enquiry into the Causes of Rebellion and Civil War in this Kingdom* (London: Printed by E. P. for R. Wilkin, 1704).

3. She opposed Whiggish views quite strongly and argued that "None can give what they have not: The People have no Authority over their own Lives, consequently they can't invest such an Authority in their Governours." And, she

continued, "it is not in the Power of the Prince and one of the Houses, to make or Abrogate any Law, without the Concurrence of the other House, so neither can it be Lawfully done by the Prince alone, or by the two Houses without the Prince" (Astell, *Causes of Rebellion*, p. 34).

4. [Mary Astell], *Some Reflections upon Marriage*, 4th ed. (London: Printed for William Parker, 1730), pp. 133–35. Further references to *Reflections* are from this edition and are noted by page number in the text.

5. René Descartes, "Discourse on Methods," in *The Rationalists* (Garden City, N.Y.: Dolphin Books, n.d.), p. 85–97, 153–59.

6. The conflict between Astell's Christianity and her political conservatism on the one side, and her feminism on the other, are made clear in this work, as well. In *Christian Religion*, speaking of male domination, she noted: "I could never understand why we are bred Cowards; sure it can never be because our Masters are afraid we shou'd Rebel, for Courage wou'd enable us to endure their Injuries, to forgive and to despise them" (p. 104). Yet, when speaking of a general rebellion, she emphasized its societal harm: "For Rebellion and Disobedience, besides the hurt they do to Society, the Injustice, Confusion, and Irreparable Injuries that attend them; are highly aggravated, and become Sins of the deepest die, by that open Contempt of GOD from whence they spring" (p. 176).

7. Florence M. Smith, *Mary Astell* (New York: Columbia University Press, 1912), p. 2.

8. Ibid., p. 3.

9. Ibid., p. 6.

10. Ibid., p. 8.

11. Ibid., p. 15.

12. John Norris and Mary Astell, *Letters concerning the love of God. Between the Author of the Proposal to the Ladies and Mr. Norris, where his late Discourse, shewing that it ought to be intire and exclusive of all other Loves, is further cleared and justified* (London, 1695), p. 3. Further references to the *Letters* are from this edition and are noted by page number in the text.

13. Norris, "Preface," *Letters*, n.p.

14. Astell, "Preface," *Letters*, n.p.

15. Ibid.

16. [Astell], *Serious Proposal*, pp. 2–3, 11–14. Further references are noted by page number in the text.

17. [Mary Astell], *A Serious Proposal to the Ladies: Part II* (London: Printed for Richard Wilkin, 1697), p. 4. Further references are to this edition and are noted by page number in the text.

18. The following citation appears in the margin alongside this comment, "Les Princip. de la Philof. de M. Des Cartes. Pt. I 45," and earlier (p. 119) she described Descartes as a very judicious writer "to whose Ingenious Remarks and Rules I am much obliged."

19. Florence Smith, *Astell*, pp. 70–76.

20. Ibid.

21. Ibid.

22. Ibid., pp. 27–29.

23. Ibid., p. 15.

24. Although Astell seldom argued along historical lines either to explain or decry women's oppression, she made clear in the following instances that she understood the importance of omitting women from history and was herself aware of contemporary accounts of women's valiant or public actions. "Considering how much the Tyranny, shall I say, or the Superior Force of Men, keeps Women from Acting in the World, or doing things considerable, and remembering withal the Conciseness of the Sacred Story, no small Part of it is bestow'd in transmitting the History of Women" (pp. 159–60). In England, she conceded, women were subject to their husbands under law, "Though in remoter Regions, if Travellers rightly inform us, the Succession to the Crown is intail'd in the Female Line" (pp. 166–68).

25. E. O. James, "The Saxon Nymph," *Times Literary Supplement*, 28 Sept. 1933, p. 646. Despite the title, the article is a serious attempt to evaluate Elstob's intellectual contribution to Anglo-Saxon studies and is particularly useful because the author devoted a substantial portion of the article to Elstob's view of women. Another modern evaluation appears in David Douglas's *English Scholars, 1660–1730* (London: Eyre & Spottiswoode, [1951]). It is, however, less useful than the *TLS* article because Douglas borrows everything from James except his conclusion.

26. Ballard MS, fols. 59 and 60, Oxford University.

27. Ibid.

28. Ibid., fol. 67.

29. Ibid.

30. Ibid., fols. 38 and 89.

31. Ibid., fol. 89.

32. James, "Saxon Nymph," p. 646.

33. Elizabeth Elstob, "Epistle Dedicatory," *An English-Saxon Homily on the Birth-day of St. Gregory* (London, 1709). Further references to this work are to this edition.

34. James, "Saxon Nymph," p. 646.

35. "Dedication," *An Essay in Defence of the Female Sex*. Written by a Lady. 2d ed. (London: Printed for A. Roper and E. Wilkerson, 1696), n.p.; ibid., pp. 2–4. Further references are to this edition and will be noted by page number in the text. The *Defence* has been attributed to Astell, but its much sharper, less religious tone does not blend easily with the remainder of her works. Judith Drake may be the better choice because her brother was an academic, and the *Defence* contains a sharp and intimate attack on scholars, as if the author were familiar with the academic setting.

CHAPTER V

"Beyond the Chalk Advance"
The Feminist Poets, 1690–1720

> They let us learn to work, to dance, or sing,
> Or any such like trivial thing,
> Which to their profit may Increase or Pleasure bring,
> But they refuse to let us know
> What sacred Sciences doth impart
> Or the mysteriousness of Art.
> In learning's pleasing Paths deny'd to go,
> From knowledge banish'd and their Schools;
> We seem design'd alone for useful Fools
> And foils for their ill shapen sense, condemned to prise
> And think 'em truly wise,
> Being not allow'd their Follies to despise,
> Thus we from Ignorance to Wonder run.[1]

This section from the anonymous 1683 poem, *The Emulation,* offered in fact a resumé of the major themes of Astell's work and the *Defence:* men saw to it that women learned to be frivolous and ornamental—and learned little else—so that women would not have any chance to question their prerogatives, their pride, and their "superiority."

The pervasiveness of such feminist themes in the poetry women wrote between 1690 and 1730 showed most clearly that substantial numbers of English women were aware of this "secret" of male hegemony. Poetry, with its emotional sensitivity, subtlety, and autobiographical basis, was a form of writing that illuminated especially well individual mood and motivation. The writings of four turn-of-the-century feminist poets—Anne, Countess of Winchilsea; Lady Mary Chudleigh; Elizabeth Singer Rowe; and Sarah Fyge Egerton—certainly fit this pattern and made clear how deeply feminist ideas and attitudes had infiltrated women's circles by this time. Their verses revealed much of their individual desires, personal loyalties, and social relationships with other women and men, while the large number of poems each wrote provided a multifaceted perspective on these personal views. There resulted a rich personal picture of the poet and of the relation of feminism to her emotions and commitments.

Writing at the end of the seventeenth century and the beginning of the eighteenth, these writers inherited a richly complex poetic tradition. From the sixteenth and seventeenth centuries there were strongly pastoral strains which emphasized the joys of rural life and the escape from society's restrictions to more "natural" behavior. Here poetic traditions describing Platonic friendships were often central, in the guise of characters given classical pastoral names, a device which easily combined feminists' stress on female friendship with their desire for a refuge in nature.[2] Some were also heirs to the tough-minded, sharp-tongued wit of the Restoration poets and playwrights in whose work the battle of the sexes loomed large. This tradition, as well as the social and cosmic satires best known through Dryden and Pope, sometimes gave edge to feminist poets' social observations and especially their portraits of men.

A nonpoetic tradition also informed the substance if not the format of their writing. Young at a time when feminist views were first readily available, these women were familiar with the publications of the duchess of Newcastle and Aphra Behn. That they read Astell was clear from the similar language and even identical phrases employed in her writing and their poetry. Some similar emphases ran through their verse but each poet developed personal themes within the context of the varying traditions they shared. As a group their feminism was clear; as individuals they were involved with differing issues.

I

English women, in larger numbers than before, began to write poetry at the turn of the eighteenth century. Of the latter seventeenth-century women Myra Reynolds chronicles in *The Learned Lady in England,*

1650–1760, at least two-thirds wrote verse, though not always exclusively. One reason was probably the influence of two female poets of substantial fame who wrote earlier in the century, Aphra Behn (1640–89) and Katherine Philips, "The Matchless Orinda" (1631–64).[3]

Aphra Behn was the most financially successful of later seventeenth-century female authors. Although most renowned for her string of Restoration comedies, she wrote novels and poetry as well. Although unsure of her biography, most scholars agree that she was born in Wye and early lived an adventurous life, accompanying a relative who was appointed lieutenant-general of Surinam. Her novel *Oroonoko* was based on these youthful experiences, which guaranteed that she would retain an air of mystery and adventure about her following her return to England. Married to a Dutch merchant, Behn, unlike other contemporary feminist writers, delighted in court society, where she reportedly amused Charles II with her witty descriptions of her many travels. Her adventures included her serving as a spy for Charles in Holland during England's war with that naion, when she rightly, though ineffectively, informed the king about an imminent invasion.

Following her husband's death she again circulated in London society, where her voluminous writings supported her comfortably, seemingly the first English woman to live off the proceeds from her writings. During the mid-1670s, after early rejections, she produced a number of her plays on the London stage. Tory audiences especially appreciated her embroidering anti-Puritan views upon the typically bawdy Restoration comedy. Her comedies, though popular, earned her some public ridicule because she used suggestive dialogue and compromising situations, as did contemporary male playwrights. Her translation of Fontenelle's work and her more generous treatment of some female characters suggested some feminist sensibilities, but her explicit imitation of the style and content of male playwrights combined with her role in court society made her a woman who, perhaps from economic necessity, conformed to rather than conflicted with her age. Without doubt her success and her vigorous intelligence encouraged young women to write, but her questionable reputation made it difficult for them to follow openly in her footsteps.

A much safer model was Katherine Philips, though her poetic talents were not great. Philips received praise normally reserved for either a genius or a member of the peerage, perhaps because she could be represented as the model female poet. She was modest and discreet in her choice of subjects and emphasized feeling and friendship rather than the passionate love that Behn stressed. She preferred, or pretended to prefer, to keep her writing a secret, though her themes of pious friendship and moral rectitude could offend no one.

A literary society composed of many of the intellects of the day, including Margaret Cavendish, developed around Philips. Both men and women were members of the society, and much of her poetry was written to praise the talents of its members. It was a precursor to the later groupings around feminist poets, even though the latter's membership was normally limited to women.[4] Philips's reputation was unsurpassed for a brief period during the mid-seventeenth century, and it continued with some force into the eighteenth. This conspicuous success probably owed something to Philips's feigning what was considered properly retiring female behavior regarding her poetry. She wrote that when she learned of the supposedly unauthorized printing of some of her poems, "really it hath cost me a sharp fit of sickness."[5] She then agreed to a subsequent edition, allegedly more accurate, "with the same reluctancy as I would cut off a Limb to save my Life." These images of reluctant self-sacrifice in going public were clear in a letter to Sir Charles Coterell. "I am so far from expecting applause for anything I scribble, that I can hardly expect pardon; and sometime I think that employment so far above my reach, and unfit for my Sex, that I am going to resolve against it for ever," she insisted modestly. Had she been able to recapture "those fugitive Papers that have escaped my hands" she would have destroyed them. Indeed, she told Coterell, who was assisting in the poems' republication, she regretted that she had not resisted her "incorrigible inclination to that folly of rhyming" even though intended "only for my own amusement in a retir'd life."[6]

Partly Philips's posture was that of poetic commitment to pastoral escape from social considerations; partly it was that of a woman who wanted to take on, by cajolery rather than by assault, an artistic role generally reserved for men. Certainly hers was a case where pretended acquiescence in society's female stereotype was an aid to circumventing common exclusions. Whatever her real motives, Philips provided a model for future feminist poets in her themes of friendship and retreat. Many of her best poems centered on her literary circle, especially the women friends within it, such as "To my excellent Lucasia on our Friendship":

> I did not live until this time,
>   Crown'd my felicity,
> When I could say without a crime,
>   I am not Thine, but Thee.
> This carcass breath'd, and walkt and slept,
>   So that the world believ'd
> There was a soul the Motions kept;
>   But they were all deceiv'd.

This was the convention of pastoral friendship, for which the world was always well lost, but there was something striking in Philips's description of herself as an object merely advancing mechanically until her friendship with a woman gave human dimension to her life. She proceeded to make clear what she gladly gave up for her friend:

> No Bridegrooms nor crown's-conquerors mirth
>   To mine compar'd can be:
> They have but pieces of this Earth
>   I've all the world in thee.
> Then let our Flames still light, and shine,
>   And no false fear controul,
> As inocent as our Design
>   Immortal as our Soul (pp. 51–52).

This suggested in part the platonic blending of two perfect souls that was at the heart of the feminist friendship poetry, but the images of gladly giving up the joys of bridegroom or of crown, those symbols of male familial and political domination, for the "flame" of female friendship suggested the incipient feminism that such ideas could take on, especially when given a somewhat more earthy and sensual cast later in the century.

Philips also represented the feminists' desire to escape the hustle and bustle of day-to-day existence and to retreat with a perfect friend to a socially isolated spot.[7] In "Invitation to the Country," for example, Philips attempted to lure "Rosania" away from the city.

> Kings may be slaves by their own passions hurld,
> But who commands himself, commands the World.
> When no distractions doth the soule arrest:
> There heav'n and earth open to our view,

There we search nature, and its author too;
Possessed with freedome and a reall state
Look down on vice, on vanity, and fate.
There (my Rosania) will we, mingling souls,
Pitty the folly which the world controuls
And all these Grandeurs which ye most do prize
    We either can enjoy or will despise (pp. 103–4).

Again the ideas were conventional-pastoral but, put in women's mouths, the desire for "freedom and a reall state," the wish to circumvent the "folly which the world controuls" and to work out life by truer and fairer standards took on some subversive connotations.

Katherine Philips, sometimes regarded as the only acceptable women poet, represented a "respectable" example to which the feminists could turn when justifying women's writings. The caution of her public stance, and the perfect acceptability of her poetic vein, made her a natural figure for the feminists to emulate. And she illustrated, to those attuned to concern about women's social lot, the way feminist implications could be engrafted on traditional poetic forms and sentiments.

II

Katherine Philips and her circle influenced the informal associations of the later feminist poets. Reynolds's description of the literary society associated with Elizabeth Singer Rowe suggested the kind of groupings of intellectual women who supported each other's poetic work; they were, of course, not so different from that group of Chelsea intellectuals which included Mary Astell, Elizabeth Elstob, and, during her early life, Mary Wortley Montagu. There were comic overtones to these groups with their fanciful names and the fulsome and often fanciful praise they lavished on each other's poetry and personal qualities. However, in an age which combined a flair for theatrics with a strong admiration of the ways and wisdom of the ancients, such groups, male and female, were not uncommon. For example, Heneage Finch, Earl of Winchilsea, who was something of an antiquarian, formed a Druid society with some of his friends in which they addressed each other under Druidic titles. But underneath these silly trappings, such groups represented a need for companionship and mutual support, a need doubtless more generally intense among women.[8]

Just as Mary Astell viewed a college for women as a kind of earthly paradise, so the feminist poets emphasized women friends. They rarely wrote about men and even more rarely wrote affectionately. Even Anne Finch, Countess of Winchilsea, whose marriage was a close and affectionate one, commonly made poetry of her friendships with other women. These poets also seldom expressed the admiration for masculine accomplishment shown by Katherine Philips and Anne Killigrew, Dryden's student.[9] Feminists have rarely developed their ideas without being drawn further from men and closer to women, and the seventeenth-century feminist poets were no exception.

These women poets were also willing to take issue publicly with those who perpetuated sexual stereotypes. Lady Mary Chudleigh's poetic attack on a sermon by John Sprint that taught women marital obedience was the most obvious example of these women's willingness to take to task openly their sex's detractors, but there were many other instances. Winchilsea's epilogue to Nicholas Rowe's play about Jane Shore (on her sufferings as a discarded mistress of the king) had the leading actress tartly question this male vision of Shore's career because, rather than showing anything of the heroine's beauty and vigor, he brought her on only "to mortify and whine." The actress teasingly announced that, had she known this was to be her lot, instead of playing the role she would have "staid at home, and drank my tea." She then concluded with a mocking rebuke of society's many double standards:

> By men indeed a better fate is known
> The pretty fellow, that has youth outgrown,
> Who nothing knew, but how his cloaths did sit,
> Transforms to a *Free-thinker* and a *Wit;*
>
> . . . .
>
> And so would I have had our mistress Shore
> To make a figure, till she pleas'd no more.
> But if you better like her present sorrow,
> Pray let me see you here again to-morrow,
> And should the house be throng'd the Poet's day,
> Whate'er he makes us women do or say,
> You'll not believe, that he'll go fast and pray.[10]

These sallies were light, but, as often in the age's theatrical epilogues, they sharply undercut some of the social pieties, and in this instance sexual roles, upheld in the featured drama.

III

All four poets—Anne, Countess of Winchilsea; Lady Mary Chudleigh; Elizabeth Singer Rowe; and Sarah Fyge Egerton—shared feminist views and a willingness to defend their sex, but their poetic and feminist emphases varied. Winchilsea and Chudleigh most wholly followed in the pastoral paths Philips had opened. Aristocratic and, like Mary Astell, devoted Anglicans, these two women tended to stress the pleasures of female friendship and of intellectual and moral contemplation.

Anne Winchilsea's views blended most easily with Mary Astell's. She was a High-Church Tory, close to James II and greatly disturbed over his being deposed. As an early maid of honor to Mary of Modena, she had formed a particularly close relationship to the future queen. Both she and her husband, Heneage Finch, found it impossible to take part in the courts of William and Mary and Queen Anne. Heneage became a non-juror, and he and Anne went into retirement at Eastwell, first as guests of Charles, nephew of Heneage and third earl of Winchilsea, and later as master and mistress after Finch succeeded his nephew to the title.[11] The secluded life, necessary because of Finch's exclusion from the court, was also highly agreeable to their scholarly and introspective natures. Their marriage was by all accounts a happy one, and Heneage Finch's lauda-tory comments about his wife's work were reminiscent of those of the duke of Newcastle. Thirty-nine years following his wedding Finch noted in his private journal, "May 15, 1684. Most blessed day." He also copied into his journal a tract's opinion that to describe justly the countess of Winchilsea's qualities required "a masterly pen like her own," but that she "was the most faithfull servant to her Royall Mistresse, the best wife to her noble Lord, and in every other relation public and private so illustrious an example of all moral and divine virtues." Such were her "extraordinary endowments . . . that the Court of England never bred a more accomplished Lady nor the Church of England a better Christian."[12] That Anne returned this affection was evident from the poems she wrote to her husband, often at his request, when he was away. In "A Letter to Dafnis April: 2d 1685," she says:

> This to the Crown, and blessing of my life,
> The much lov'd husband, of a happy wife.
> To him, whose constant passion found the art
> To win a stubborn, and ungratefull heart;

And to the World, by tend'rest proof discovers
They err, who say that husbands can't be lovers (pp. 19–20).

Although Wilchilsea was noted as a wit—with some justification, as the *Jane Shore* epilogue shows—while she was still at court, in her later years she was penitent about those earlier trivial days. Much of her poetry was devoted to attacking just such light attitudes, and most especially their baneful influence on the lives of women. This rejection of court life, when monarchical change cut her and her husband off from it, probably influenced her glorification of the simpler pleasures of nature and of female friendship, themes frequently repeated in her poetry. For instance her "Friendship between Ephelia and Ardelia," dedicated to her close friend Catherine Cavendish, the granddaugher of the first duke of Newcastle, offered this bloated definition of their affection:

Eph. What Friendship is, Ardelia shew.
Ard. 'Tis to love, as I love You.
Eph. This Account, so short (tho' kind)
     Suits not my enquiring Mind,
     Therefore farther now repeat;
     What is Friendship when compleat?
Ard. 'Tis to share all Joy and Grief;
     'Tis to lend all due Relief
     From the Tongue, the Heart, the Hand;
     'Tis to mortgage House and Land;
     For a Friend be sold a Slave:
     'Tis to die upon a Grave,
     If a Friend therin do lie.
Eph. This indeed, tho' carry'd high,
     This, tho' more than e'er was done
     Underneath the rolling Sun,
     This has all been said before.
     Can Ardelia say no more?
Ard. Words indeed no more can shew:
     But, 'tis to love, as I love you (p. 46).

In many of her verses, Winchilsea expressed such ideas more deftly and vigorously. In a later verse about another personal friend, "To the Painter of an ill-drawn Picture of Cleone, the Honorable Mrs. Tynne," Winchilsea wrote that she missed "the Look that captivates my Heart" and the evidence of those personal qualities that had won her admiration and love (p. 59). The union of admiration and affection, so central to platonic friendship, Winchilsea presented most succinctly in "An Epistle from Ardelia to Mrs. Randolph in Answer to her Poem upon her Verse":

> Since Friendship, like Devotion clears the Mind,
> Where every thought, is heighten'd and refin'd (p. 96).

For this feminist poet friendship was less a passion than a means to reach understanding of God and his creation. As in much of feminist verse, the friendship of women became a way of moving toward knowledge and religious truth while circumventing those male figures socially entrusted with the keys to such understanding.

Winchilsea, like Philips, expressed trepidation at making her poetry public, and at the pursuit of fame this implied. Yet her real craving for recognition created the kind of internal doubts that many female writers felt. They were outlined best in Winchilsea's only preface, "The Introduction," written in both prose and verse. Here she explained how she had long been uneasy about showing her "uncorrect Rime" but equally unable to refrain from writing or revealing her verses until finally, "wearied with uncertainty, and irresolution, I rather chuse to be harden'd in an errour, then to be still att the trouble of endeavouring to over come it." Though she no longer denied herself "the pleasure of writing," or of sharing that writing with friends she still felt "great satisfaction" that she was not "so far abandon'd by my prudence, as out of a mistaken vanity, to lett any attempts of mine in Poetry shew themselves whilst I liv'd in such a publick Place as the Court, where every one wou'd have made their remarks upon a Versifying Maid of Honour, and far the greater number with prejudice, if not comtempt" (pp. 7–8).

But with her later isolation, she could indulge her poetic inclinations. Winchilsea's nature poetry, greatly admired by the romantic poets and academic critics, owed much to her personal isolation at Eastwell, where with the encouragement of husband and friends, she wrote extensively about its beauties.

> A pleasing Wonder thro' my fancy moves,
> Smooth as her lawnes, and lofty as her Groves.
> Boundlesse my Genius seems, when my free sight,
> Finds only distant skys to stop her flight (p. 8).

In concluding her "Introduction" Winchilsea noted that people had praised "the great reservednesse of Mrs. Philips" in moral tone and expressed her fear that she would not be able to live up to this high standard. Her poems were too much on frivolous topics or on love, she admitted, but she assured her readers that she had terminated her translation of the *Aminta* of Tasso because of its lack of moral seriousness, even though convinced, "itt must be as soft and full of beautys, as ever anything of that nature was" (p. 10).

Her desire for fame, however, spurred Winchilsea's feminism. It was only a pitiful prejudice, she believed, which denied her and other women writers their rightful acclaim. She claimed in her "Introduction" that the ridicule of critics was part of the general scheme to keep intelligent women from intruding "on the rights of men."

> They tell us, we mistake our sex and way;
> Good breeding, fassion, dancing, dressing, play
> Are the accomplishments we shou'd desire;
> To write, or read, or think, or to enquire
> Wou'd cloud our beauty, and exhaust our time,
> And interrupt the Conquests of our prime:
> Whilst the dull manage, of a servile house
> Is held by some, our utmost art, and use.

She noted, as had others, that in the past women had been allowed to use their minds:

> How are we fal'n, fal'n, by mistaken rules,
> And Education's, more than Nature's, fools,
> Debarr'd from all improve-ments of the mind,
> And to be dull, expected and dessigned.

And these general expectations about what women should do encumbered all who tried a different course:

> And if some one wou'd Soar above the rest,
> With warmer fancy, and ambition press't,
> So strong, th' opposing faction still appears,
> The hopes to thrive, can ne're outweigh the fears.
> Be caution'd then my Muse, and still retir'd;
> Nor be despis'd, aiming to be admir'd.

Pastoral retirement was the only protection in such a situation, but here it became a mark of defeat instead of the perfect content the tradition emphasized.

Conscious of wants, still with contracted wing,
To some few freinds, and to thy sorrows sing;
For groves of Lawrell, thou wert never meant;
Be dark enough my shades, be thou there content (pp. 4–6).

The pervasiveness of Winchilsea's feminism and its relation to society's bounds to female creativity came through in the closing lines of her
"Poem, Occasion'd by the Sight of the 4th Epistle Lib. Epist: 1. of
Horace." The poem described the wisdom of Horace; the poetic genius
of his translator, Mr. Rowe; and the poetic sensitivity of Richard Thorn-
hill, Esq., the recipient of this translation and a translator of Horace
himself. None of these men had given much attention to women, she
noted with little warning, and ended her poem:

Happy You three! happy the Race of Men!
Born to inform or to correct the Pen
To proffitts pleasures freedom and command,
Whilst we beside you but as Cyphers stand
T' increase your Numbers and to swell th' account
Of your delights which from our charms amount
And sadly are by this distinction taught
That since the Fall (by our seducement wrought)
Ours is the greater losse as ours the greater Fault (pp. 98–100).

This was a biting feminism that, in praising Horace, would condemn the
male monopoly of knowledge and the subordination of women to their
pleasure, ostensibly because a woman had first eaten of the tree of
knowledge.

Winchilsea's own happy marriage did not blind her to the reality of
wedded life for most women. Her anger against women's oppression was
not restricted to curbs on artistic creativity but encompassed a broad
view of the generally "unequal fetters" of marriage:

Free as Nature's first intention
    Was to make us, I'll be found
Nor by subtle Man's invention
    Yield to be in fetters bound
By one that walks a freer round.
    Marriage does not but slightly tye Men
        Whilst't close Pris'ners we remain (pp. 150–51).

The phrase "yield to be" suggested women had some choice, but, unless firmly aware of such realities, women were likely to find themselves "close Pris'ners" in the homes society decreed as their proper destination. Mary Chudleigh, who was married unhappily to a man she didn't love and whose children died young, had more personal experience than Winchilsea of what a prison marriage could be for women. This gave a greater emotional intensity to her idealization of pastoral retreat and female friendship and contributed to her almost total exclusion of men from her poetic vision. Her *Poems on Several Occasions*[13] included over 230 pages of verse, but there were only two poems written to individual men—one praising Dryden's translation of Virgil and the other expressing thanks to a physician who saved her daughter's life. She wrote loving verses to her daughter and mother, but there were no poems to husband, father, or any male relative or friend.

Her favorite theme, elaborated in numerous poems, was the joys of female friendship, based on shared moral goodness and similar intellectual pursuits. Chudleigh's intense desire for such friendship gave some fire to this platonic formula, which Philips had made popular in the late seventeenth century. "To Clorissa" represented clearly Chudleigh's desire to discover a woman whose interests would mesh with her own and to find for both of them a retreat from the cares of the world. The poet first pleaded that she might flee to Clorissa's bosom in "sacred friendship," and then extolled the beauties of a solitary life:

> When all alone in some belov'd Retreat,
> Remote from Noise, from Bus'ness, and from Strife,
> Those constant curst Attendants of the Great;
> I freely can with my own Thoughts converse,
>   And cloath them in ignoble Verse,
> 'Tis then I tast the most delicious Feast of Life.

Chudleigh went on to make clear how, in such a secluded spot, she (or other women) could develop her intellectual capacity.

> There, uncontroul'd I can my self survey,
>   And from Observers free,
>   My intellectual Pow'rs display,
> And all th' opening Scenes of beauteous Nature see:
> Form bright Ideas, and enrich my Mind,
> Enlarge my knowledge, and each Error find;
> Inspect each Action, ev'ry Word dissect,
> And on the Failures of my life reflect.

In this isolation wisdom from books and contemplation would flow if those things were shared with Clorissa:

You've, sure, a double Title to my Love,
    And I my Fate shall bless,
For giving me a Friend, in whom I find
    United, all the Graces of the Female kind.
                . . . .
Thus, of a thousand Sweets possest,
    We'll live in one another's Breast:
When present, talk the flying Hours away,
When absent, thus, our tender Thoughts convey (pp. 22–25).

And this heavenly friendship would be finally transferred to heaven itself where their "delight" would be eternal. "The Choice, A Dialogue between Emilia and Marissa" presented a similarly idyllic picture of the eternal unity of kindred female spirits:

Mar. No, thou lov'd Darling of my Heart,
    We'll never, never, never part:
Those Virtues which our Souls combine,
    Shall ever in our Union shine (p. 115).

The excessive quality of these pictures of the "Sweets of Love" and eternal agreement was counteracted by the need Chudleigh felt to substitute for her unhappy real life an ideal poetic one. In one sense, the poems were intellectual constructs of the one great desire of her life—the attainment of mental, moral, and personal fulfillment. The paramount concern was self-development, which required both escape from the injustices of the ordinary world and the support of female friendship. One senses that the reaching out for a poetic formulation that might fill a psychic and social void was often more important than the friendship itself.[14]

Chudleigh did not retreat from John Sprint's arguments for female subordination, but turned her disagreement into a major battle in the general feminist campaign against those who would rob women of basic human rights. She wrote two replies, *The Female Advocate* in prose and *The Ladies' defence* in verse. Sprint was a Nonconformist minister who preached a wedding sermon in 1699 on the necessity of wifely obedience. It was not difficult to understand why this heavy-handed demand for total submission infuriated feminists. In it Chudleigh probably saw the ridiculously extreme statement of those conventions that bound her, and which she could never fully escape or even with perfect comfort attack in their usual moderate form.

The *DNB* has no entry for John Sprint, but gives a brief summary of his father's life.[15] John Sprint, Sr., was a theologian of Puritan leanings, a graduate of Christ Church, Cambridge, who was forced to read his submission in convocation for preaching against the ceremonies of the church while at the university. The son seemingly inherited his stubborn spirit, for his father in his submission did not justify Anglican ritual, but merely argued that disagreement over ceremony was not a sufficient cause to abandon one's ministry. Both of his sons followed him into the ministry, and John was ejected from his living at Hampstead in 1622. Such is the bare surviving outline of his life. This much suggested, though, that Mary Chudleigh, a strong Anglican, differed with Sprint on issues other than his unacceptable views of women. In "The Ladies' defence," a lengthy satirical fable which attacked Sprint, Chudleigh referred to him as "parson" and played up his theological naiveté and lowly ecclesiastical position. She clearly thought women were being told what to do by an inferior creature.[16]

Sprint's sermon, originally unpublished, circulated enough privately to generate angry reaction. Sprint then published it to defend himself against attack by "some ill-natur'd Females." In his "Epistle to the Reader" he outlined his reasons for printing it, for "tho' I should purchase the Character of a Block-head, yet I hope I shall get the advantage of convincing the World that I am not such an impudent Villain as my waspish Accusers have reported me to be. Be it known unto thee Reader, whosoever thou art, that I have not met with one Woman among all my Accusers whose Husband is able to give her the Character of a dutiful and obedient wife."[17] Such comments hardly mollified the anger of the feminists or of his more conventional critics, nor did his insistence that "Good wives" liked his work and only wished he would extend his comments to the role of husbands. He promised to expand his scope in this direction whenever "imperious Wives" heeded his warning and no longer refused to believe "their Husbands love them well, unless they will obey them too." Women clearly were the main problem, and their "Guilt which makes them so uneasy" could only be removed by "a speedy Repentance and Reformation." Otherwise he hoped his words would haunt them to Judgment Day "and there witness against them, not only as Traitors to their Husbands, whose Authority they usurp, but as

Rebels to the Great Monarch of the World, whose Sacred Laws they impiously violate."[18] This no doubt brought scant comfort to Mary Chudleigh.

In *The Female Advocate* Chudleigh constructed an attack against Sprint that was less a direct refutation of his simpleminded arguments than a satire on the repetition and simplicity of his demand for female obedience. Sprint's work was vulnerable to such attack for it was only an extended explanation of his biblical text, "But she that is Married Careth for the things of the World, how she may please her Husband. I Corinthians 7:34."[19] He proceeded to elaborate on the meaning of this verse by defining the biblical use of "caring." Chudleigh ridiculed his definition of this "hard and obscure word" which, she wrote, "(take notice Ladies) signifies more than ordinary Care, and implies a dividing of the Mind into divers thoughts, casting this way and that way, and every way, how to give best Content, that is to say, Fetch and bring, Go and she goeth, Come and she Cometh; to the Right, to the Left, as you were, and so on."[20] Next, she noted that Sprint's biblical reference omitted the preceding verse which read, "He that is married careth for the things of the World, how he may please his Wife," and she added that in the Greek edition the same word was used for "careth" in each instance.[21]

It was not difficult to better Sprint because he espoused commonplace views so clumsily. After presenting numerous examples of the necessity for female subservience he ended with a comforting thought for men, which, had he not written it, could surely have been taken for a satire on his work. First, God had ordained that, if women "love, honour and obey" their husbands, they would "do what becomes good Wives, and indeed what is, or should be at least sufficient to pleasure your husbands." He next drew from this the happy implications for men, both married and single: "You may from this Doctrine learn how great a Friend Religion is to the Comfort and Happiness of Man in this Life, in the Institution whereof God hath not only wisely consulted the Interest of his own Honour and Glory, but hath graciously condescended to adapt its Precepts to the Comfort and Happiness of Man in every State and condition of Life."[22]

Chudleigh's personal unhappiness perhaps prevented her from taking his writings lightly despite their obvious obtuseness. To Sprint's strangely straightforward explanation that woman's duty was "harder" because the "Precepts for Ruling and Governing are more taking, and have a more pleasing relish, than those which enjoyn Subjection and

Obedience,"[23] Chudleigh angrily retorted: "Insolent Man! To preach us gravely into Slavery and Chains, and then deride and banter us, as the Babylonians did the captive Jews when they had 'em fast in their power."[24]

Chudleigh expanded her attack on Sprint in *The Ladies defence*[25] to include a broader feminist vision. This fable depicted the characters of Sir John Brute, the recalcitrant antifeminist; Sir William Loveall, the chivalric defender of women; Melissa, the feminist and Chudleigh's spokeswoman; and the parson, Sprint. As the dialogue developed, Brute and the parson took sides against Melissa and Loveall. Chudleigh skillfully interwove Brute's personal distaste for the clergy with his praise of Sprint's ideas.

> Welcome, thou brave Defender of our Right;
> 'Till now, I thought you knew not how to Write:
> Dull heavy Morals did your Pens imploy;
> And all your business was to pall our Joy
>
> . . . .
>
> Till now, none of your Tribe were ever kind,
> Good Humour is alone to you Confin'd;
> You, who against those Terrours of our Lives,
> Those worst of Plagues, those Furies call'd our Wives,
> Have shew'd your Anger in a Strain Divine,
> Resentment sparkles in each poignant Line (p. 1).

Brute turned to Loveall for support, but he was on the other side:

> Then wonder not to hear me take their Part,
> And plead for the dear Idols of my Heart.
> Spightful Invectives shou'd no Patrons find,
> They are the Shame, and Venome of the Mind (p. 2).

Melissa then attacked the "Narcissus-like" quality of men's assumptions of superiority and the notion that they are "By Learning rais'd above humanity,"—and especially above women:

> Must Men command, and we alone obey,
> As if design'd for Arbitrary Sway:
> Born petty Monarchs, and, like Homer's Gods,
> See all subjected to their haughty Nods? (p. 3).

The men could not understand Melissa's unhappiness with women's lot, and the parson was at a loss to discover the reason for her hate. He expresses himself in words that must have come close to the common-place view of Chudleigh's own, and other women's, marital troubles:

> Why all this Rage? we merit not your hate;
> 'Tis you alone disturb the Marriage State:
> If to your Lords you strict Allegiance pay'd,
> And their Commands submissively obey'd:
> If like wise Eastern Slaves with trembling Awe
> You watch'd their Looks, and made their Will your Law,
> And wou'd both Kindness and Protection gain
> And find your duteous Care was not in vain (p. 6).

Even Loveall was puzzled at Melissa's dissatisfaction, except as it applied specifically to Brute and the parson. The parson continued his condescending commonplaces about women's behavior, Brute argued that nothing could be done with them, and Loveall praised the lovely and gentle qualities of women. However, as Melissa pressed for women's entrance into men's world of learning Loveall ceased to support her cause. Women, if they had learning, would admire only themselves so that:

> All our Addresses wou'd be then in vain,
> And we no longer in your Hearts shou'd Reign.

Few marriages would occur, he complained, if only "Men of Sense" dared to love.

> While You are ignorant, We are secure,
> A little Pain will your Esteem procure.
> Nonsense well Cloath'd will pass for solid Sense,
> And well pronounc'd, for matchless Eloquence:
> Boldness for Learning, and a foreign Air
> For nicest Breeding with th' admiring Fair (p. 16).

In passing from the crudities of Brute and Sprint to the conventionalities of Loveall, Chudleigh made her strongest case against the vapidity of cultural values that transformed what was despicable in human conduct, both male and female, into its farcical parody.

The fable ended with a request that men begin to educate women and to become aware themselves of the empty forms that passed for wisdom and propriety in their time. The pedantic scholar, the incompe-tent physician who killed while using foreign words, and the merchant who cheated and flattered his customers simultaneously all were products of the artificial learning of the day. The feminist was alone in her defense of women at the end of the fable, but she had expanded her concern to men and called upon them, as well as her own sex, to follow the path of truth and goodness. The fable argued that men kept women ignorant because their self-contented pride blinded them to true wisdom themselves.[26]

The note of a sad and complex understanding in *The Ladies defence* disappeared in Chudleigh's other specifically feminist poem, "To the Ladies." However truly wise and rewarding it would be for men to relinquish their control over women, Chudleigh had no delusions that they would do so. Hence women had to choose between marriage and the pursuit of knowledge and fulfillment. "To the Ladies," in *Poems on Several Occasions,* began by claiming that "wife and servant are the same," and ended in a bitter warning to young women:

> Then shun, oh! shun that wretched State,
> And all the fawning Flatt'rers hate:
> Value your selves, and Men despise,
> You must be proud, if you'll be wise (p. 40).

Her strong belief that all types of men—beaux, clergymen, and gentlemen—were fundamentally untrustworthy on the issue of developing women's potential, and her view of the unequal and unfair structure of marriage in seventeenth-century England, led her to argue that only single women could freely pursue intellectual interests.

IV

While the personal poetry of Winchilsea and Chudleigh adhered closely to the pastoral pattern of Philips, with its emphasis on idealized female friendship and on retreat from society toward a personal idyll, other feminist poets emphasized other traditions. Elizabeth Singer Rowe engrafted onto these concerns much more interest in exploring heterosexual relationships and the positive influence of passion on human conduct. Sarah Fyge Egerton showed no interest in the sentimentalities of the pastoral tradition. Her poetry was determinedly tough-minded and even bitter toward the world in general and men in particular. Literarily the most original and vigorous of these writers, Egerton seldom talked of love, and her negative, antimale feminism was unsoftened by any affection expressed for women.

Elizabeth Singer Rowe's feminism grew not from the personal unhappiness that motivated Chudleigh's but from the encouragement and loyal support of parents, husband, relatives, and a large circle of friends, especially women friends. The *Life of Elizabeth Singer Rowe*, written by Rowe's brother-in-law, Theophilus Rowe, attached to a 1739 edition of her and her husband's writings, was clearly a eulogy to Rowe and her husband, but there was much sincerity in the rhetoric. Elizabeth Singer Rowe apparently was surrounded by men who adored her and appreciated her talent throughout her life. The first, and perhaps most important, was her father. Theophilus Rowe described the Reverend Walter Singer as a man "of inflexible adherence to his principles, and at the same time a truly catholic spirit." [27] By all accounts, including his daughter's, he was a truly kind and understanding man who spent his time in prayer, study, or ministering to the needs of the less fortunate, characteristics noted and appreciated by those above his rank.[28] In a letter to a friend she explained that she had had "ease and plenty to the extent of my wishes," because of "my father's indulgence." "I ask nothing of Heaven but the good old man's life. The perfect sanctity of his life, and the benevolence of his temper, make him a refuge to all in distress, to the widow and fatherless: The people load him with blessings and prayers whenever he goes abroad; which he never does but to reconcile his neighbours, or to right the injur'd and oppressed; the rest of his hours are entirely devoted to his private devotions, and to books, which are his perpetual entertainment." [29] Her mother had died some years before her father, and Elizabeth was particularly close to him in later life. One of her younger sisters died in childhood; the other, a student of medicine, died at age twenty, so that Elizabeth and her father were the only family members alive for much of her adult life.[30]

Her father encouraged both her painting and her poetry, but the latter proved "her favourite employment" and "most distinguishing excellence." [31] The quality of her verse came to the attention of the Thynne family when she was less than twenty, and they asked her to visit them. At their Somerset estate, Longleat, Henry Thynne, son of Viscount Weymouth, taught her Italian and French, and she proved to be an apt pupil with a growing reputation as a charming and witty young woman. Masculine attention followed, and the poet Matthew Prior wrote her letters stating his desire to marry her, but she remained single until 1710 when, at the age of thirty-six, she wed twenty-three-year-old Thomas Rowe.

Thomas Rowe's character was in general outline much like that of the duke of Newcastle and the earl of Winchilsea—the two other husbands of seventeenth-century feminists about whom there is substantial information. All three men, the duke perhaps less seriously, were interested in intellectual pursuits, and all, pleased with their wives' accomplishments, encouraged their writings and intellectual pursuits. Thomas Rowe believed that Elizabeth Singer was a truly remarkable individual and seemingly was somewhat in awe of her throughout their marriage, although he himself had been a child prodigy and apparently one of the most brilliant young students in England. However his own attainments did not lessen his admiration for those of his learned wife.[32]

The affection expressed in Thomas Rowe's poetry did not cease with marriage. His brother stated that Rowe always "knew how to value that treasure of wit, softness and virtue, which the divine providence had given to his arms in the most lovely of women." Not only did he try to repay the happiness she gave him, but "the esteem and tenderness he had for her is inexpressible, and possession seemed scarce to have abated the fondness and admiration of the lover."[33] It is intriguing that Rowe spoke of her as "youth's liveliest bloom," even though she was thirteen years older than he was. Their marriage followed the pattern that Defoe outlined in *Conjugal Lewdness:* a rational attraction cemented by virtue and deep mutual respect.[34]

There is, on the surface at least, little doubt that Elizabeth Singer Rowe was a truly impressive woman. She was generally praised, and her brother-in-law's biography made clear that he was as fond of her as his brother had been. He was particularly pleased that "she continued to the last moments of her life to express the highest veneration and affection to his [Thomas Rowe's] memory, and a particular regard and esteem for his relations, several of whom she honour'd with a long and most intimate friendship." That he participated in this "intimate friendship" Theophilus Rowe's eulogy to her showed:

> O friend! O sister! . . .
>
>   . . . .
>
> . . . in thee I mourn
> Life's fondest joy—ah! never to return!

No more these eyes on thy lov'd form shall gaze,
Where more than beauty glow'd in ev'ry grace.[35]

The author hoped for a meeting in heaven, though he said he could not aspire to her certain spiritual rank.

Female friends as well as male relatives gave Elizabeth Singer Rowe ample support. The nature of this backing, and its ideological underpinnings, was clear in the introductory essay that Elizabeth Johnson wrote for Rowe's poems. Johnson was pleased to introduce her friend's work to the public for social as much as personal reasons. The quality of the verse proved "our Sex has some Excuse for a little Vanity, when they have so good reason for't, and such a Champion among themselves."[36] This theme of feminist pride led into a lengthy analysis of women's male-enforced inferior status, so that women could "only Kiss the Foot that hurts us." Men admittedly had the "Brutal Advantages of Strength" as well as "Custom on their side," and women would not mind men's ruling if they did it better and "could keep quiet among themselves." But, for Johnson as for other feminists, it was too much when men pretended to "monopolize Sence, too" and "won't let us say our Souls are our own." Some men even tried to persuade women, Johnson sarcastically said in her introduction, that females "are no more reasonable creatures, than themselves, or their fellow Animals."

This was, sharply stated, the commonplace argument of seventeenth-century feminists, but Johnson, perhaps because of the nonconforming background of Rowe's feminism, gave her history of oppression, especially of women's minds, a political cast. Women, she continues, were not "so compleatly passive" to put up with injustice indefinitely: "We complain, and we think with reason that our Fundamental Constitutions are destroyed; that here's a plain and an open design to render us meer Slaves, perfect Turkish Wives, without Properties, or Sense or Souls; and are forc'd to Protest against it, and appeal to all the World, whether these are not, notorious Violations on the Liberties on Freeborn English Women?" Such rhetoric about the rights of freeborn English women obviously derived from the seventeenth-century dissenting and Whig traditions. Yet Johnson's example of slavery referred not to disenfranchised Englishmen, but rather to Turkish wives. The position of women was central to Johnson's argument, but the political connotations she gave this concern, unprecedented at this time, suggested the major areas left unexplored both because of the Anglican-Tory orientation of most seventeenth-century feminists and because of the greater immediacy of women's subordination within the home.[37]

This introduction and, to a lesser degree, the second poetic one by another woman friend, made clear how natural it had become to turn praise for one female's contribution into feminist argument. These introductions became much more than mere well-wishing among acquaintances; they were really arguments that placed particular accomplishments in the context of society's failure to reward women artists properly and, more broadly, to treat all women fairly.

Johnson's introductory concern was much less with literary than with feminist matters, though she praised Rowe's "vivacity of thought" and "purity of language." She also gave an interesting list of Rowe's poetic predecessors: Sappho, Behn, Schurman, and Orinda (Philips). The inclusion of Sappho and Behn suggested the more passionate—in contrast to pastoral—quality of Rowe's poetry compared to that of Winchilsea or Chudleigh. The second introductory preface to *Poems on Several Occasions*, however, suggested the relation of these various emphases more exactly:

> Sappho and Behn reform'd, in thee revive,
> In thee we see the Chast Orinda live.

The pastoral idyll of female friendship developed by Philips was the prevailing strain in Rowe's poetry, but it had to compete with more sensual and witty strands drawn from other Restoration sources. In "The Female Passion," for example, Rowe dealt with heterosexual attraction and the "love's battles" at the heart of much of the best Restoration drama with witty resignation. Despite "a thousand great resolves" and determined efforts to have "honour and Pride" stand guard,

> One dart from his insulting eyes,
>   Eyes I'm undone to meet,
> Throws all my boasting faculties
>   At the lov'd Tyrant's feet.
> In vain alas, 'tis all in vain,
>   To struggle with my fate,
> I'm sure I ne're shall cease to love,
>   How much less can I hate! (pp. 30–31).

Rowe here presented the tyranny of love and the comedy that grew from its ability to circumvent people's best rational guard in much the same way Congreve did in his plays, but her feminism gave somewhat different connotations to the struggle. For her the tyrant was not simply love but the loved one, and capitulation to the charms of the opposite sex not merely a personal but a social fate.

Perhaps because of these differences, her poetry emphasized escape from love's bonds rather than succumbing to them, though often with a similar sense of loss. In "A Farewell to Love," the last poem in the volume, Rowe decided

> Well, since in spight of all that Love can do,
>   The dangerous steps of Honour thoul't pursue,
> I'll just grow Wise and Philosophical too.

Growing wise, however, took effort and substantial reinforcement from "Pride and Resentment," against "the Slavery of Man" and "the Lords of Nature."

> No more such wild Fantastick things shall Charm:
> My breast; nor these Serener Thoughts Alarm.
> No more for Farce; I'll make a Lover Creep
> And look as Scurvy as if he had bit a Sheep.

This comic turning of the tables on lovers, now scurvy and creeping, was followed by a pastoral section that at once played with the ludicrous qualities of much escapist verse, but also reminded men, in a more serious vein, that when she gave up love she realized that Cupid had "lost a politician in thy State."

> Like bright Diana now I'll range the Woods,
> And haunt the silent Shades and silver Floods.
> I'll find out the Remotest Paths I can,
> To shun th' Offensive, Hated Face of Man.
> Where I'll indulge my Liberty and Bliss,
> And no Endimyon shall obtain a Kiss (pp. 65–69).

What Winchilsea and Chudleigh described as the ideal setting, Rowe treated similarly but with rhetoric that made clear the comic exaggeration of the ideal of perfect happiness in the most remote of spots. Obviously she had not easily or completely put away "the hated face of

Man" or his embraces, despite her determination to leave Cupid to mourn. She wrote in "The Reply to Mr.———":

> Even Theron's lively and Inticing Eyes,
> Tho' arm'd with flames, I can at last despise;
> With all the Genuine Charms and Courtly Arts,
> By which your Treacherous Sex invade our Hearts
> (pp. 59–61).[38]

The charms of the opposite sex were for Rowe both genuine and treacherous, but there was also real desire for escape in the lines that follow:

> No more those little Things contract my breast
> By diviner Excellence possest;
>
>   . . . .
>
> For the mad Venome's quite expelled my veins,
> And calmer Reason now Triumphant Reigns.

Here the characterization of love as a "mad venome" that drew one to little things and away from one's full potential in calm reason and spiritual excellence gave a tone of desire for escape. Passages like this made clear Rowe's understanding, despite the unusual supportiveness of the men to whom she was closest, of how love created for women not just a controlling personal relationship but one which substituted a subordinate and supportive role for full human development.

The tensions apparent here existed in somewhat different guise in Rowe's many poems to and about women friends. In some of the more traditional ones like "Platonic Love" there was the hope for a pure and lasting friendship that was free of conflict in a way that heterosexual ties never could be. Yet these relationships Rowe often idealized much less than Winchilsea and Chudleigh, as in "To my Lady Carteret":

> Too great your Power, and too soft my Breast:
> The charming Inspiration to resist:
> But Oh in what bold strain shall I begin,
> To breathe th' unusual Potent Instinct in?

Here Rowe described a "potent instinct" of attraction that was not the abstraction of female friendship in the Philipsean pastoral tradition, and went on to describe its very physical source:

> A Form more fine, more accurately wrought,
> Was n'er conceiv'd by a Poetick Thought?
> So mild your eyes, so beautiful and bright,
> That lovelier eyes did ne'r salute the Light (pp. 14–15).

The honesty of Rowe's attraction to both men and women was clear, but in her poetry heterosexual attraction required resistance while the charms of female friendship offered lasting support. In the poem "To Celinda" Rowe began with a description of attraction rather like that in her verses to Lady Carteret:

> I can't, Celinda, say I love,
> But rather I adore,
> With transported eyes I view,
> Your shining merits o're.

But here she went on to emphasize the moral-intellectual qualities at the heart of female pastoral poetry:

> A flame so spotless and serene
> A vertue so refin'd;
> And thoughts as great, as e're was yet
> Graspt by a female mind.

And to this hope, Rowe tied her half-serious, half-mocking recognition that escape from men was necessary if this idyll were to take place:

> Then let's, my dear Celinda thus
> Blest in our selves contemn
> The treacherous and deluding Arts,
> Of those base things call'd men (pp. 27–28).

The richness of Rowe's vision grew from her recognition of the attraction of physical beauty and sexual passion, and her comic sense of the oversentimentalization of the pastoral tradition. Yet she appreciated as well its essentially serious social point if a woman's spiritual and rational resources were to be developed. Many of her poems combined a need for men with a realization of the consequences of fulfilling such a need. To her, love meant pleasure and slavery, but the alternative had its losses and its comic aspects as well. There was a real point in her friend's introduction to her poetry where Sappho and Behn, the poets of love's passion, were said to be "reformed" toward Orinda.

In 1715 the death of her husband from consumption allowed Elizabeth Rowe an actual retreat, to Frome where she had lived as a child. Here she wrote her *Letters Moral and Entertaining* and her *Friendship in Death*, the latter volume comprising "correspondence" between the living and the dead. Her husband's early demise, as well as perhaps the deaths of her mother and sisters at young ages, prompted the emphasis on death in these meditational and religious tracts, which admonished the young to avoid vice and pleasure and to pursue noble acts. She left her retreat occasionally at the request of her old friend, the countess of Hertford, the daughter of the Thynnes of Longleat. The possibility of death seemed to weigh heavily upon her mind, and when her own death was imminent, she wrote poems to those especially close to her, including the countess of Hertford and her mother-in-law.[39]

Whatever the reason for Elizabeth Singer Rowe's retreat from the world in the years following her husband's death, it had nothing to do with the enmity of friends or relatives. Her many admirers, both male and female, encouraged her work, and this made particularly striking her final choice of the pastoral retreat that her poetry alternately satirized and accepted as necessary for women's full rational and spiritual development. The tension was partly within herself, making it difficult for her to dismiss male attraction and adulation, even though she recognized that such affection carried with it an unequal submission for women. She wrote no more touching resumé of her personal and poetic vision than the lines in "The Reply to Mr.———" suggesting that she would not choose to be reunited with her husband:

> Nor would I for my late splendid Chain
> Forgo this Charming Liberty again;
> Which with so sweet a Calmness fill my Breast
> As cannot in Words, no not in thine Exprest (p. 61).

v

Sarah Egerton showed none of Elizabeth Rowe's ambiguous and half-amused gentleness toward either men or the female pastoral tradition. She shared something of Rowe's passionate nature and her intelligence, but both characteristics were wedded to a vein of sharp-eyed, cynical anger rather than half-playful wit and self-mockery. Unfortunately, there were only hints in her poetry as to the reasons for such anger. Her work was rejected early by her father and she appeared to have been, if her verse were reasonably autobiographical, especially afflicted with inconstant lovers, an assumption that will have to suffice given the lack of biographical information.[40]

Egerton presumably had a number of influential friends and supporters, including Lord Halifax, to whom she dedicated her volume, but she shared her ideas and verse with a circle of women friends predominantly. She noted their support and linked it to the publication of her work: "They never were abroad before, nor e'er seen but by my own Sex, some of which have favour'd me with their Complements, and I was too much of a Woman to refuse them." That this was a close group of mutually supportive feminists was made clear in the introductory verses four friends wrote for Egerton's volume. The first two, both called "To Mrs. S. E. on her Poems," tied Egerton's literary efforts to those of other women and to masculine suppression of female efforts generally:

> No more let haughty Man with fierce disdain,
> Despise the Product of a Female brain,
> But read thy Works, there view thy spacious Mind,
> Thy Reason clear, thy Fancy unconfin'd,
> And with due Honours celebrate thy Name.

In this attack on male presumption, the accomplishments of one woman served to prove the abilities of all. The poet went on to connect the specific case with the general pattern.

> Mankind has long upheld the Learned Sway,
> And Tyrant Custom forc'd us to obey.
> Thought, Art, and Science did to them belong,
> And to assert our Selves was deem'd a Wrong
> But we are justify'd by thy immortal Song.[41]

Egerton was, S. C. continued, a "Champion for our Sex" destined to show "ambitious man" with his "scholastick rules" just "what Womankind can do."

The characteristics of Egerton's verse were also accurately set out by E. C. in "To my Ingenious Friend Mrs. S. E. on her Poems":

> And when her Muse Satyrick would appear,
> 'Tis without air of Spite, and yet severe.
> Then in deep Thought reflects on human kind,
> And traces Fate thro' her mysterious Wind.

Satire, severity, deep thought, a passionate concern with fate's "mysterious wind"—such were the qualities to praise in Egerton's work, concerns generally deemed "unwomanly" and hence harmful to her career. Yet Egerton's friends praised her work specifically because it emphasized themes considered beyond the modest sphere of a proper woman poet. These opening verses suggested the prevalence of feminist ideas in groups of intellectual women. The arguments and the language of feminists like Astell had become, such evidence hinted, fairly commonplace truisms to significant numbers of educated women.

Sarah Egerton's literary support and talent in no way lessened her anger, as she demonstrated in "Satyr against the Muses":

> By my abandon'd Muse, I'm not inspir'd,
> Provok'd by Malice, and with Rage I'm fir'd.
> Fly, fly, my Muse from my distracted Breast,
> Who e'er has thee, must be with plagues possesst (p. 14).

The power of her poetry owed much to this sense of rage—and of skepticism about solutions, specifically those which other feminists had idealized. She saw no way out of her and other women's dilemmas in the platonic friendships and personal or intellectual meditation that attracted Mary Astell and earlier feminist poets. Her poem "On Friendship" was very different from what Philips, Winchilsea, or Chudleigh wrote on the subject:

> Friendship (the pursuit of noble Minds)
> Passion in abstract, void of all designs;
> Each generous Pen, doth celebrate thy Fame,
> And yet, I doubt, thou'rt nothing but a Name.

Egerton here not only mocked the idea of perfect friendship which, like other human relations, was bound to become merely a matter "of vulgar Commerce, or Debate." She also pinpointed the appeal of the sentimental escapism that lay behind the vision of female pastorals:

> Sure, like the Chymick Stone, it was design'd,
> But to imploy the curious searching Mind,
> In the pursuit of what none e'er shall find (pp. 1–2).

Egerton found no more help for unhappiness in her writing than in the support of friends. For Chudleigh and Winchilsea writing was a release from a dull and trifling existence, but Egerton saw that poetry's inducement to look deeply destroyed innocence without supplying answers. Seldom has a poet more soundly attacked the muse which had made her "not only Poor, but wretched too." She continued in "On Friendship":

> Happly I liv'd, for almost Eight years time;
> Curs'd by your Skill, you taught me then to Rhim:
> The Jingling noise, shed its dark Influence,
> On my then pleased, unwary Innocence.
> I scarce have had one happy Moment since.

With her uncompromising views, poetry aroused not release or peace but "all the Spite and Rage of Womankind":

> Curses, in vain, on Poets I bestow;
> I'm sure, the greatest is, that they are so:
> Fate, send worse if thou cans't, but Rescue me
> From trifling torturing wretched Poetry (pp. 14–16).

Egerton's was a nightmare vision in which anger was the deepest honesty, especially toward those things that promised happiness. Poetry was "Jingling noise," all the more irritating because it was the vehicle through which one saw and into which one poured the "Rage of Womankind."

Egerton expressed her passion and anger more fervently than any other feminist in part because she had no comforting solace, either personal or social. Efforts at writing heightened rather than dissipated her understanding of woman's subordination and her consequent rage. "The Liberty" presented one of the clearest statements of feminist resistance to a meaningless life, but one that went much further in its rejection of social mores than did other such works. The first lines were very much in keeping with the ideas and language of her feminist contemporaries:

> Shall I be one, of those obsequious Fools,
> That square there lives, by Customs scanty Rules;
> Condemn'd for ever, to the puny Curse,
> Of Precepts taught, at Boarding-school, or Nurse,
> That all the business of my Life must be,
> Foolish, dull Trifling, Formality.
> Confin'd to a strict Magick complaisance,
> And round a Circle, of nice visits Dance,
> Nor for my Life beyond the Chalk advance (p. 19).

This catalogue of the emptiness of women's ordained life, in which the social and the mystical were joined, was powerfully stated but still similar to what other feminists had said. However, Egerton's rejection went beyond criticism of the usual restraints on women who wished to think and write, both in defiant tone and in social scope. Public criticism was a "Bug-bear" that frightened only children:

> Whatever is not vicious, I dare do,
> I'll never to the Idol Custom bow,
> Unless it suits my own Humour too.
> Some boast their Fetters, of Formality,
> Fancy they ornamental Bracelets be,
> I'm sure their Gyves, and Manacles to me.
> To their dull fulsome Rules, I'd not be ty'd,
> For all the Flattery that exalts their Pride (p. 20).

The formal rules of society handcuffed women under the guise of making them ornamental, and this justified that the honest woman be a law unto herself.

> My daring Pen, will bolder Sallies make,
> And like myself, an uncheck'd freedom take;
> Not chain'd to the nice Order of my Sex,
> And with restraint my wishing Soul perplex;
> I'll blush at Sin, and not what some call Shame,
> Secure my Virtue, slight precarious Fame.
> This Corage speaks me, Brave, 'tis surely worse,
> To keep those Rules, which privately we Curse
> And I'll appeal, to all the formal Saints,
> With what reluctance they indure restraints (p. 21).

It is not totally clear how far this rejection of social customs went or what direction it took. Egerton spoke of remaining moral, while defining morality in her terms, not those of society: "Whatever is not vicious, I dare do." In a society where even the taint of an unchaste character was sufficient to damn a woman's reputation, Egerton was damning such false modesty, if not conventional notions of chastity.

By implication at least her argument went further than that of Defoe in his "Academy for Women," in the *Essay upon Projects* (1697), where women's formal modesty was contrasted with an internal understanding or justification for proper behavior. Defoe quoted an anonymous poem:

Custom with Women 'stead of Virtue rules;
It leads the Wisest, and commands the Fools:
For this alone, when Inclinations reign,
Tho' Virtue's fled, will Acts of Vice restrain.
Only by Custom 'tis that Virtue lives,
And love requires to be ask'd, before it gives.[42]

This mockery of custom, the awareness of the emptiness of formal rules that feminist sensibility nurtured, led Egerton to assert that both honesty and courage demanded that people openly break "those Rules, which privately we Curse."

The roots of Egerton's anger and her feminism came early. At fourteen she wrote a poem, "The Female Advocate," which led to her sharpest sense of male injustice. The poem outlined her understanding of feminist issues while yet an adolescent, and as an adult Egerton described in another poem ("To the Lady Cambell, with a Female Advocate") her father's reaction to the earlier verse:

Scarce fourteen Years, when I the piece begun,
And in less time than fourteen days 'twas done;
Without design of Publication writ,
And Innocence supply'd the want of Wit.
But ah! my Poetry, did fatal prove,
And robb'd me of a tender Father's Love;
(I thought that only Men, who writ for Fame,
Or sung lewd Stories, to unlawful Flame,
Were punish'd for, their proud or wanton Crime.
But Children too, must suffer if they'll Rhyme) (p. 22).

The poem ended with a rarely sentimental argument that, if the Lady Cambell enjoyed the poem, it would compensate for "all my Sorrows past." Yet there was sincerity in the description of this small event that "cost me more than all the World can give," a sense of stinging injustice and bitter reaction that radiated through Egerton's better poems. That she was a "female advocate" at fourteen offered good evidence for the widespread dissemination of feminist ideas, and their ready availability might account for her uncompromising vision. She was a second-generation feminist, in effect, in whom expectation or hope of change gave place to the kind of bitterness that existed, more quietly, in Mary Astell's last prefaces.

This adolescent hurt at her father's rejection of her verse and her ideas did not lead Egerton away from men but into uneasy relationships with them. And what Rowe handled with playful if sometimes bitter-sweet grace took on biting sarcasm and passionate intensity in Egerton's verse. If Rowe's heterosexual poetry showed Behn reformed by Philips, Egerton's suggested Behn unreformed and made more passionate by a deep-seated feminism.

"As light and heat compose the genial sun," Egerton wrote in "To One Who Said I Must Not Love," "So Love and I essentially are one." In her dedication of *Poems on Several Occasions* to Lord Halifax, the poet wrote a justification of her concentration on this theme, an argument which suggested both her feminism and the unusual tack it often took. She trusted that Halifax agreed with her that, if love were no crime, writing about it could be none. "Besides our Sex is confin'd to so narrow a sphere of action, that things of greater Consequence seldom fall within our Notices," she wrote, "so that Love seems the only proper Theme (if any can be so) for a Woman's Pen." Passionate love, rather than being an unsuitable topic for a female poet, Egerton insisted, was the only one about which women could well speak, given their systematic exclusion from the public and practical concerns of their age.

Her light and satiric poetry on heterosexual relations was often fairly conventional in its scope and its targets, though biting enough. For example in "To Orabella, Marry'd to an old Man," Egerton took aim at a stock figure of Restoration ridicule, the ancient husband with the young wife. "What strong Persuasions made you thus to wed," she asked the young woman, "with such a carcass scandalize your Bed?":

> A moving Skeleton he seems to be,
> Nature's antienest Anatomy.
> Worth Observation, hang him up therefore
> In Gresham College, and I'll ask no more (pp. 36–37).

The element of brutality here and Egerton's stress that Orabella should have married a youth "of equal Mind" gave some personal stamp to the verse but, like most of her comic poetry, it remained fairly conventional.

Egerton's more serious and personal poetry dealing with men was more original in sentiment and language, the harshness and the passion of her accounts seeming to war with the orderly rhythms and couplets that she used to encase the ideas. In them Egerton wavered between a youthful pride in her share of lovers and a criticism of male inconstancy. But the strongest and most striking verses expressed her anger. In "To Philaster," for example, she berated a former lover who was now searching for a new nymph "who longs to know how 'tis and what Men swear," but, she warned, his new lover would get only "the forc'd-kind Complaisance you now bestow," because Egerton, as his first love, received the "native Sweetness" of early innocence. She concluded with this threat:

> Perjur'd imposing Youth, cheat who you will,
> Supply defect of Truth with amorous Skill;
> Yet thy Address must needs insipid be
> For the first Ardour of thy Soul was all possess'd by me
>
> (pp. 34–35).

The proud anger here, and the frank desire for vengeance, made this unusual in the poetry of slighted love, but even more surprising was the way that Egerton appropriated the usual male idea of associating original sexual conquest with permanent possession. This was a step beyond the boundaries of other seventeenth-century feminist writings.

Egerton's poetry on marriage, like that on love, was fairly conventional, if unusually vigorous, in its more objective, argumentative form, but took on peculiar twists and power when most closely related to her personal feelings and experiences. Egerton's "The Emulation" stated the usual feminist case against "Tyrant Custom" strikingly:

> From the first dawn of Life, unto the Grave,
> Poor Womankind's in every State, a Slave.
> The Nurse, the Mistress, Parent and the Swain,
> For Love she must, there's none escape that Pain.

For Egerton love, as well as custom, tied women to the social roles in which women's slavery occurred, and the most important of these was marriage where husbands

> . . . with insulting Tyranny
> Can have ill Manners justify'd by Law;
> For Men all join to keep the Wife in awe.
> Moses who first our Freedom did rebuke
> Was married when he writ the Pentateuch.

Here Egerton's freedom from the intensity of Anglican conviction that

Astell, Chudleigh, and Winchilsea shared allowed her to relate injustices to women more broadly to the Judeo-Christian tradition than others could have comfortably done. She was also more tough-minded about the inevitable sexual power struggle than they, about woman's desire for power and man's fear of losing it:

> They're Wise to keep us Slaves, for well they know,
> If we were loose, we soon should make them, so.
> We yield like vanquish'd Kings whom Fetters bind,
> When chance of War is to Usurpers kind:
> Submit in Form; but they'd our Thoughts controul,
> And lay restraints on the impassive Soul:
> They fear we should excel their sluggish Parts,
> Should we attempt the Sciences and Arts (pp. 108–9).

Here was not merely custom but conspiracy, an intentional effort by men of "sluggish parts" to keep women securely bound. And this was a wise move on the part of men, for women submitted only "in Form" and quietly awaited the opportunity to turn the tables on the usurpers. Such a vision left little room for compromise.

Whatever the validity of this picture, "The Emulation" lacked the personal twists and passion of Egerton's verse at its best. If no one else wrote so personally about the tyranny of love in relation to the tyranny of marriage, it may have been because love's pull was especially strong. She had wanted to escape the involvement of love, as she said in "To One Who Said I Must Not Love":

> E'er your Advice, a thousand ways I try'd
> To ease the inherent Pain, but 'twas deny'd;
> Tho' I resolv'd, and griev'd, and almost dy'd.
> Then I would needs dilate the mighty Flame,
> Play the Coquet, hazard my dearest Fame.

Egerton's passionate involvement in the game of love offered no retreat into pastoral friendship or even into the mock-pastoral games Rowe used to handle it. Marriage seemed the only escape:

> Weary'd at last, curst Hymen's Aid I chose;
> But find the fetter'd Soul has no Repose.
> Now I'm a double Slave to Love and Vows:
> As if my former Sufferings were too small,
> I've made the guiltless Torture—Criminal.

Surely this was the ultimate attack on marriage, not by a woman abused within the relationship but by one who found herself "a double slave" to both love and vows. And she had also become "criminal" by turning her formerly "guiltless" passion into the torment of marriage. The unequal relationship of marriage, with its inevitable tensions and irritations, made for bitterness not because love and respect were lacking but because they were present.

> Each vital String cracks with th' unequal Strife,
> Departing Love racks like Departing Life (pp. 42–43).

Sarah Egerton's being racked with love and an unflinching honesty that clutched at the harshest aspects of human dilemmas gave a startlingly grim dimension to her feminism, a darkly passionate quality to her verse that seems at times closer to Sylvia Plath's work than Anne Winchilsea's. Thus the amount of support women gave her work was even more remarkable. Other feminists shared her desire for autonomy in their lives, but no one else suggested just how far away from conventional social and sexual relations this objective might lead, nor with what ambiguous results. It was almost as if Egerton were daring those who might try to limit what she could do with her life or her mind, or who might try to make too simplistic a solution to women's needs, whether for friendship or retreat.

The strands of feminism among these poets were impressive. While not leading to a new interpretation of women's position, they revealed a rich and varied literature arguing, crying, and raging against women's various prisons. The poets provide a fitting climax to seventeenth-century feminism, which began with the duchess of Newcastle's unexpected critique of women's lives, in which feminist perception was offset by her numerous attacks upon her sex. Mary Astell, in the latter part of the century, argued vigorously that women's deficiencies were not innate but socially induced, an assumption that had become standard by the time the feminist poets wrote. Astell, to a greater extent than the earlier feminists, linked all aspects of women's lives together in a pattern of subjugation. Domineering husbands, male-dominated institutions, and a society which wanted women to remain docile and to entertain themselves with trifles were partners in the oppression of women.

The feminist poets built on this understanding and enriched it with their personal longings. They felt less need to argue their case than to find words for it, to express their problems and their hopes in evocative terms. Anne Winchilsea and Lady Mary Chudleigh particularly shared Astell's Tory-Anglican principles and her stress on female friendship as an alternative to male domination. In a basic sense their use of the female pastoral was a poetic and personal equivalent to the female college, a setting where women's mutual support would make possible women's full development.

Elizabeth Singer Rowe and Sarah Egerton, in part because feminist ideas were so generally acceptable in their separate circles of female friends and in part because of their relative freedom from the Anglican-Tory vision of most feminists of the day, carried feminism into some new areas, especially into a franker handling of heterosexual relations and of the relation of passion to women's freedom. Elizabeth Johnson's introduction to Rowe's poems connected feminism to the English radical political tradition, perhaps because of Rowe's closer ties to dissenting circles. And Sarah Egerton endowed her feminism with a passionate and uncompromising skepticism that gave the ideology a personally radical cast it had in no other writer's works.

Concern about women was central to their work, the real theme of introductions and verses on every conceivable subject. They each had distinct interests—Anne Winchilsea's nature poetry, Lady Mary Chudleigh's feud with John Sprint, Elizabeth Rowe's use of mock-pastoral wit, and Sarah Egerton's passionate skepticism—but each one continually returned to the plight of women. The manner in which these poets viewed the success or failure of their own lives, or the benevolence or vindictiveness of society, was inextricably tied to their view of women as a sociological group.

NOTES

1. *Triumphs of Female Wit, in some Pindarick Odes; or, The Emulation* (London: Printed for T. Malthus, 1683), pp. 2–3.
2. Analyses of the pastoral tradition in English poetry are numerous. They, however, ignore the connection between the literary theme of female friendship and retreat and the growth of feminist ideas in the seventeenth century. Pastoral themes usually treated include the shepherd as a pastoral subject, nature as a source of spiritual and poetic rebirth, and a general criticism of worldly hustle

and bustle; the latter theme was also important in feminist pastorals of the late 1600s. For general discussions of this tradition consult James E. Congleton's *Theories of Pastoral Poetry in England, 1684–1798* (1952; reprint ed., New York: Haskell House, 1968); John F. A. Heath-Stubbs, *The Pastoral* (London: Oxford University Press, 1969); and a more recent account that analyzes its broad philosophical implications, Richard Feingold's *Nature & Society* (New Brunswick, N.J.: Rutgers University Press, 1978).

3. For a brief biographical account of Katherine Philips see the *Dictionary of National Biography*, 45: 177–78, and the introduction to Katherine Philips, *Selected Poems, The Orinda Booklets*, ed. Louise I. Guiney, vol. 1 (Hull: J. R. Tutin, 1905). Further references to this work are referred to by page number in the text. Finally, for the glowing accounts of her character and writings by her contemporaries see the introductory poems to Katherine Philips, *Poems By the . . . Matchless Orinda* (London: Printed by J. M. for H. Herringman, 1667). For an account of Aphra Behn's life see the *Dictionary of National Biography*, 4: 129–31, and *Life and Memoirs of Mrs. Behn. Written by One of the Fair Sex* (London: For S. Briscoe, 1656). (The latter 68-page essay was included in a seventeenth-century edition of her work).

4. Myra Reynolds, *Learned Lady*, p. 57. "In her day Orinda was not only prized as a poet, but she was considered the highest example, the prophet and expounder, of true friendship. Much of her verse was called forth by her Society of Friendship. The chief members of this circle were 'Antenor' (Mr. Philips), 'Lucasia' (Miss Anne Owen), 'Rosania' (Miss Mary Aubrey), 'Regina' (Mrs. John Collier), 'Palaemon' (Jeremy Taylor), 'Silvander' (Sir Edward Dring), 'Policrite' (Lady Margaret Cavendish), 'Celimena' (Miss E. Boyl), 'Cassandra' (Mrs. C. P., her dear sister), and 'Critender' (Mr. J. B.). 'Ardellia,' 'Phillis,' and 'Pastora' remain unidentified."

5. Ibid., pp. 55–58.

6. Ibid., pp. 58–59. Philips was an unusual choice for a famous and successful female poet. She lacked wealth and good looks and was "married to an ordinary, rather dull man." She was quite "housewifely" herself and was simply "a virtuous, sane, orderly, thrifty woman."

7. Ibid., p. 158. "One interesting fact with regard to these early poems is the indication we have of a kind of poetical commerce maintained among the members of a group of persons similarly inclined to verse."

8. Such closeness among female poets is representative of relationships among women friends in later centuries as well. An important discussion of female friendships can be found in Carroll Smith-Rosenberg's "The Female World of Love and Ritual: Relations between Women in Nineteenth-Century America," *Signs: A Journal of Women and Society* 1 (1975): 1–29.

9. Killigrew's poetry is included in the following collection: *Poems*, intro. by Richard Morton (1686; reprint ed., Gainesville, Fla.: Scholars' Facsimilies and Reprints, 1967).

10. Anne, Countess of Winchilsea, "Epilogue to the Tragedy of Jane Shore," *The Poems of Anne, Countess of Winchilsea*, ed. Myra Reynolds (Chica-

go: University of Chicago Press, 1902). Further references to Winchilsea's poetry are to this edition and are noted by page numbers in the text.

11. Reynolds, Introduction to Winchilsea, *Poems*, pp. xxxiv–xxxvi. The Finches lived a life of scholarly retreat and each was able to follow his/her individual intellectual interests; his ran to antiquarianism and hers to poetry.

12. Ibid., p. li.

13. Lady Mary Chudleigh, *Poems on Several Occasions, together with the "Song of the Three Children Paraphras'd"* (London: Printed by W. B. Lintott, 1703). Further references to this work will be noted by page number in the text.

14. Reynolds, *Learned Lady*, p. 162. Marissa was Lady Chudleigh's pen name, but there are few clues as to who her friends were. It would require a massive, and likely futile, search through repetitious fanciful names to produce even a partial list of these lost women.

15. There seems to be no separate biography of John Sprint, either father or son, beyond the materials included in the *Dictionary of National Biography*.

16. The feminists' love of scholarship often made them disdainful of the ignorant or superficially knowledgeable.

17. John Sprint, "Epistle to the Reader," *The Bride-Womans Counseller, Being a Sermon Preach'd at a Wedding, May 11th, 1699 at Sherbourn in Dorsetshire* (n.p., 1699).

18. Ibid.

19. Ibid., title page.

20. [Lady Mary Chudleigh], *The Female Advocate; or, A Plea for the just liberty of the Tender Sex, and particularly of Married Women* (London, 1700), pp. 9–10.

21. Ibid., p. 10.

22. Sprint, *Bride-Womans Counseller*, p. 14.

23. Ibid., p. 14.

24. Chudleigh, *Female Advocate*, p. 14.

25. [Lady Mary Chudleigh], *The Ladies defence: or, "The Bride-Womans Counseller" Answer'd* (London: Printed for John Deeve, 1701). Further references to *Ladies defence* are from this edition and are noted by page number in the text.

26. These latter, more charitable views, are quite comparable to the opinion expressed in "A History of the Athenian Society," in *A Supplement to the Athenian Oracle, Being a Collection of the Remaining Questions and Answers in the Old "Athenian Mercuries. . . . " To which is prefix'd the "History of the Athenian Society"* (London: Printed for Andrew Bell, 1710). For a more complete discussion of these views see the Conclusion. However, it should not be forgotten that the feminists' resentment against the professions had a bitter side as well. This view was expressed well by Anne Winchilsea in the following verse:

> No more Vapours, your belov'd Disease,
> Your Ignorance's Skreen, your what-you-please
> With which you cheat poor Females of their lives
> Whilst men dispute not, so it rid their wives.

In Winchilsea's "For the Better," *Miscellany Poems on Several Occasions* (London, 1713), p. 138.

27. Elizabeth Singer Rowe, *The Miscellaneous Works in Prose and Verse of Mrs. Elizabeth Singer Rowe, to which are added, "Poems on Several Occasions" by Mr. Thomas Rowe*, ed. Theophilus Rowe, 2 vols. (London, 1749), 1: v. Near the end of Theophilus Rowe's biography he includes Anne, Countess of Winchilsea's name first in a listing of Elizabeth Singer Rowe's close friends (p. xcvi).

28. Ibid., pp. v–vi. The Rev. Singer was "held in high esteem, even by persons of superior rank: My Lord Weymouth, who was reckon'd a very good judge of men, not only writing to him, but honoring him with his visits; as did the devout Bishop Kenn very frequently, sometimes once a week."

29. Ibid.

30. Ibid., pp. vii–xv.

31. Ibid., p. xv.

32. Ibid., pp. xix–xx. His biographer described Thomas Rowe as follows: "His superior genius, insatiable thirst after knowledge, made themselves taken notice of at an age when the generality of mankind have scarcely outgrown the merely sensitive life. He was able to *read* as soon almost as he could *speak*; had such a pleasure in books, as to take none at all in the diversions which children are usually so fond of."

33. Ibid., p. xxx. Rowe expressed a nonsensual love in his courtship poetry to his future wife.

> Youth's liveliest bloom a never fading grace,
> And more than beauty sparkles in her face;
> Yet the bright form creates no loose desires,
> At once she gives, and purifies our fires,
> And passions chaste as her own soul inspires;
> Her soul, heaven's noblest workmanship, design'd
> To bless the ruin'd age, and succour lost mankind.
> To prop abandon'd virtue's sinking cause,
> And snatch from vice its undeserved applause.

34. Defoe's work will be discussed in the concluding chapter.

35. Theophilus Rowe, "On the Death of Mrs. Elizabeth Rowe," in Rowe, *Miscellaneous Works*, pp. cxxi–cxxvii, liii, xliv–xlvi.

36. Elizabeth Johnson, "Preface to the Reader," [Elizabeth Singer Rowe], *Poems on Several Occasions* (London, 1696), n.p. Further references to this work are noted by page number in the text.

37. For a growing awareness of the political implications of the legal subordination of seventeenth-century women see an early eighteenth-century tract written by an anonymous woman and reprinted in 1735, *The Hardships of the English Laws in Relation to Wives. With an explanation of the Original Curse of Subjection passed upon the Woman. In an humble address to the Legislature* (London and Dublin: Reprinted by and for G. Faulkner, 1735).

38. "Theron" was a fanciful name Rowe used for her deceased husband.

39. Rowe, *Miscellaneous Works*, pp. liii, xliv–xlvi.

40. Except for Lady Mary Chudleigh, it is difficult to find a single seventeenth-century feminist who had an unhappy marriage, although Egerton did speak of difficulties with suitors.

41. S[arah] E[gerton], *Poems on Several Occasions, together with a Pastoral* (London: Printed by J. Nutt [1706]), n.p.; S. C., "To Mrs. S. E. on her incomparable Poems," ibid. In "On my Wedding Day," Egerton indicates she was a widow in the following line: "Dismale as I, black as the Weeds I wear." However, her sorrow at widowhood did not prevent her noting her reluctance to wed originally and her continual doubts about marriage. "If my first Offering had been Free-Will, / I then perhaps might have enjoy'd thee still" (pp. 70–72). Further references to Egerton's work are from this 1706 edition and are noted by page number in the text.

42. Daniel Defoe, "An Academy for Women," *An Essay upon Projects* (1697; reprint ed., Menston, England: Scholar Press, Ltd., 1969), p. 282.

Conclusion

Influences and Limitations of Seventeenth-Century Feminism

These early English feminists were largely forgotten both because the social effect of their thought was limited and because its historical influence was truncated. Around the turn of the century, their stress on women's rational ability and on the uneven distribution of power within marriage permeated other thought briefly, but the ties between feminist and general social thought in the period remained slight, at least as compared with what women's advocates hoped to accomplish. And while this early feminism's stress on women as a sociological group was to remain a permanent contribution, the views of Mary Astell and others were largely forgotten when Mary Wollstonecraft, a century later, revived the movement with a more political cast. The seventeenth-century movement was not only ahead of its time but hedged in by intellectual and social realities that helped at once to engender the ideas and to insure that they would little prosper.

I

The ideas of seventeenth-century feminists were traceable in other ideas of the age. Though, as always, cause and effect, influence and result were not easily segregated, certainly some of the writings of the 1690s and early 1700s showed some themes and concerns common to the feminists. Individual men in the 1690s wrote defenses of women, notably William

Walsh, *A Dialogue Concerning Women* (1691), and Nahum Tate, poet laureate, playwright, and contributor to the *Athenian Mercury*, *A Present for the Ladies* (1693). These two works were less important for their originality than as indicators of a certain general interest in aspects of feminism. Walsh's book borrowed much from Poulain de la Barre's, especially in its discussion of women's education and masculine motives for female exclusion, while Tate drew heavily on Agrippa's views about the excellency of the female sex. Poulain and Agrippa were sources that later women feminists drew on also, and, if uninventive, the works of Tate and Walsh doubtless gave exposure to, as well as showed general concern with, the issue of women's place in society. Tate's book, given his social and literary prominence, was perhaps the best proof of some establishment susceptibility to feminist concerns in the age.[1]

A more significant literary figure who shared feminists' interests, and with greater originality, was Daniel Defoe. Defoe acknowledged Mary Astell's influence on his "Academy for Women," in his 1697 *Essay upon Projects*, but the plan of education he outlined for women was more wholly secular than Astell's and less tied to the kind of philanthropic work often associated with women's special sphere, even though it did include more of the normal finishing-school trappings. Defoe's *Conjugal Lewdness; or, Matrimonial Whoredom*, published in 1727 but written in the 1690s, offered a feminist view of the need for fairer relationships within marriage. It criticized the use of women, either before or after the wedding ceremony, exclusively for the sexual pleasure of men. And his *Moll Flanders*, while far from a feminist tract, took its heart from the uneven social conditions a woman faced, and her resilience, competence, and intelligence in meeting the various hard knocks fate and society visited upon her.[2]

While a handful of men took at least partially feminist positions in books, others did so, even more ambiguously, in periodicals and compilations. In the latter cases, the motivation was apparently as much profit as promotion of social justice, but perhaps the baser motive suggested the greater feminist success. Feminists had helped create a female audience large enough and intellectual enough to support publications that took seriously women's mental capacities and interests. *The Athenian Mercury*, which began publication in 1690, *The Ladies Diary*, which appeared during the first three decades of the eighteenth century, and *The Ladies Library*, a compilation of items of interest to women published by Richard Steele in 1714, all took modified feminist stances in their pursuit of an increasingly large female reading public. These works focused much of their attention on questions relevant to women's education and general status within society. The *Mercury* and the *Diary* received and printed numerous letters to the editors, poems, and queries (both personal and academic) from women. Their editors made it clear that women were a welcomed and substantial portion of their reading public, and they specifically addressed issues to them. The feminists cannot be given the total credit for this increase in women's intellectual interests, but the questions asked and the letters submitted made it clear that their writings were well known both to the female readers and to the men editing periodicals geared, in part or generally, toward women.[3]

John Dunton, in the first issue of the *Athenian Mercury*, did not specifically mention women among those readers he encouraged to submit questions or enigmas on topics of general, mathematical, or scientific interest. However, in number 13 (1697) Dunton, in an advertisement, replied affirmatively to a young woman who asked if her sex were welcome to submit questions. By issue 18 of the *Athenian Mercury*, Dunton made clear that women had responded broadly to this offer. "The Questions we receive from the Fair Sex are both *pressing* and *numerous*," he wrote, and agreed to set aside an issue each month "to satisfy Questions of that Nature" because he realized women "have a very *strong* party in the World."[4] That that "party" was now strong enough to be heard, and to have an issue devoted solely to its interests, in a popular intellectual periodical was a victory for women.

Although the entire series of the *Athenian Mercury* is not currently available, compilations include all the questions submitted to this late seventeenth-century periodical. A three-volume compilation, *The Athenian Oracle*, published in 1703–4, included selected questions from the original *Mercuries* of the 1690s, as did *A Supplement to the Athenian Oracle*, printed in 1710, which included the "remaining questions and answers in the old Athenian Mercuries" and *The History of the Athenian Society* by a member of the society.[5] All of these attest to the popularity of the publications of the Athenian Society as well as to their commitment to including women among their readers and correspondents.

The *History* made clear the basic goal of the society and also suggested why women were included. It wanted to convey specialized knowledge to a general public, to popularize not only "experimental Improvement of Natural Knowledge" but also "all other Sciences to all Men, as well as to both Sexes." The *History* credited the Baconians, the Royal Society, and Descartes with revolutionizing scholarship, but criticized them for not sharing their new insights more broadly. "Tis true it was great to cast off Authoritys, and to have recourse alone to Reason and Experiment, the only sure Foundation of all Learning," but these changes left the public, for the most part, still in the dark. "But tho the Treasure of Knowledge increas'd so vastly," the author noted, "Yet the Possessors of this Treasure did not grow much more numerous than of old." The *Athenian Mercury* wanted to bridge the gap between the few who were aware of the new learning and the many outside the universities and the Royal Society who were not.[6]

For obvious reasons, in pursuing this goal of more general education the *Athenian Mercury* faced some of the same opposition that the feminists aroused. The author of the *History* knew that some "plodding grave Gentleman" who had spent many years learning Latin, Greek, or Hebrew might be upset that now the kernel he had gained through so much work was "given to every illiterate Fellow." Such an attitude, however, was both petty and a serious impediment to England's intellectual advance. Such egotistic "Desire of Honour and Veneration, and to be esteem'd something more than Men, has been the Cause of the small Progress of Learning in former Ages" and now "ought to be cast away."[7] The views of the society's historian here paralleled the criticism of pretentious intellectuals that the duchess of Newcastle and Mary Astell voiced, and the related argument that formal learning too often stressed dead tongues over live ideas was a staple of feminist educational critiques.

The author of the *History* tied this concern over expanding awareness of knowledge generally to women's deserving equal access to education and learning. Women, he argued, had "as nice a Sense of things, and as good Judgments too, as most Men," despite little chance or encouragement for them to utilize these skills. " 'Tis true, that here in *England* the Women are kept from all Learning," he wrote in words similar to Astell's, so that it was truly remarkable that "there are a great many, who in spite of the Tyranny of Custom will steal some Minutes from the Needle to improve their Minds." He argued that the *Mercury* had not provided science or philosophy watered down for female readers, but rather had shown its faith in abilities that English women had earlier demonstrated.[8]

Its historian represented fairly the *Athenian Mercury*'s attitudes toward women's intellectual potential. For example, the editors replied tartly to a questioner who wondered whether women's minds could be improved by learning. The man noted that he had just read "A little tract"—probably Astell's—that "very much encourages Women to be Studious," but from his own experience he doubted them capable of it. The *Mercury* took him sorely to task for such a view. Men had taken advantage of the superior status with which God had entrusted them because "absolute power is often Accompanied with Tyranny." As a part of their domination, men retained "the Authority of making Laws," which they used to reduce women "into a perpetual Wardship, which is a real Servitude." Now this correspondent and most of his fellow men would unjustly deprive them of "the greatest of all Goods; to wit, that of the Mind."[9] In such a way the *Athenian Mercury* did much to spread the viewpoint that advanced intellectual opportunity for women was both just and beneficial.

Yet even this reply suggested the limitations of the *Mercury*'s support of women. They should have every chance to learn, but the fact that God had ordained general male dominance circumscribed any advance within the home, church, or state. Working within this limited framework, John Dunton, Samuel Wesley, Richard Sault, and John Norris composed the Athenian Society and together answered most of the inquiries to their journal, but often called on educated contemporaries to aid them with a particular question. Dunton acted as general editor, and in this capacity included verses by a number of feminist poets, and Norris had, of course, earlier published his correspondence with Mary Astell. Still, some of the *Mercury*'s opinions showed the limitations of vision even among those educated men with the most advanced intellectual hopes for women.

The *Mercury*'s authors sometimes handled women's questions by equivocation. In one of the earliest issues devoted to women, for example, they decided that marriage was both a "Divine Right" and a political institution, without touching on the thorny issues really at question. On religious issues, the periodical was especially conservative. In responding to a question about women's ability to prophesy, the *Mercury* noted that women might do so in song or prayer but not in teaching "because that

Office is plainly restrained to the *Men.*" Women were incapable of "a Doctrine or an Interpretation," the editors believed, because these belonged to "Man's Province." [10]

At times the *Mercury* connected women's inferior position within the church to her inferior position within the home. A man should prophesy with his head uncovered "*because the Head of every Man is Christ,*" but a woman who did so dishonored not only Christ, but her husband as well, "who is her Political or Oeconomical Head." Women in church with their heads uncovered showed that they paid no attention to the Scriptures, where Paul admonished that uncovered hair harkened back to heathen goddesses, and also that "they regarded not their Duty and Subjection" to their husbands. [11] It was perhaps such reflections as these that led Mary Astell, strong Anglican that she was, to argue with the usual interpretation given to Paul's letter to the Corinthians.

John Tripper, the editor of the *Ladies Diary*, was of a different stripe than the intellectually enthusiastic authors of the *Mercury*. His annual *Diary* made clear that he set up the journal because a broad female reading public enabled him to make a profit from his venture. Tripper included in his almanacs material which he believed would hold particular interest for women, such as "The History of Famous Women," explanations of scientific phenomena, and enigmas and mathematical questions for readers to decipher. Although Tripper called the work *The Ladies Diary* to attract women, its appeal was not limited to one sex. As many men as women sent in solutions to the enigmas, and men in considerably greater numbers answered the mathematical questions. Readers were encouraged to send in their own enigmas and puzzles, and those women posing questions or answering them appeared to be a cross section of the middle- and upper-class female population, not exclusively from the gentle classes or from London. Tripper listed names of those who successfully answered all or some of the enigmas and questions given in a single volume, but could not do so completely because there were always "several others, who desired that their names not be made publick." [12]

Because of growing interest in the almanac, Tripper increased its publication from an annual to a monthly basis in 1711. He also raised the requirements for readers receiving prizes—normally twelve to twenty free copies of the *Diary*; winners had to answer all of the enigmas and questions included in a particular issue. Too many of his readers had been giving correct responses, and he felt compelled to change his standards "upon receiving several letters from several Ladies that my Enigmas were so easy, they could find them out almost at the first reading." [13]

Although Tripper's *Diary* filled an obvious void in the reading materials available to educated women and provided them with the scientific and mathematical questions they seldom faced in school, Tripper himself had little personal interest in the education of women. His views were made clear in a 1710 advertisement announcing the publication of a new almanac directed toward men. "Having endeavoured for these six years past, to entertain WOMEN by this Diary," Tripper wrote, "I design this Year, 1710 to present the MEN with a new Almanack also to promote their real and true Interest." In *Great Britain's Diary or the Union Almanack*, he assured the gentlemen, "all Useless and impertinent Amusements will be laid aside, and nothing inserted but what tends to promote TRADE and BUSINESS." [14] Tripper was no educational reformer interested in spreading learning to women but an enterprising businessman who recognized the profit to be made from the growing numbers of educated women and their hunger for mental stimulation, a wholly unidealistic testimonial that some feminist concerns were taking root.

Richard Steele's motives for publication of *The Ladies Library* fell somewhere between those of the authors of the *Mercury* and Tripper's. In his introductory comments, Steele stressed that he supported the expansion of female learning, but his three-volume compilation of writings was obviously put together haphazardly. It was, in many ways, an unusual mixture of the types of writings assumed to be of interest to women. It had the tenor of mid-seventeenth-century guidebooks leading women along the proper moral, domestic, and religious paths, yet it included as well materials which were highly critical of women's traditional guides and role. The work borrowed from a number of contemporary texts, including feminist ones. For instance, the materials in the chapter on "Ignorance" were taken from Astell's *Serious Proposal to the Ladies*, though she was nowhere given credit, and Steele's third volume on religion also used materials from her work. [15]

Steele claimed the *Library* was "written by a lady" and that he merely acted as "Gentleman-Usher" to both the compiler and the female reader. Probably there was no lady author, but that Steele chose this facade suggested a belief that women would more readily accept a woman writer. Certainly he felt obliged to make clear that although "the Words Man and Men are made use of" when he referred to matters of interest to both sexes, this did not mean "that the Work is not principally intended for the Information of the Fair Sex."[16]

The introduction by the alleged female compiler of the collection which followed Steele's was more strongly feminist. "She" had little respect for society's attitudes about women's education and found it hard personally to avoid "such Enquiries as by general Custom my Sex is debarr'd from" or "a strong Propensity to Reading." The author of this introduction was especially incensed by what contemporary authors— she quoted Milton, Dryden, and Otway—had to say about the general nature of women and wondered that any "of these Men had any such Relations as Mothers, Wives or Sisters."[17] If male authors did not mean their views as "a Reproach Upon Women as such" then they should not have spoken of "general Calumnies without Exception." "She" also attacked the solemnity of guidebooks on the subject of women's affectation, coquetry, and falsehood: "Dissertations for the Conduct of Life are as gravely composed upon these Topicks, as if they were as infallible as mathematical Truths."[18]

Whatever these periodicals reflected of feminist influence, they obviously suggested a better-educated portion of the female population, at least among the middle and upper classes. Certainly feminists wrote amidst and encouraged a broad movement in support of the spread of knowledge at this time. But it was only the feminists who continually reminded their readers of the special needs of women for greater educational opportunity.

The Society for Promoting Christian Knowledge, the Athenian Society, and other similar organizations working to expand learning throughout England, Scotland, and Wales claimed the dual goals of teaching Christian tenets and good working habits to the poor and expanding the knowledge of those unable to attend grammar schools or universities. Their focus was primarily middle- and working-class males, although the Athenian Society did speak of providing information to both sexes, and girls were educated in the charity schools established by the SPCK, as well as boys. However, concern for the female sex often appeared as an afterthought.[19]

Whether this afterthought would have gained what support it did without feminist agitation is impossible to say. Certainly the charity school movement provided a number of outlets for those interested in female education. Middle- and upper-class women furthered its cause by providing funds for girls' charity schools, while women with some academic training served as teachers, so that a limited number of poor girls gained an elementary education. Yet contemporary feminists gave little heed to these educational efforts, in part because of their own class biases, but also because these schools, especially the ones for girls, reinforced more than questioned traditional sex roles.

The charity schools generally aimed at social control as well as uplift, and for girls it was especially obvious that education was of secondary importance. Although the boys devoted a large portion of the school day to learning trades or doing manual labor, they spent considerably less time doing so than the girls. As the historian of the charity school movement noted, vocational instruction "was the predominant element" in the girls' curriculum. Boys learned to write and cast accounts, but girls seldom were taught academic subjects other than reading. "Plain needlework, knitting, sometimes spinning, and, when possible, housewifery took their place, that the girls might be prepared specifically for one type of work, never adequately supplied, that of domestic service." [20]

Because of differences in career possibilities, boys were apprenticed, giving them some hope for social advance, in much larger numbers than girls. A 1733 report summarizing the progress of the charity schools in London and Westminster from 1700 stated that "out of 20,000 children instructed in the metropolitan schools since the beginning of the century, 7,139 boys had been put out to apprentice, and 3,377 to service; while of the girls 1,383 had been apprenticed and 3,873 put to service." Further, there was some small chance that "the occasional bright lad of parts" might be able to rise from his station and "proceed to the grammar school or university." Such was not possible for the girls. [21]

There was little evidence, then, that the feminists' views supporting advanced education for women filtered down to the working classes, or that feminists concerned themselves about this problem. Given the social biases of charity school education, it would have been hard for those concerned with women's interests to be wholeheartedly enthusiastic about the cause. Yet, no matter how restrictive charity school education was for girls, they were at least included. And spokesmen for the schools like White Kennett specifically pointed out that one of the failings of sixteenth- and seventeenth-century grammar schools was their exclusion of girls.[22] The feminists' concern with questions of higher education, as well as with the educational needs of women of their own class, blinded them to the inequitable and inadequate training available for poor girls, but perhaps their ideas provided support for the partial inclusion of women in other people's educational projects.

II

The lack of clear links between this early form of feminism and the later movements owed something to both its inability to suggest broader political goals and the sentimental tendencies of eighteenth-century thought that undercut these writers' rationalist argument. The class and doctrinal views of most early English feminists created a significant lacuna in their thought if not in their social concern. They generally ignored the political dimension of women's oppression outside the family. The one group of early feminists to connect the status of women with politics was that around poet Elizabeth Rowe, whose ties were to Whig and dissenting circles. The Tory and Anglican loyalties of most feminists in these years clearly circumscribed their willingness to relate their central social concern to that body of political theory commonly used to question traditions in the seventeenth and early eighteenth centuries.

The omission was not one-sided however. If feminists neglected to consider how Whig political theory might have broadened and abetted their central social concern, this political theory wholly ignored women's interests. Traditionally the English revolutions of the seventeenth century have been seen as promoting or protecting individual rights or liberties against absolute power; more recently and realistically the events have been tied to securing greater power for limited groups from which the majority was excluded.[23] In both interpretations, lack of interest in women's position suggested the basic truth that women as a social category remained apart from either individuals or groups destined to benefit. The "rights of citizens" in the seventeenth century might include, depending on who was arguing, those of freeholders, family heads, or, in some radical opinion, even of Englishmen generally. They never included those of women. Women as members of victorious classes or groups might benefit, but they were "virtually" represented in the changes by their menfolk rather than directly permitted, in theory at least, any greater exercise of their rights.[24]

Formal political theory also proved scant help for feminists. The doctrines of Robert Filmer, whose classical defense of monarchy appealed most to old-fashioned Tories, founded kingly power and the subject's obedience on unquestioned paternal authority, a position antithetical to feminism. On the other hand, Locke's codification of the Whig alternative theory made independent property-holding the crucial determinant of the rights of citizenship, in a way that debarred women more completely from real power than had the medieval notion of position conferring status. Seventeenth-century feminists' concentration on familial power grew in large part from the insight that the duchess of Newcastle first expressed and others developed: that women were not of the nation but of the household, were subjects not of the monarch but of their husbands. Seventeenth-century conceptions had to be transformed toward an idea of inalienable rights, especially by the American and French Revolutions, before feminists could wield them to demand their political rights.

To a degree, the seventeenth-century feminists not only did not but could not tie their cause to a political theory, as Mary Wollstonecraft found it natural to do in 1792. For her, as for those who shared her beliefs a century earlier, women's "inferiority" was the product of male and social oppression to be ended partly by equal education, but also by a redistribution of power among the sexes based on women's equal rights.[25] And another century passed before Emmeline Pankurst organized an effective political movement based on "the fact—a very simple fact—that women are human beings" endowed with basic and equal rights which only political enfranchisement and power could protect. "We found," Pankhurst noted, "that all the fine phrases about freedom and liberty were entirely for male consumption."[26] It took a great struggle to have these phrases applied to women, but because of two centuries of political development the words and their implications were readily found and recognized.

Seventeenth-century feminism's stress on reason, even more than its neglect of politics, helped truncate the continuing influence of its thought. For these feminists reason provided the equalizing agent between men and women, and as eighteenth-century doctrines of feeling waxed and women gravitated toward defining themselves in a separate but equal sphere of sensibility, religion, and aestheticism, their feminist argument fell into disuse. As intellectual modes shifted, women chose or had thrust upon them different strategies that offered more immediate satisfaction and protection but at the price of greater compromises.

Marjorie Nicolson's analyses of the appeal of Descartes for Platonist Henry More, a contemporary of the later feminists, suggested much about their commitment to reason, the psychological as well as the intellectual satisfaction they found in it. Nicolson noted the "sense of withdrawal" in both More and Descartes. The Frenchman "shut himself away from the world in order to find the meaning of the world," and his English follower found similar satisfaction in Christ's College, where he sought truth in two elements—"the phenomena of nature and the rational mind of man." Analyzing these phenomena in isolation from the general intellectual debates of the day allowed him a sense of freedom and control he could obtain in no other way. "Descartes offered him at the time when he most needed it, intellectual assurance of the validity of his own feelings in regard to the nature of man and the phenomena of the universe."[27]

This description of More's reaction to contemporary intellectual currents suggested that feminists shared much with other seventeenth-century intellectuals who were trying to reconcile rationalism with Christianity. Yet their institutional isolation was greater than that of any male contemporary, as was their need for some kind of rational retreat which would allow them to assert intellectual control over their environment and to circumvent the household duties, the child-rearing, the social gatherings that were their prescribed lot. The emphasis on the supremacy of the individual mind was not merely an intellectual tenet on the part of feminists but also the result of their painful understanding of what alternatives existed for women who did not isolate themselves for the purpose of study.

The excitement and optimism feminist writers exuded over rationalism is understandable only within this context of the freeing of the individual mind from its traditional limitations. In a very general way, Descartes, and the broad seventeenth-century enthusiasm for reason and experimentation, freed feminists by breaking the barriers against the educated woman in a way that piecemeal changes in England's educational structure never could. It was difficult to become excited about the few additional secondary schools being opened to girls during the second half of the century or over the small numbers of poor girls who were able to learn reading and household skills through the auspices of the charity schools during the late seventeenth and early eighteenth centuries.[28] But the use of the individual mind was a cause that could excite feminist authors, could provide them with an absolute value—the equal rational powers of men and women—which they could use as a tool to carve new lives for themselves and as a rallying cry to encourage their sisters to a totally different kind of life.

The most creative literary work of the feminists' age, its social comedy, revealed something of the impact of feminist ideas in both a negative and a positive sense. The stage laughed at "learned ladies" as it long had, but now two new types became prominent objects of scorn: the woman writer and the woman scientist. Pretentious, fundamentally ignorant, easily taken in by surface learning, they flounced about the stage using complicated words and foreign languages inaccurately. Scorning women's domestic concerns, they were led by their pretensions into ridicule, trouble, and often the arms of imposters to learning.[29] George Farquhar's "Bissare," who accepted a man she greatly disliked because he quoted in Latin from Virgil, or Colley Cibber's "Sophronia," "sage and haughty Prude" who was "half mad with her Learning and Philosophy," were typical.[30]

These women were part of a more general dramatic tradition, the comic scorn lavished on anyone, male or female, who pretended to specialized learning. Congreve's "Foresight" and a host of other males were as badly misled by and abused for their pretensions to understanding as the ladies. Yet the common satire took a different strain when applied to women, condemning them not only as pompous and silly but also as members of their sex stepping out of their proper bounds. When "Lady Science" was abandoned by a false Oxford don in *The Humours of Oxford* of 1730, she admitted she deserved to suffer "for affecting to move into a Sphere that did not belong to me," and was lectured: "People of either Sex, Madam, are generally imposed on, when they concern themselves with what is properly the Business of the other. The Dressing-Room, not the Study, is the lady's Province—and a Woman makes as ridiculous a Figure, poring over Globes, or thro' a Telescope, as a Man would with a Pair of *Preserves* mending lace."[31]

If some comic learned ladies suggested Restoration awareness of feminist aspirations in a negative sense, the heroines of many plays, especially those of the 1690s when the feminist writings peaked, represented a broad acceptance of much of what the feminists said about the unequal position of women in the marriage game. John Vanbrugh's *The Provok'd Wife* (1697) set up a situation in which a wife was driven to near infidelity by a husband, his ardor cooled by marriage, whose conduct became that of irritable boorishness. In a witty equivalent to Astell's argument about abused wives, the wife argued well her right, before men if not God, to reject her vows given her mistreatment. The husband's name, Sir John Brute, adequately defined his character—so well indeed that Lady Mary Chudleigh appropriated the sobriquet in her feminist reply to John Sprint's sermon on female obedience.[32]

In the age's greatest comedies, those of William Congreve, heroines showed shrewd awareness of the pitfalls that marriage held for women and carefully protected themselves, as far as possible, from future problems. Angelica in *Love for Love* (1695) tests her suitor in every way possible before marriage, knowing the harder test comes later. Millamant in *The Way of the World* enters into a prenuptial agreement with her lover in which both try to fend off future difficulties while Mrs. Fainall—another abused wife—is saved from ruin because she was wise enough to convey her property to another before she married. The spirit of these plays is witty and cynical rather than serious and reformative, as in the feminist tracts on marriage, but the idea is the same: caution and intelligence were women's only protection in the socially unequal battle of the sexes.[33]

The sentimental and moralistic elements which remained subordinate in Restoration comedy became more pronounced in many eighteenth-century literary dealings with women. By the time Richard Steele wrote *The Conscious Lovers* (1722), less than a decade after he edited *The Ladies Library*, the heroine acted with a very unworldly moralism and sensibility that forced providence to replace reasonable calculation as her protector. Though feminists may have deemed that Vanbrugh and Congreve dealt flippantly with serious female dilemmas, they were closer to these playwrights than to the moral world that came to predominate in the eighteenth century where, speaking very broadly, Pamela, Clarissa, and their literary sisters less battled men with equal minds than subdued them with superior moral sensibilities. The choice that historian Nancy Cott sees for women at the end of the eighteenth century—between moving toward overt equality and accepting a separate and allegedly equal women's sphere—was also made in the early decades of the eighteenth century.[34]

In most ways the small victories for intellectual women in the first half of the eighteenth century were part of a larger compromise. Literary gatherings flourished, like the one where Lady Mary Wortley Montagu attracted some of the best male and female talents of the age, yet her contact with the great minds of the age was more through correspondence than through a formal salon. She helped to usher in the age of the bluestocking, when some women gained attention and prestige from their efforts in literature and thought. On the surface, then, women with intellectual interests during the 1700s had an advantage over those living during the second half of the previous century, but these advantages were paid for in acceptance of a secondary status in their literary world and by relinquishing an independent female perspective. In fact, literary men who mixed with women in the salons penned some of the sharpest statements against females who did not recognize their proper place.[35]

The seventeenth-century feminists were notably isolated, in ideals and in fact, from the mainstream of the male literary world, and this exclusion gave them the freedom to speak their minds more fully on sexual relationships than could the bluestockings, who held an uncertain position within the inner sanctum of London literary circles. The restraint placed upon women who had gained this partial acceptance was made clear in the letters of Lady Mary Wortley Montagu.

During her youth she had been an acquaintance of Mary Astell's and a strong supporter of her projected women's college, noting angrily that there was "hardly a character in the World more Despicable or more liable to universal ridicule than that of a Learned Woman," and that women were "permitted no Books but such as tend to the weakening and Effeminateing the Mind." After she married and as she grew older she did not give up her desire "to improve our Reason"[36] but softened her insistence on women's needs. Having experienced ridicule and holding her position through grace and tact, she warned young women that they should display their knowledge only with caution. Concerning her granddaughter's education, Montagu wrote to her daughter, "The second caution to be given her (and which is most absolutely necessary) is to conceal whatever Learning she attains, with as much solicitude as she would hide crookedness or lameness."[37] Montagu had not changed her views on the proper education of women as she grew older; in this same letter she outlined a rigorous curriculum for her granddaughter's study. But now she felt women could safely be intelligent only by overtly accepting rather than fighting society's discriminations.

Montagu's cautious injunctions for success matched the sense of dispiritedness about women's chances for equal educational opportunity that plagued more demanding feminists like Astell and Elstob in their last years. The reality behind this dispiritedness probably accounted for the high percentage of eighteenth-century intellectual women represented in the *DNB* who gained prominence by their ties to men rather than by their own work, in contrast to the pattern for seventeenth-century females.

There is no clear chain of thought from the seventeenth-century feminists to the modern movement. Even Astell's writings, sometimes included in eighteenth-century women's collections, apparently had no direct influence on later feminist thinkers. Their ideas may have died with them, or have been resurrected only by individual women reading them in isolation in later centuries. Yet their failure to achieve their goals or to influence later thought does not detract from the vigor of their contribution and the proof it offers of the often forgotten emergence of feminist hopes and theories in former ages.

These early feminists developed a central tenet that later women would have to rediscover to create an ideology to attack female subordination. In some ways their demands were limited, and they gave too much attention to education and too little to political or economic issues, but the questions they emphasized were the most relevant and practical for themselves and for their age, and these they always put in the context of a sound understanding of women as a discreet group confined by social subordination and defined by male oppression. They understood thoroughly what John Stuart Mill was to argue in the nineteenth century: "What in unenlightened societies, colour, race, religion, or in the case of a conquered country, nationality, are to some men, sex is to all women; a peremptory exclusion from almost all honourable occupations, but either such as cannot be fulfilled by others, or such as those others do not think worthy of their acceptance." [38]

That this social insight found such a small audience and achieved so little clear result is sad, but there is something heartening too in seeing something of feminism's resilience and variety in the questioning intelligence of the duchess of Newcastle, the sharp observations of Hannah

Woolley or the author of the *Defence of the Female Sex*, the intellectual enthusiasm of Bathsua Makin and Elizabeth Elstob, the poetic wistfulness of Anne Winchilsea, Lady Mary Chudleigh, and Elizabeth Singer Rowe, the passionate intensity and anger of Sarah Fyge Egerton, and the rational vigor of Mary Astell. They were the worthy, if largely forgotten, English founders of a continuing cause.

NOTES

1. Nahum Tate, *A Present for the Ladies*, 2d ed. (London, 1693); William Walsh, *A Dialogue Concerning Women, Being a Defence of the Sex* (London, 1691). John Dryden wrote a preface for Walsh's work in which he called his age a time in which heroines rather than heroes dominated.

2. The similarity between Astell's and Defoe's ideas was made clear in an opening statement to "An Academy for Women": "I have often thought of it as one of the most barbarous Customs in the world, considering us as a Civiliz'd and a Christian Countrey, that we deny the advantages of Learning to women. We reproach the Sex every day with Folly and Impertinence, while I am confident, had they the advantages of Education equal to us, they wou'd be guilty of less than ourselves" (Daniel Defoe, "An Academy for Women," *An Essay upon Projects* [1697; reprint ed., Menston, England: Scholar Press, 1969], p. 282). Daniel Defoe, *Conjugal Lewdness; or, Matrimonial Whoredom. A Treatise Concerning the Use and Abuse of the Marriage Bed* (1727; reprint ed., Gainesville, Fla.: Scholars' Facsimiles and Reprints, 1967). In this work Defoe argued against premarital sex and against men's using their wives merely as sexual objects before and after the wedding ceremony. For a current edition of *Moll Flanders* based on the text of the first edition and including useful notes and bibliography see Daniel Defoe, *Moll Flanders*, ed. G. A. Starr (Oxford: Oxford University Press, 1976).

3. *The Athenian Gazette; or, Casuistical Mercury, Resolving all the most Nice and Curious Questions proposed by the Ingenious: From Tuesday, March 17th to Saturday, May 30th, 1691*, vol. 1 (London: Printed for John Dunton, 1691); *Athenian News; or, Dunton's Oracle. In 3000 several Posts. To which is added, "The . . . Athenian Mercury" Resolving the Most Nice and Curious Questions propos'd by the Ingenious of either Sex* (London: Printed by T. Darrock . . . and Sold by J. Morphew . . . at most Booksellers Shops in Town and Country, 1710) (the last phrase indicates the popularity of the *Mercury*); *The Ladies Diary; or, The Womens Almanack for the Year of our Lord, 1707 . . . Containing many Delightful and Entertaining Particulars, particularly adapted for the Use and Diversion of the Fair-Sex*, No. 4 (London: J. Wilde, 1707), *The Ladies Library*, 3 vols. (London: Published by Mr. Steele, printed for Jacob Tonson, 1714).

4. *Athenian Gazette*, Nos. 13 (Tues., May 5, 1691) and 18 (Sat., May 23, 1691), n.p.

5. *A Supplement to the Athenian Oracle, Being a Collection of the Remaining Questions and Answers in the Old "Athenian Mercuries . . ." To which is prefix'd the "History of the Athenian Society"* (London: Printed for Andrew Bell, 1710).

6. Ibid., pp. 8–9.

7. Ibid., pp. 9–10.

8. Ibid., pp. 52–53. Although the author of this piece has not been positively identified as John Norris, one of the members of the Athenian Society and a correspondent of Mary Astell's, it is not too far-fetched to assume that the following reference, made after an extensive list of French, Spanish, Italian, and English female scholars, is to her, "I could name another that surpasses all these, if I fear'd not to offend her Modesty, by publishing her Name."

9. *The Athenian Oracle. Being an Entire Collection of all the Valuable Questions and Answers in the Old Athenian Mercuries*, 2d ed. (London: Printed for Andrew Bell, 1704), I:382.

10. Ibid., p. 97.

11. Ibid., pp. 98–100.

12. *Ladies Diary*, No. 7 (1710), n. p.

13. *Ladies Diary*, No. 9 (1712), n. p.

14. *Ladies Diary*, No. 7.

15. "Ignorance," *Ladies Library*, I:438–524. The language Steele used reads : "Thus Ignorance, and a narrow Education, lay the Foundation of Vice, and Imitation and Custom rear it up" (p. 441), while Astell used these words: "Thus ignorance and a narrow Education lay the Foundation of Vice, and Imitation and Custom rear it up," in the first volume of the *Serious Proposal* (p. 75); further, Steele wrote: "Tis Custom therefore, that Tyrant Custom, which is the grand Motive to all those irrational Choices which we daily see made in the World," while Astell had written earlier, "Tis custom therefore, that Tyrant Custom, which is the grand motive to all those irrational choices which we daily see made in the World" (p. 46). Although Steele failed to credit Astell for her earlier work, his use of her views gave them an even wider circulation during the early eighteenth century. His entire chapter was not lifted word for word, but it was all essentially Astell's work.

16. "Preface," *Ladies Library*.

17. "Introduction," *Ladies Library*, pp. 1–3.

18. Ibid. pp. 3–5.

19. There were a number of printed reports published during the early eighteenth century outlining the progress of the charity schools. These are useful in describing the nature of individual schools, and they tell us much about the different treatment afforded girls and boys in these schools. One is struck first by the much larger numbers of boys educated and the greater number of all-boy than all-girl schools; girls were more apt to be educated in coeducational institutions. Further, as noted in Jones's figures, boys were apprenticed in much larger

numbers and were more apt to have their clothing paid for as well. M. G. Jones, *The Charity School Movement: A Study of Eighteenth-Century Puritanism in Action* (Cambridge: Cambridge University Press, 1938), pp. 51–53. *An Account of the Methods Whereby the Charity-Schools have been Erected and Managed. . . . Together with a Proposal of Enlarging their Number* [London, 1705]. This report concluded with a financial statement on the London and Westminster schools in May 1705. Other than confirming the predominance of boys' schools and the more frequent selection of boys for apprenticeships, it indicated that girls' schools relied more on weekly church contributions and small donations and less on permanent and substantial endowments. A typical entry reveals such differences: for Brightelmeston, Sussex, it notes "Fifty Boys taught to Read, Write, Cast Account, and the Art of Navigation: The Subscription is about £47 per Ann. There is also a School for 20 Girls," in *An Account of Charity-Schools in Great Britain and Ireland . . . and of the Methods whereby they were set up, and are governed,* 10th ed. (London: Printed and sold by Joseph Downing, 1711), p. 11. It is noted that 1,096 boys and 467 girls were apprenticed from the London charity schools, and a report from a Warwickshire school for twenty girls described their curriculum as "taught to Read, Knit, Sew and to Spin Linen and Jersey, and carefully instructed in the Principles of Religion, etc." These reports provide evidence, as well, for the distinction in salaries between male and female teachers: in an Oxfordshire school the master was paid £25 and the mistress £12 10s. per year, while at a Colchester school the master was paid £30 per annum including a dwelling, while the mistress was given £15, plus a house and coals (pp. 11–22).

 20. M. G. Jones, *Charity School Movement,* pp. 80–84, 89–95; White Kennett, *The Charity of Schools for Poor Children, Recommended in a Sermon . . .* The Anniversary Meeting of about Three Thousand of the Poor Children, Boys and Girls (London: Printed and sold by Joseph Downing and John Churchill, 1706). Kennett made clear in this sermon the desire for social control which underlay the charity school movement: "All Government must subsist by Unity, Order, and Peace. Now if Children by timely Discipline, are made tractable and obedient to the Advice and Authority, of their Parents and Teachers, they are then fitted to the Hands of other lawful Rulers; and the Church and the State will be as quiet as were the Family and the School" (p. 11).

 21. M. G. Jones, *Charity School Movement,* pp. 51, 73. W. A. L. Vincent, *The Grammar Schools: Their Continuing Tradition, 1660–1714* (London: John Murray, 1969), notes that small numbers of girls attended isolated grammar schools during the seventeenth century, and that school founders did not always explicitly exclude them. However, by the end of the century they were no longer in attendance, and where they had attended, such as Rivington in Lancashire, they had not "stayed more than a year or two and the likelihood is that their education and school days did not normally extend beyond the time needed to acquire proficiency in reading and writing" (pp. 46–48).

 22. Kennett, *Charity of Schools,* p 12. Kennett noted that the charitable impulse during the sixteenth and seventeenth centuries normally found its outlet

through the establishment of a grammar school, but such institutions failed to meet the needs of poor children. "The Masters of those schools set up for Greek and Latin only; and so their Dispensation excluded one Sex altogether, and was indeed too high for the meaner Boys, born to the Spade and the Plough."

23. Almost any of those works discussing the political thought of the Civil War period analyzes its development of individual political obligation, but perhaps the classic formulation of its importance for later democratic principles was G. P. Gooch's *English Democratic Ideas of the Seventeenth Century,* 2d ed. (Cambridge: Cambridge University Press, 1954); from the perspective of economic individualism C. B. MacPherson's more recent work, *The Political Theory of Possessive Individualism,* has become the standard interpretation; Michael Walzer, in his *Revolution of the Saints,* argued that the Puritans were a truly revolutionary group and that this fact had been overlooked because past scholars had stressed their individualistic rather than group-based efforts. Christopher Hill, *The World Turned Upside Down,* focuses on the radical revolutionaries.

24. For the most thorough discussions of this question see MacPherson's *Possessive Individualism* and Hill's *World Turned Upside Down.*

25. Mary Wollstonecraft, *A Vindication of the Rights of Woman*; John Stuart Mill, *On the Subjection of Women* (1869; reprint ed., London: J. M. Dent and Sons, 1970), p. 154. A recent article has contrasted Mary Astell and Mary Wollstonecraft and found little similarity between them. Regina Janes, "Mary, Mary, Quite Contrary; or, Mary Astell and Mary Wollstonecraft Compared," in *Studies in Eighteenth-Century Culture* (Madison: University of Wisconsin Press, 1976), pp. 121–40. Janes argues that Astell looked "back towards monastic establishments and passive obedience to established authority both religious and secular." Wollstonecraft, on the other hand, would have women "advance, instead of retarding, the progress of those glorious principles that give a substance to morality" (p. 124). Astell is criticized for not rejecting Christian strictures on women's potential, and Wollstonecraft is praised for adopting the natural-rights doctrine of the French Revolution. Both women relied upon the ideas of the period to form their views about women and Astell, of course, explicitly rejected passive obedience for women. Whatever the limitations of Astell's feminism, it is difficult to accept Janes's evaluation of her: "Astell's work shows no new ideas or new ordering of thought consequent upon a new intellectual discovery" (p. 125).

26. Emmeline Pankhurst, "When Civil War Is Waged by Women," in *Feminism: The Essential Historical Writings,* ed. Miriam Schneir (New York: Random House, 1972), pp. 298–99.

27. Marjorie Nicolson, "The Early State of Cartesianism in England," *Studies in Philology* 25 (1929): 364–65.

28. For the limited expansion of girls' primary and secondary education during the seventeenth century see Josephine Kamm's *Hope Deferred,* pp. 68–82; Nicolson discussed the importance of Cartesian thought for the development of the self (especially among the young) in seventeenth-century England. This influence was not merely to the thinking self, but to the increase in autobio-

graphical writings during the 1600s. "It was in its supposed insistence upon the 'thinking self' as the evidence of existence that Cartesianism appealed particularly to the youthful. From his works enthusiasts read an exultation of individual thought as the criterion of existence which Descartes was far from intending" (p. 371). Also, "How much did the compelling autobiographical account of Descartes in his Principles have to do with the interest in psychological autobiography in the late seventeenth century, and with the growth of the psychological novel? The influence of Descartes upon the philosophy of 'mad Madge of Newcastle,' for instance is clear; but how much had that influence to do with her extraordinary autobiographical fragment?" (p. 372).

29. Jean Elizabeth Gagen, *The New Woman: Her Emergence in English Drama, 1660–1730* (New York: Twayne Publishers, 1954). Gagen's work is a thorough survey of the changing condition of female characters on the Restoration stage. As the century progressed, women spoke more of learning and demanded more personal rights, especially widows and daughters, who, on stage, refused to marry against their wishes and thereby lose their independence.

30. George Farquhar, *The Inconstant; or, The way to win him. A Comedy, As it is Acted in the Theatre Royal in Drury-Lane* (London: Printed for J. Knapton, G. Strahan and B. Lintott, 1702), Act II, p. 14; Colley Cibber, *The Refusal; or, The Ladies Philosophy. A Comedy*, 3rd ed. (London: Printed for J. Tonson, J. Watts and J. Woodward, 1735), Act I, p. 9.

31. Quoted in Gagen, *New Woman*, p. 65.

32. John Vanbrugh, *The Provok'd Wife*, in *Twelve Famous Plays of the Restoration and Eighteenth Century*, intro. by Cecil A. Moore (New York: Modern Library, 1933), pp. 348–49. Although the wife defends her right to seek a lover, the bantering tone distinguishes Vanbrugh's presentation from the feminists' displeasure with marriage.

33. William Congreve, *The Way of the World*, in *Twelve Famous Plays*, pp. 494–96; Congreve, *Love for Love*, ibid, pp. 328–29. In *Love for Love* Angelica demonstrates that she realizes the political implications of marriage for women, yet her solution—to take a witty man for a lover and not a husband—separates her from feminists who did not argue that men's power would disappear if wedding vows were omitted. She says: "She that marries a fool, Sir Sampson, forfeits the reputation of her honesty or understanding: and she that marries a very witty man is a slave to the severity and insolent conduct of her husband."

34. Numerous articles have appeared within the last decade discussing Fanny Burney and other early eighteenth-century novelists. For a listing of these works consult the general bibliographies in each volume of *Women and Literature*.

35. For a general discussion of the role of the salon in English literary society see Chauncey Brewster Tinker, *The Salon and English Letters: Chapters on the Interrelations of Literature and Society in the Age of Johnson* (1915; reprint ed., New York: Gordian Press, 1967). Tinker's work is useful only for creating a list of those in attendance at the salons; it includes little serious analysis of the role of educated women in society. The debate over women's proper role in

the salons and an analysis of whether their presence there aided or hurt their general position within society is discussed in Lougee's *Paradis des Femmes*; in P. J. Miller's "Women's Education, 'Self-Improvement,' and Social Mobility—A Late Eighteenth Century Debate," *British Journal of Education Studies* 20 (1973): 302–14; and in Katherine Bodard Silver's "Salon, Foyer, Bureau: Women and the Professions in France," in *Clio's Consciousness Raised*, ed. Lois Banner and Mary Hartman (New York: Harper and Row, 1974). In *Bonds of Womanhood* Nancy Cott demonstrates that the charitable and church activities that drew women together in the early nineteenth century seldom led them to feminist efforts. Based as they were on views similar to Hannah More's—who was a product of the English salon—these charitable efforts were not predicated on either similarities or equality between the sexes. For Hannah More's limited views on women's education see her *Strictures on the Modern System of Female Education* (1799; reprint ed., New York: Garland Publishing, 1974). The opening sentences set the tone of her work: "The chief end to be proposed in cultivating the understanding of women, is to qualify them for the practical purposes of life. Their knowledge is not often like the learning of men, to be reproduced in some literary composition, nor even in any learned profession; but it is to come out in conduct" (p. 1). This conduct, More expounded throughout her work, was based on women's general moral and social responsibilities.

Although the heyday of the English salon occurred during the second half of the eighteenth century, the association between Lady Mary Wortley Montagu, the literary figures of her age, and the court established those intellectual and social links that came to characterize the formal salon of the later eighteenth century. Tinker, *Salon*, pp. 100–101.

36. Lady Mary Wortley Montagu, *The Complete Letters of Lady Mary Wortley Montagu*, ed. Robert Halsband (Oxford: At the Clarendon Press, 1965), 1: 44–45.

37. Ibid., 3:22. These arguments are made in a letter to Bishop Gilbert Burnet, dated 20 July 1710.

38. John Stuart Mill and Harriet Taylor Mill, *Essays on Sex Equality*, ed. Alice Rossi (Chicago: University of Chicago Press, 1970), p. 316.

Selected Bibliography

Primary Sources

An Account of Charity-Schools in Great Britain and Ireland . . . and of the Methods whereby they were set up, and are governed. 10th ed. London: Printed and sold by Joseph Downing, 1711.

An Account of the Methods Whereby the Charity-Schools have been Erected and Managed. . . . Together with a Proposal of Enlarging their Number. [London, 1705.]

AGRIPPA, HENRY CORNELIUS. *Female Pre-eminence; or, The Dignity and excellency of that Sex, above the male.* London, 1670.

———. *The Glory of Women; or, A Looking-glasse for ladies.* London, 1652.

———. *A Treatise of the Nobilitie and Excellencye of Woman Kynde.* Tr. D. Clapham. N.p., 1542.

ASTELL, MARY. *The Case of Moderation and Occasional Communion, Represented by way of Caution to the True Sons of the Church of England.* London: Printed for R. Wilkin, 1705.

———. *The Christian Religion, As Profess'd by a Daughter of the Church of England.* London: Printed by S. H. for R. Wilkin, 1705.

———. *An Impartial Enquiry into the Causes of Rebellion and Civil War in this Kingdom.* London: Printed by E. P. for R. Wilkin, 1704.

[———.] *The Second Part: Serious Proposal to the Ladies.* London, 1701.

[———.] *A Serious Proposal to the Ladies, For the Advancement of their true and greatest Interest. By a lover of her Sex.* London, 1694.

———. *A Serious Proposal to the Ladies: Part II.* London: Printed for Richard Wilkin, 1697.

[———.] *A Serious Proposal to the Ladies: Part Two.* 1701. Reprint. New York: Source Book Press, 1970.

[———.] *Some Reflections upon Marriage.* 4th ed. London: Printed for William Parker, 1730.

[———.] *Some Reflections upon Marriage.* 1730. Reprint. New York: Source Book Press, 1970.

[———.] *Some Reflections upon Marriage, Occasion'd by the Duke and Dutchess of Mazarine's Case.* London, 1700.

The Athenian Gazette; or, Casuistical Mercury, Resolving all the most Nice and Curious Questions proposed by the Ingenious: From Tuesday, March 17th to Saturday, May 30th, 1691. London: Printed for John Dunton, 1691.

Athenian News; or, Dunton's Oracle. In 3000 several Posts. To which is added, *"The . . . Athenian Mercury" Resolving the Most Nice and Curious Questions propos'd by the Ingenious of either Sex.* London: Printed by T. Darrock . . . and Sold by J. Morphew, 1710.

The Athenian Oracle. Being an Entire Collection of all the Valuable Questions and Answers in the Old "Athenian Mercuries." 3 vols. 2d ed. London: Printed for Andrew Bell, 1704.

AYLMER, JOHN. *An Harbarow for faithful and trewe Subjects.* London, 1559.

BAXTER, RICHARD. *The Catechizing of Families: A Teacher of Householders How to Teach Their Households.* London: T. Parkhurst, 1683.

———. *A Christian Directory; or, A Summ of Practical Theologie, and Cases of Conscience.* 2d ed. London: Printed by Rob't White, for Nevil Simmons, 1678.

BEHN, APHRA. *The Histories and Novels of the late Ingenious Mrs. Behn . . . Together with the Life and Memoirs of Mrs. Behn. Written by one of the Fair Sex.* London: For S. Briscoe, 1696.

———. Translator's Preface to *A Discovery of New Worlds*, by Bernard de Fontenelle. London, 1688.

BRATHWAIT, RICHARD. *The English Gentleman: Containing Sundry excellent Rules or exquisite Observations . . . How to demeane or Accomodate himself in the manage of publicke or private Affaires.* London: John Haviland, 1630.

———. *The English Gentlewoman, drawne out to the Body.* London: B. Alsop and T. Fawcet, 1631.

BULLINGER, HEINRICH. *The Christen State of Matrimonye.* N.p., 1541.

CELLIER, ELIZABETH. "A Scheme for the Foundation of a Royal Hospital and Raising a Revenue of Five or Six Thousand Pounds a year, by and for the Maintenance of a Corporation of skilful Midwives, of such Foundlings, or Exposed Children, as shall be admitted therein." In *Harleian Miscellany* IV: 142–46. London: White and Company, 1809.

———. *To Dr. . . . An Answer to his Queres, concerning the College of Midwives.* London, 1687/8.

CHUDLEIGH, LADY MARY. *Essays upon Several Subjects in Prose and Verse.* London: T. H. for R. Bonwicke, W. Freeman, T. Goodwin, 1710.

[———.] *The Female Advocate; or, A Plea for the just liberty of the Tender Sex, and particularly of Married Women.* London, 1700.

[———.] *The Ladies defence; or, "The Bride-Womans Counseller" Answer'd.* London: Printed for John Deeve, 1701.

———. *Poems on Several Occasions, together with the "Song of the Three Children Paraphras'd."* London: Printed by W. B. Lintott, 1703.

CIBBER, COLLEY. *The Refusal; or, The Ladies Philosophy. A Comedy.* 3rd ed. London: Printed for J. Tonson, J. Watts and J. Woodward, 1735.

CONGREVE, WILLIAM. *Love for Love*. In *Twelve Famous Plays of the Restoration and Eighteenth Century*. Introduction by Cecil A. Moore. New York: Modern Library, 1933.

———. *The Way of the World*. In *Twelve Famous Plays of the Restoration and Eighteenth Century*. Introduction by Cecil A. Moore. New York: Modern Library, 1933.

DEFOE, DANIEL. *Conjugal Lewdness; or, Matrimonial Whoredom. A Treatise Concerning the Use and Abuse of the Marriage Bed*. 1727. Reprint. Gainesville, Fla.: Scholars' Facsimiles and Reprints, 1967.

———. *An Essay upon Projects*. 1697. Reprint. Menston, England: Scholar Press, 1969.

———. *Moll Flanders*. Edited by G. A. Starr. Oxford: Oxford University Press, 1976.

DESCARTES, RENÉ. "Discourse on Method." In *The Rationalists*. Garden City, N.Y.: Dolphin Books, n.d.

E[GERTON], S[ARAH]. *Poems on Several Occasions, together with a Pastoral*. London: Printed by J. Nutt, [1706].

ELSTOB, ELIZABETH. *An English-Saxon Homily on the Birth-day of St. Gregory*. London, 1709.

ELYOT, SIR THOMAS. *The Defence of Good Women*. London, 1545.

An Essay in Defence of the Female Sex. Written by a Lady. 2d ed. London: Printed for A. Roper and E. Wilkerson, 1696.

FARQUHAR, GEORGE. *The Inconstant; or, The way to win him. A Comedy, As it is Acted in the Theatre Royal in Drury-Lane*. London: Printed for J. Knapton, G. Strahan and B. Lintott, 1702.

FARWORTH, RICHARD. *A Woman forbidden to Speak in the Church, The grounds examined, the mystery opened, the Truth cleared, and the ignorance both of Priests, and People discovered*. London: Giles Calvert, 1654.

FOX, GEORGE. *The Woman learning in silence; or, The misterie of the Womans subjection to her husband: as also, the daughter prophesying . . . .* London, 1656.

FOX, MARGARET FELL. *A Brief Collection of Remarkable Passages . . . Relating to the Birth, Education, Life . . . of . . . Margaret Fell . . . Fox*. London: Printed and Sold by J. Sowle, 1710.

———. *Women's Speaking Justified*. London, 1666.

[GOSYNHYLL, EDWARD.] *The Prayse of all Women, Called Mulieru pean*. [n.p., 1542?]

[———.], [attr.] *Scholehouse of Women*. London, 1560.

GOUGE, WILLIAM. *Of Domesticall Duties. Eight Treatises*. London: Printed by John Haviland for William Bladen, 1622.

HALIFAX, GEORGE SAVILE, Marquis of. *The Lady's New-Years Gift; or, Advice to a Daughter*. London, 1688.

The Hardships of the English Laws in Relation to Wives. With an explanation of the original Curse of Subjection passed upon the Woman. In an humble address to the Legislature. London and Dublin: Reprinted by and for G. Faulkner, 1735.

HOBBES, THOMAS. *The English Works of Thomas Hobbes of Malmesbury.* Edited by Sir William Molesworth. *Philosophical Rudiments Concerning Government and Society,* vol. 2. 1841. Reprint. Aalen: Scientia Verlag, 1962.

JAMES I. *King James's Instructions to his Dearest Sonne, Henry the Prince.* London: M. Flesher, 1682.

KENNETT, WHITE. *The Charity of Schools for Poor Children, Recommended in a Sermon* . . . The Anniversary Meeting of about Three Thousand of the Poor Children, Boys and Girls. London: Printed and sold by Joseph Downing and John Churchill, 1706.

KILLIGREW, ANNE. *Poems.* Introduction by Richard Morton. 1686. Reprint. Gainesville, Fla.: Scholars' Facsimiles and Reprints, 1967.

The Ladies Diary; or, The Womens Almanack for the Year of Our Lord, . . . *Containing many Delightful and Entertaining Particulars, particularly adapted for the Use and Diversion of the Fair-Sex.* London: J. Wilde, 1707, 1710, 1712.

The Ladies Library. 3 vols. London: Published by Mr. Steele, printed for Jacob Tonson, 1714.

A Lady's Religion: in a Letter to the Honourable my Lady Howard. By a Divine of the Church of England. 2d ed. London: For A. and J. Churchill, 1704.

The Leveller Tracts. Edited by William Haller and Godfrey Davies. New York: Columbia University Press, 1944.

LILBURNE, JOHN. *The Freemans Freedome Vindicated.* [London, 1646.]

LOCKE, JOHN. *Two Treatises of Government.* Edited by Peter Laslett. 2d ed. Cambridge: Cambridge University Press, 1963.

MAKIN, BATHSUA. *An Essay to Revive the Antient Education of Gentlewomen, in Religion, Maners, Art, and Tongues.* London: Printed by J. D. to be sold by Tho. Parkhurst, 1674.

MILL, JOHN STUART. *On the Subjection of Women.* 1869. Reprint. London: J. M. Dent and Sons, 1970.

MILL, JOHN STUART, and MILL, HARRIET TAYLOR. *Essays on Sex Equality.* Edited by Alice Rossi. Chicago: University of Chicago Press, 1970.

Minute Book of the Men's Meeting of the Society of Friends in Bristol, 1667–1686. Bristol Record Society's Publications, 25, edited by Russel Mortimer. Bristol: Bristol Record Society, 1971.

MONTAGU, LADY MARY WORTLEY. *The Complete Letters of Lady Mary Wortley Montagu.* Edited by Robert Halsband. 3 vols. Oxford: At the Clarendon Press, 1965.

MORE, HANNAH. *Strictures on the Modern System of Female Education.* 1799. Reprint. New York: Garland Publishing, 1974.

MORE, THOMAS. *Utopia.* Introduction by the Rev. T. F. Dibdin. London: William Bulmer, 1808.

218 REASON'S DISCIPLES

MULCASTER, RICHARD. *The Educational Writings of Richard Mulcaster.* Edited by James Oliphant. Glasgow: James Maclehose and Sons, 1903.

NEWCASTLE, MARGARET CAVENDISH, Duchess of. *The Description of a new World called The Blazing-World.* London: Printed by A. Maxwell, 1668.

——. *The Grounds of Natural Philosophy.* London, 1668.

——. *The Life of William Cavendish, Duke of Newcastle, to which is added the true relation of my birth, breeding, and Life.* Edited by C. H. Firth. London, 1886.

——. *Natures Pictures drawn by Fancies Pencil to the Life.* London: For J. Martin and J. Allestrye, 1656.

——. *Observations upon Experimental Philosophy.* London: A. Maxwell, 1666.

——. *CCXI Sociable Letters.* London: Printed by W. Wilson, 1664.

——. *Orations of Divers Sorts.* 2d ed. London: Ptd. by A. Maxwell, 1668.

——. *Philosophical and Physical Opinions.* London: Ptd. by William Wilson, 1663.

——. *Philosophical Letters . . . Some Opinions in Natural Philosophy.* London, 1664.

——. *Playes.* London: Prd. by A. Warren for John Martyn, 1662.

——. *Plays, Never before Printed.* London: Printed by A. Maxwell, 1668.

——. *Poems and Fancies.* 1653. Facsimile reproduction. London: Scolar Press, 1972.

——. *The Worlds Olio.* London: Printed for J. Martin and J. Allestree, 1655.

NEWCASTLE, WILLIAM CAVENDISH, Marquis of. *The Phanseys of William Cavendish, Marquis of Newcastle, addressed to Margaret Lucas and her Letters in Reply.* Edited by Douglas Grant. London: Nonesuch Press, 1956.

NICOLSON, MARJORIE, ed. *Conway Letters: The Correspondence of Anne, Viscountess Conway, Henry More, and Their Friends, 1642–1684.* New Haven, Conn.: Yale University Press, 1930.

NORRIS, JOHN, and ASTELL, MARY. *Letters concerning the love of God.* Between the Author of the Proposal to the Ladies and Mr. Norris, where his late Discourse, shewing that it ought to be intire and exclusive of all other Loves, is further cleared and justified. London, 1695.

OSBORNE, DOROTHY. *Letters.* Edited by G. C. Moore Smith. Oxford: Clarendon Press, 1928.

Oxford: Oxford University. Ballard Manuscript.

PHILIPS, KATHERINE. *Poems By the . . . Matchless Orinda.* London: Printed by J. M. for H. Herringman, 1667.

——. *Selected Poems, The Orinda Booklets.* Edited by Louise I. Guiney. Vol. 1. Hull: J. R. Tutin, 1905.

[POULAIN DE LA BARRE, FRANCOIS.] *The Woman as Good as the Man; or, The Equality of Both Sexes.* Translated by A. L. London, 1677.

ROWE, ELIZABETH SINGER. *The Miscellaneous Works in Prose and Verse of Mrs. Elizabeth Singer Rowe, to which are added, "Poems on Several Occasions" by Mr. Thomas Rowe.* Edited by Theophilus Rowe. 2 vols. London, 1749.

——. *Poems on Several Occasions.* London, 1696.

SHARP, JANE. *Complete Midwife's Companion; or, The Art of Midwifery Improved.* London, 1725.
———. *The Midwives Book. Or the whole Art of Midwifery.* London: Printed for Simon Miller, 1671.

SOWERNAM, ESTER. *Ester hath hang'd Haman; or, An Answere to a lewd Pamphlet, entituled, "The Arraignment of Women."* London, 1617.

SPRINT, JOHN. *The Bride-Womans Counseller, Being a Sermon Preach'd at a Wedding, May 11th, 1699 at Sherbourn in Dorsetshire.* N.p., 1699.

A Supplement to the Athenian Oracle, Being a Collection of the Remaining Questions and Answers in the Old "Athenian Mercuries. . . ." To which is prefix'd the "History of the Athenian Society." London: Printed for Andrew Bell, 1710.

[SWETNAM, JOSEPH.] *The Arraignment of Lewde, idle, forward, and unconstant Women: . . . Pleasant for Married Men, profitable for young Men, and hurtful to none.* London: Edward Allde for Thomas Archer, 1615.

TATE, NAHUM. *A Present for the Ladies.* 2d ed. London, 1693.

Triumphs of Female Wit, in some Pindarick Odes; or, The Emulation. London: Printed for T. Malthus, 1683.

VANBRUGH, JOHN. *The Provok'd Wife.* In *Twelve Famous Plays of the Restoration and Eighteenth Century.* Introduction by Cecil A. Moore. New York: Modern Library, 1933.

VIVES, JUAN. *The Instruction of a Christian Woman.* In *Vives and the Renascence Education of Women,* edited by Foster Watson. New York: Longmans, Green and Co., 1912.

WALSH, WILLIAM. *A Dialogue Concerning Women, Being a Defence of the Sex.* London, 1691.

WINCHILSEA, ANNE, Countess of. *Miscellany Poems on Several Occasions.* London, 1713.
———. *The Poems of Anne, Countess of Winchilsea.* Edited by Myra Reynolds. Chicago: University of Chicago Press, 1902.
———. *Selected Poems of Anne Finch, Countess of Winchilsea.* Edited by Katharine Rogers. New York: Frederick Ungar Publishing Co., 1979.

WINSTANLEY, GERARD. *The True Levellers Standard Advanced; or, The State of Community opened, and Presented to the Sons of Men.* London, 1649.

WOLLSTONECRAFT, MARY. *A Vindication of the Rights of Woman.* New York: Norton, [1967].

WOOLLEY, HANNAH. *The Gentlewoman's Companion; or A Guide to the Female Sex.* London: Printed by A. Maxwell for Dorman Newman, 1673.
———. *The Queen-like Closet . . . stored with . . . Receipts for Preserving, Candying and Cookery.* 3rd ed. London: Printed for Richard Lowndes, 1675.

Secondary Sources

AVELING, J. H. *The Chamberlens and the Midwifery Forceps.* London: J. & A. Churchill, 1882.

BALLARD, GEORGE. *Memoirs of Several Ladies of Great Britain . . . Celebrated for their Writings or Skill in the Learned Languages*. Oxford: Printed by W. Jackson, 1752.

BELL, SUSAN GROAG. "Christine de Pisan (1364–1430): Humanism and the Problem of a Studious Woman." *Feminist Studies* 3 (1976): 173–84.

BERG, BARBARA J. *The Remembered Gate: Origins of American Feminism: The Woman and the City, 1800–1860*. New York: Oxford University Press, 1978.

BOWDEN, P. J. *The Wool Trade in Tudor and Stuart England*. London: Macmillan and Co., 1962.

BRINK, J. R. "Bathsua Makin: Educator and Linguist (English, 1608?–1675?)." In *Female Scholars: A Tradition of Learned Women before 1800*, edited by J. R. Brink. Montreal: Eden Press, 1980.

BUSH, DOUGLAS. *The Renaissance and English Humanism*. Toronto: University of Toronto Press, 1939.

BUTLER, MELISSA A. "Early Liberal Roots of Feminism: John Locke and the Attack on Patriarchy." *American Political Science Review* 72 (Mar. 1978): 135–50.

BUTTERFIELD, HERBERT. *The Origins of Modern Science, 1300–1800*. London: G. Bell, 1949.

CAMDEN, CARROLL. *The Elizabethan Woman*. Houston, Tex.: Elsevier Press, 1952.

CHAFE, WILLIAM H. *Women and Equality: Changing Patterns in American Culture*. New York: Oxford University Press, 1977.

CHARLTON, KENNETH. *Education in Renaissance England*. London: Routledge and Kegan Paul, 1965.

CHOJNACK, STANLEY. "Patrician Women in Early Renaissance Venice." *Studies in the Renaissance* 21 (1974): 176–203.

CLARK, ALICE. *Working Life of Women in the Seventeenth Century*. 1919. Reprint. London: Frank Cass and Co., 1968.

CONGLETON, JAMES E. *Theories of Pastoral Poetry in England, 1684–1798*. 1952. Reprint. New York: Haskell House, 1968.

COTT, NANCY. *The Bonds of Womanhood: "Woman's Sphere" in New England, 1780–1835*. New Haven, Conn.: Yale University Press, 1977.

CRESSY, DAVID. "Educational Opportunity in Tudor and Stuart England." *History of Education Quarterly* 16 (Fall 1976): 301–20.

———. "Literacy in Seventeenth-Century England: More Evidence." *Journal of Interdisciplinary History* 8 (Summer 1977): 141–50.

CURTIS, MARK H. *Oxford and Cambridge in Transition, 1558–1642*. Oxford: Clarendon Press, 1959.

DAVIES, KATHLEEN M. " 'The Sacred Condition of Equality'—How Original Were Puritan Doctrines on Marriage?" *Social History* 5 (May 1977): 563–80.

DAVIS, J. C. "The Levellers and Democracy." *Past and Present* 40 (July 1968): 174–80.

DAVIS, NATALIE Z. "Women's History in Transition: The European Case." *Feminist Studies* 3(1976): 83–103.

DAVIS, RALPH. *The Rise of the Atlantic Economies.* Ithaca, N.Y.: Cornell University Press, 1973.

————. *The Rise of the English Shipping Industry.* London: Macmillan and Co., 1962.

DOUGLAS, DAVID. *English Scholars, 1660–1730.* London: Eyre & Spottiswoode [1951].

DUBOIS, ELLEN C. *Feminism and Suffrage: The Emergence of an Independent Women's Movement in America, 1848–1869.* Ithaca, N.Y.: Cornell University Press, 1978.

ELTON, G. R. *Reform and Reformation: England, 1509–1558.* Cambridge, Mass.: Harvard University Press, 1977.

FEINGOLD, RICHARD. *Nature & Society.* New Brunswick, N.J.: Rutgers University Press, 1978.

FLEXNER, ELEANOR. *Century of Struggle: The Woman's Rights Movement in the United States.* Cambridge, Mass.: Harvard University Press, 1959.

————. *Mary Wollstonecraft: A Biography.* Baltimore: Penguin Books, 1972.

FORBES, THOMAS R. "The Regulation of English Midwives in the Sixteenth and Seventeenth Centuries." *Medical History* 8 (1964): 235–43.

FREEMAN, JO. *The Politics of Women's Liberation.* New York: McKay, 1975.

GAGEN, JEAN ELIZABETH. *The New Woman: Her Emergence in English Drama, 1660–1730.* New York: Twayne Publishers, 1954.

GARDINER, DOROTHY. *English Girlhood at School: A Study of Women's Education through Twelve Centuries.* Oxford: Oxford University Press, 1929.

GASKIN, KATHERINE. "Age at First Marriage in Europe before 1850: A Survey of Family Reconstitution Data." *Journal of Family History* 2 (1978): 23–36.

GEORGE, MARGARET. *One Woman's "Situation": A Study of Mary Wollstonecraft.* Urbana: University of Illinois Press, 1970.

GLANZ, LENORE MARIE. "The Legal Position of English Women under the Early Stuart Kings and the Interregnum, 1603–1660." Ph.D. dissertation, Loyola University of Chicago, 1973.

GOOCH, G. P. *English Democratic Ideas of the Seventeenth Century.* 2d ed. Cambridge: Cambridge University Press, 1954.

GOODY, JACK. "Inheritance, Property and Women: Some Comparative Considerations." In *Family and Inheritance: Rural Society in Western Europe,* edited by Jack Goody et al. New York: Cambridge University Press, 1976.

GRANT, DOUGLAS. *Margaret the First: A Biography of Margaret Cavendish, Duchess of Newcastle, 1623–1673.* London: Ruper Hart-Davis, 1957.

GREEN, MARY ELIZABETH. "Elizabeth Elstob: The Saxon Nymph (English, 1683–1765)." In *Female Scholars: A Tradition of Learned Women before 1800,* edited by J. R. Brink. Montreal: Eden Press, 1980.

GURR, TED R. *Why Men Rebel.* Princeton, N.J.: Princeton University Press, 1970.

HAJNAL, J. "European Marriage Patterns in Perspective: The Uniqueness of the European Pattern." In *Population in History,* edited by D. V. Glass and D. E. C. Eversley. Chicago: Aldine, 1965.

HALLER, WILLIAM. *The Rise of Puritanism, 1570–1640.* New York: Columbia University Press, 1938.

HEATH-STUBBS, JOHN F. A. *The Pastoral.* London: Oxford University Press, 1969.

HERLIHY, DAVID. *The Renaissance Family in Italy.* St. Louis: Forum Press, 1972.

HIGGINS, PATRICIA. "The Reactions of Women, with Special Reference to Women Petitioners." In *Politics, Religion and the English Revolution, 1640–1649,* edited by Brian Manning. London: Edward Arnold, 1973.

HILL, CHRISTOPHER. *Milton and the English Revolution.* New York: Viking Press, 1977.

———. *The World Turned Upside Down: Radical Ideas during the English Revolution.* New York: Viking Press, 1972.

HOGREFE, PEARL. *Tudor Women.* Ames: Iowa State University, 1975.

HOLDSWORTH, WILLIAM. *Hisotry of English Law.* 9 vols. London: Methuen and Co., 1923–31.

HUFTON, OLWEN. "Women and the Family Economy in Eighteenth-Century France." *French Historical Studies* 9 (Spring 1975): 1–22.

HUGHES, DIANE OWEN. "Urban Growth and Family Structure in Medieval Genoa." *Past and Present* 66 (Feb. 1975): 3–28.

JACK, SYBIL M., ed. *Trade and Industry in Tudor and Stuart England.* London: George Allen and Unwin, 1977.

JACOB, J. R. *Robert Boyle and the English Revolution.* New York: Burt Franklin and Co., 1977.

JACOB, MARGARET C. *The Newtonians and the English Revolution, 1689–1720.* Ithaca, N.Y.: Cornell University Press, 1976.

JAMES, E. O. "The Saxon Nymph." *Times Literary Supplement,* 28 Sept. 1933, p. 646.

JANES, REGINA. "Mary, Mary, Quite Contrary; or, Mary Astell and Mary Wollstonecraft Compared." In *Studies in Eighteenth-Century Culture.* Madison: University of Wisconsin Press, 1976.

JONES, M. G. *The Charity School Movement: A Study of Eighteenth-Century Puritanism in Action.* Cambridge: Cambridge University Press, 1938.

JONES, RICHARD F. *Ancients and Moderns.* St. Louis: Washington University Press, 1962.

KAMM, JOSEPHINE. *Hope Deferred: Girls' Education in English History.* London: Methuen and Co., 1965.

KANNER, S. BARBARA, ed. *The Women of England.* Hamden, Conn.: Archon Books, 1979.

KEARNEY, HUGH. *Scholars and Gentlemen.* Ithaca, N.Y.: Cornell University Press, 1970.

KELLY-GADOL, JOAN. "Did Women Have a Renaissance?" In *Becoming Visible:*

A History of European Women, edited by Renate Bridenthal and Claudia Koonz. Boston: Houghton-Mifflin, 1977.

KELSO, RUTH. *The Doctrine for the Lady of the Renaissance.* Urbana: University of Illinois Press, 1956.

KINNAIRD, JOAN K. "Mary Astell and the Conservative Contribution to English Feminism." *Journal of British Studies* 19 (Fall 1979): 53–75.

KUHN, THOMAS. *The Structure of Scientific Revolutions.* Chicago: University of Chicago Press, 1962.

LASLETT, PETER. *Family Life and Illicit Love in Earlier Generations.* New York: Cambridge University Press, 1977.

———. "Mean Household Size in England since the Sixteenth Century." In *Household and Family Size in Past Time,* edited by Peter Laslett and Richard Wall. Cambridge: Cambridge University Press, 1972.

LERNER, GERDA. "The Lady and the Mill Girl." *American Studies Journal* 10 (Spring 1969): 5–15.

———. "Women's Rights and American Feminism." *American Scholar* 40 (1971): 235–48.

LEVINE, DAVID. *Family Formation in an Age of Nascent Capitalism.* New York: Academic Press, 1977.

LIDDINGTON, JILL, and NORRIS, JILL. *"One Hand Tied Behind Us": The Rise of the Women's Suffrage Movement.* London: Virago Press, 1978.

LOUGEE, CAROLYN. *Le Paradis des Femmes: Women, Salons, and Social Stratification in Seventeenth-Century France.* Princeton, N.J.: Princeton University Press, 1976.

LUCAS, HENRY S. *The Renaissance and the Reformation.* 2d ed. New York: Harper and Brothers, 1960.

MCBRIDE, THERESA M. *The Domestic Revolution: The Modernization of Household Service in England and France, 1820–1920.* New York: Holmes and Meier, 1976.

MCCONICA, JAMES K. *English Humanists and Reformation Policies under Henry VIII and Edward VI.* Oxford: Oxford University Press, 1965.

MCEWEN, GILBERT D. *The Oracle of the Coffee House, John Dunton's "Athenian Mercury."* San Marino, Calif.: Huntington Library, 1972.

MACFARLANE, ALAN. *The Family Life of Ralph Josselin, A Seventeenth Century Clergyman: An Essay in Historical Anthropology.* New York: W. W. Norton and Co., 1970.

———. *The Origins of English Individualism: The Family, Property and Social Transition.* New York: Cambridge University Press, 1979.

MCGUIRE, MARY ANN. "Margaret Cavendish, Duchess of Newcastle, on the Nature and Status of Women." *International Journal of Women's Studies* 1 (1978): 193–206.

MACPHERSON, C. B. *The Political Theory of Possessive Individualism: Hobbes to Locke.* Oxford: Clarendon Press, 1962.

MASON, SHIRLENE. *Daniel Defoe and the Status of Women.* St. Albans, Vt.: Eden Press, 1978.

MELDER, KEITH. *Beginnings of Sisterhood: The American Woman's Rights Movement, 1800–1850*. New York: Schocken Books, 1977.

MEYER, GERALD DENNIS. *The Scientific Lady in England, 1650–1760*. Berkeley: University of California Press, 1955.

MILLER, P. J. "Women's Education, 'Self-Improvement,' and Social Mobility—A Late Eighteenth Century Debate." *British Journal of Education Studies* 20 (1973): 302–14.

MILLETT, KATE. *Sexual Politics*. New York: Doubleday and Co., 1970.

MORGAN, VICTOR. "Cambridge University and the 'Country' 1560–1640." In *Oxford and Cambridge from the 14th to the Early 19th Century. The University in Society*, edited by Lawrence Stone, vol. 1. Princeton, N.J.: Princeton University Press, 1974.

NICOLSON, MARJORIE. "The Early State of Cartesianism in England." *Studies in Philology* 25 (1929): 364–65.

NORTON, MARY BETH. *Women of America*. Boston: Houghton-Mifflin, 1978.

O'DAY, ROSEMARY. *The English Clergy: The Emergence and Consolidation of a Profession, 1558–1642*. [Leicester]: Leicester University Press, 1979.

PANKHURST, EMMELINE. "When Civil War Is Waged by Women." In *Feminism: The Essential Historical Writings*, edited by Miriam Schneir. New York: Random House, 1972.

PERRY, HENRY T. E. *The First Duchess of Newcastle and Her Husband as Figures in Literary History*. Cambridge, Mass.: Harvard University Press, 1919.

PETRELLI, RICHARD L. "The Regulation of French Midwifery in the *Ancien Regime*." *Journal of the History of Medicine and Allied Sciences* 26 (1971): 276–92.

POCOCK, J. G. A. *The Ancient Constitution and the Feudal Law*. Cambridge: At the University Press, 1957.

POPE-HENNESSEY, UNA BIRCH. *Anna van Schurman, Artist, Scholar, Saint*. London: Longmans, Co., 1909.

POWELL, CHILTON. *English Domestic Relations, 1487–1653*. New York: Columbia University Press, 1916.

POWER, EILEEN. *Medieval Women*. Edited by M. M. Postan. New York: Cambridge University Press, 1976.

PURVER, MARGERY. *The Royal Society*. Cambridge, Mass.: MIT Press, 1967.

REYNOLDS, ERNEST EDWIN. *Margaret Roper: Eldest Daughter of St. Thomas More*. New York: P. J. Kennedy, 1960.

REYNOLDS, MYRA. *The Learned Lady in England, 1650–1760*. Boston: Houghton-Mifflin, 1920.

ROBERTS, R. S. "The Personnel and Practice of Medicine in Tudor and Stuart England." Parts I and II. *Medical History* 6 (1962): 363–82, 8 (1964): 217–34.

ROGERS, KATHERINE. "Anne Finch, Countess of Winchilsea: An Augustan Woman Poet." In *Shakespeare's Sisters: Feminist Essays on Woman Poets*, edited by Sandra M. Gilbert and Susan Gubar. Bloomington: Indiana University Press, 1979.

ROSEN, ANDREW. *Rise up Women! The Militant Campaign of the Women's Social and Political Union, 1903–1914.* London: Routledge and Kegan Paul, 1974.

ROSS, ISABEL. *Margaret Fell, Mother of Quakerism.* London: Longman's, Green, 1949.

SADLER, JOHN E. J. A. *Comenius and the Concept of Universal Education.* London: George Allen and Unwin, 1966.

SCHLATTER, RICHARD. *The Social Ideas of Religious Leaders.* 1940. Reprint. New York: Octagon Books, 1943.

SCHOCHET, GORDON. *Patriarchalism in Political Thought: The Authoritarian Family and Political Speculation and Attitudes Especially in Seventeenth-Century England.* Oxford: Basil Blackwell, 1975.

SCHOFIELD, R. S. "The Measurement of Literacy in Pre-industrial England." In *Literacy in Traditional Societies,* edited by Jack Goody. Cambridge: Cambridge University Press, 1968.

SCHUCKING, L. L. *The Puritan Family.* New York: Schocken Books, 1969.

SEIDEL, MICHAEL A. "Poulain de la Barre's *The Woman as Good as the Man.*" *Journal of the History of Ideas* 35 (1974): 499–508.

SILVER, KATHERINE BODARD. "Salon, Foyer, Bureau: Women and the Professions in France." In *Clio's Consciousness Raised,* edited by Lois Banner and Mary Hartman. New York: Harper and Row, 1974.

SIMON, JOAN. "The Social Origins of Cambridge Students." *Past and Present* 26 (Nov. 1963): 58–67.

SMITH, FLORENCE M. *Mary Astell.* New York: Columbia University Press, 1912.

SMITH, HILDA. "Feminism and the Methodology of Women's History." In *Liberating Women's History: Theoretical and Critical Essays,* edited by Berenice A. Carroll. Urbana: University of Illinois Press, 1976.

———. "Ideology and Gynecology in Seventeenth-Century England." In *Liberating Women's History: Theoretical and Critical Essays,* edited by Berenice A. Carroll. Urbana: University of Illinois Press, 1976.

———, and CARDINALE, SUSAN, comps. *Women and the Literature of the Seventeenth Century: An Annotated Bibliography Based on Wing's Short-Title Catalogue.* Westport, Conn.: Greenwood Press, forthcoming.

SMITH-ROSENBERG, CARROLL. "The Female World of Love and Ritual: Relations between Women in Nineteenth-Century America." *Signs: A Journal of Women and Society* 1 (1975): 1–29.

SPENCER, HERBERT R. *The History of British Midwifery from 1650–1800.* London: John Bale, Sons, 1927.

SPUFFORD, MARGARET. *Contrasting Communities: English Villagers in the Sixteenth and Seventeenth Centuries.* New York: Cambridge University Press, 1974.

———. "Peasant Inheritance Customs and Land Distribution in Cambridgeshire from the Sixteenth to the Eighteenth Centuries." In *Family and Inheritance: Rural Society in Western Europe,* edited by Jack Goody et al. New York: Cambridge University Press, 1976.

――――. "The Schooling of the Peasantry in Cambridgeshire, 1575–1700." In *Land, Church and People,* edited by Joan Thirsk. Reading: Museum of English Rural Life, 1970.

STENTON, DORIS MARY. *The English Woman in History.* London: Routledge and Kegan Paul, 1957.

STOCK, MARIE L. "Poullain de la Barre: A Seventeenth-Century Feminist." Ph.D. dissertation, Columbia University, 1961.

STOCK, PHYLLIS. *Better than Rubies: A History of Women's Education.* New York: G. P. Putnam's Sons, 1978.

STONE, LAWRENCE. "The Education Revolution in England, 1560–1640." *Past and Present* 28 (July 1964): 41–80.

――――. *The Family, Sex and Marriage in England, 1500–1800.* New York: Harper and Row, 1977.

――――. "Literacy and Education in England, 1640–1900." *Past and Present* 42 (Feb. 1969): 69–139.

――――. "The Size and Composition of the Oxford Student Body 1580–1909." In *Oxford and Cambridge from the 14th to the Early 19th Century. The University in Society,* edited by Lawrence Stone, vol. 1. Princeton, N.J.: Princeton University Press, 1974.

THIRSK, JOAN. "The European Debate on Customs of Inheritance, 1500–1700." In *Family and Inheritance: Rural Society in Western Europe,* edited by Jack Goody et al. New York: Cambridge University Press, 1976.

――――. "Seventeenth-Century Agriculture and Social Change." In *Land, Church and People,* edited by Joan Thirsk. Reading: Museum of English Rural Life, 1970.

THOMAS, KEITH. "Women and the Civil War Sects." *Past and Present* 13 (Apr. 1958): 42–62.

THOMPSON, ROGER. *Women in Stuart England and America.* London: Routledge and Kegan Paul, 1974.

TILLEY, LOUISE, and SCOTT, JOAN. *Women, Work, and Family.* New York: Holt, Rinehart and Winston, 1978.

TINKER, CHAUNCEY BREWSTER. *The Salon and English Letters: Chapters on the Interrelations of Literature and Society in the Age of Johnson.* 1915. Reprint. New York: Gordian Press, 1967.

VEALL, DONALD. *The Popular Movement for Law Reform, 1640–1660.* Oxford: At the Clarendon Press, 1970.

VINCENT, W. A. L. *The Grammar Schools: Their Continuing Tradition, 1660–1714.* London: John Murray, 1969.

WALZER, MICHAEL. *The Revolution of the Saints.* Cambridge, Mass.: Harvard University Press, 1965.

WATSON, FOSTER, ed. *Vives and the Renascence Education of Women.* New York: Longmans, Green and Co., 1912.

WEBSTER, CHARLES. *The Great Instauration: Science, Medicine and Reform, 1626–1660.* New York: Holmes and Meier, 1975.

―――. *Samuel Hartlib and the Advancement of Learning.* Cambridge: Cambridge University Press, 1970.

WILCOX, DONALD J. *In Search of God and Self: Renaissance and Reformation Thought.* Boston: Houghton Mifflin, [1975].

WILSON, JOAN HOFF. "The Illusion of Change: Women and the American Revolution." In *The American Revolution: Explorations in the History of American Radicalism,* edited by Alfred F. Young. De Kalb: Northern Illinois University Press, 1976.

WRIGHT, LOUIS B. *Middle-Class Culture in Elizabethan England.* Ithaca, N.Y.: Cornell University Press, 1958.

WRIGLEY, E. A. "Family Limitation in Pre-Industrial England." *Economic History Review.* 2d ser. 19 (1966): 82–107.

―――. "A Simple Model of London's Importance in Changing English Society and Economy, 1650–1750." *Past and Present* 37 (July 1967): 44–70.

YOUNG, ROBERT F., ed. *Comenius in England.* Oxford: Oxford University Press, 1932.

Index

A Note on the Author

Hilda L. Smith was born in Kansas City, Missouri. She received her bachelor's degree from Southwest Missouri State University, her master's from the University of Missouri at Columbia, and her Ph.D. in history from the University of Chicago. She has taught women's history at the University of Maryland, has headed the Chesapeake Area Group of Women Historians, and has been co-president of the Coordinating Committee on Women in the Historical Profession. Currently she is the Acting Executive Director of the Maryland Committee for the Humanities. Her scholarly publications include essays on feminism and historical methodology and on gynecology in seventeenth-century England, and *Women and the Literature of the Seventeenth Century: An Annotated Bibliography Based on Wing's Short-Title Catalogue* (1982).